£1-50

MURDER ONE

Edited by Mike James

GW00631051

PAN BOOKS

First published 1999 by True Crime Library

This edition published 2005 by Pan Books
an imprint of Pan Macmillan Ltd
Pan Macmillan, 20 New Wharf Road, London N1 9RR
Basingstoke and Oxford
Associated companies throughout the world
www.panmacmillan.com

ISBN 0 330 42116 6

1 3 5 7 9 8 6 4 2

A CIP catalogue record for this book is available from
the British Library.

Printed and bound in Great Britain by
Mackays of Chatham plc, Chatham, Kent

To Brian Baker,
thanks for
everything

CONTENTS

Preface

1. Voices From Death Row   3
   L. C. Schmuhl

2. I Watched My Husband's Killer Fry   17
   Clara Morris

3. An Englishman Goes To The Chair   31
   Richard Devon

4. Horror In The Coughing Box   35
   Brian Marriner

5. On Death Row With Jesse Bishop   49
   Joseph L. Koenig

6. Two And A Half Pounds of Arsenic   61
   Jack Heise

7. Death Of A Clown   75
   W. T. Brannon

8. Letters From A Dead Man   97
   L. C. Schmuhl

9. "Burn, Bundy, Burn"   113
   Charles Cleveland

10. The Lady Cop And The Serial Killer   129
    Steven Barry

11. An Awful Spectacle Far Worse Than Hanging   147
    Martin Lomax

12. Electrocuted Twice   151
    George Courson

13. Tensions In The Household   155
    Ben Tilsley

14. The "Day You Got Me Day"   169
    Terry Ecker

15. Oklahoma's Hound From Hell   197
    Charles W. Sasser

16. Death To The Freeway Killer   209
    Lester Fox

17. Lover Of The Dead   217
    Turk Ryder

18. An Eye For An Eye   229
    Franklyn Sharpe

19. Please Put Him To Death   237
    Michael Jason

20. The Buchenwald Experience   245
    L. C. Schmuhl

PREFACE

Since 1976 when the Supreme Court revoked an earlier ruling that executions were "cruel and unusual punishment," hundreds have died in the death chambers across America.

In the past decade just over 400 people have been executed and if this rate is to continue, 1400 persons will go to the death chamber in the next 10 years. Reason enough for men and women on Death Row today to be scared. "It's like the old days," one state legislator in Virginia stated. "Then you went to Death Row to be executed, not to spend years fighting your case. We're getting it right again."

But others are concerned about this trend. Anti-capital punishment campaigners have called into question the motives behind this increase in executions. They argue that capital punishment is often wielded as a political tool with little regard for the person whose life hangs in the balance. Prosecutors, they claim, want to appear tough on crime and consequently will ask for the death penalty not because the defendant deserved it, but because it will help their political careers.

Also the same can be said of governors who deny clemency appeals because they fear criticism of being soft on crime when it comes to the next elections.

"One of the basic tenets of our criminal justice system is consistency," says Mark Krumholz in a recently published article in America, "which means that punishments for similar crimes should be of similar severity. The death penalty flagrantly violates this standard, which clearly discriminates on the basis of race, wealth and fame."

Certainly it is hard to argue with this point when looking at the statistics: an African-American who murders a Caucasian is 25 times more likely to face execution than a Caucasian who murders an African-American.

But however convincing the abolitionists are, there is a massive lobby in America in support of capital punishment.

"It's nothing to do with being a deterrent, if you want, call it revenge," a pro-execution demonstrator told a reporter. "If it were your son or daughter who'd been murdered, you'd have different views." And today the views of relatives of victims are considered more than ever when determining the punishment.

In *Murder One* a victim's widow appeared before an appeal court to assess whether a killer should live or die. "Please put him to death. He took my life. Now take his," she told the panel.

And the case of British-born Nicholas Ingram is another where relatives had a say.

Ingram had marched a husband and wife into woods, tied them to a tree, and tortured them for hours before he shot them. The woman survived and 12 years later when Ingram was executed his lawyer described the electrocution as barbaric saying his client wanted to look forward to another life, "so that he could look for something better because what had happened in this life had been so sad."

The victim's widow saw things differently. "We begged for mercy and were given none. He was judge, jury and executioner ... For years the spectre of this case has hung over me, but at last, I can now get on with my life."

And who could argue with her?

1
VOICES FROM DEATH ROW

Former deputy warden of Indiana State Prison,
L. C. Schmuhl

THE headline caught my eye the moment I opened the evening paper. Another man was coming to Death Row! Slowly shaking my head, I began to read. It was late in February, 1938, and we had trouble aplenty at Indiana's big state prison.

Only two weeks before five dangerous long-termers had sawed out of their cells, clambered over roofs to an obscure corner of the wall and dropped to freedom. Three were caught the same night by alert state police — but it didn't ease the uproar. The break had been the fourth major escape in five years and the governor's men were all over the place investigating.

I was dead tired — and now they were sending me another man for the death house.

Normally that wouldn't have been so bad — even amid the investigative uproar. Indiana, a small state, doesn't execute many men. In fact, in the 41 prior years only 50 had died on the scaffold or in the chair. But now, through a quirk of circumstances, Death Row was jackpot full. There were already seven men there waiting to die.

And an eighth was coming. Hoping fervently he wouldn't be troublesome, I skipped through the essential details of the case: "John Dee Smith ... killer of Arlie Foster, Fort Wayne restaurant owner, in a hold-up ..."

My hopes faded as I came to a startling paragraph. During final arguments to the jury, I read, Prosecutor C. Byron Hayes had called Smith a dirty coward. Smith had promptly leaped up, shouting: "A bunch of flat-footed rats framed me. I'll show 'em how to die. Death in the electric chair doesn't mean a thing to me!"

Slowly I put the paper down. So John Dee Smith was a tough guy, eh?

We'd see!

When they brought Smith in a few days later I had him delivered to my office. If he was as tough as he had appeared in print I wanted to know it and be prepared.

He stood in front of my desk, a lean, hard young man of medium height. I like to read faces, and I scanned Smith's. I saw a long, pugnacious lantern jaw that accentuated a tight, sardonic mouth. He had a good nose, small ears and nicely trimmed hair.

It was his eyes that startled me. They were a cold grey, like November skies, and now they stared straight at me with mocking impudence and even seemed to twinkle. A ghost of a matching smile touched Smith's lips.

His good humour was so real I almost smiled back before I checked myself. I think he noticed because he grinned outright and said:

"I'd like a room with southern exposure and a shower! And what's the check-out hour?"

I don't like flippant prisoners, in or out of Death Row, so I dredged up a date from my memory and snapped: "For you it's 12.05 a.m. on June 1st."

Smith grimaced, then chuckled softly. "Okay, deputy," he said. "You won that round. I'll behave."

"See that you do. It'll be easier for you."

I had planned to give Smith a sharp lecture on the folly of being mean, tough and ornery on Death Row. But I sensed that it wasn't needed. Instead, I briefed him matter-of-factly on Death Row rules. He listened soberly and alertly. When I'd finished, he grinned again.

"Fair enough," he said. "I won't give you any trouble."

We went upstairs to Death Row — 10 cells, five of them on each side of a short corridor, all of it fenced off by ceiling-high bars and a perpetually watched gate.

When the gate guard rattled a key in the lock to admit Smith, all seven men inside came to the front of their cells to peer curiously at the new arrival.

Smith let his sharp grey eyes flit from cell to cell. Then with a jaunty wave and a friendly smile, he cried:

"Hya, mugs! Roll out the carpet for another thunderbolt jockey."

I smiled in spite of myself. It was a good switch on an old gag. Around the prison, death in the chair had long been called "riding the thunderbolt."

We led Smith into his cell and I watched him closely, wondering if his bravado was real or phoney. It seemed genuine. I went back to my office, wondering how long it would last.

In the busy weeks that followed I had little time for Smith or any of the other men on Death Row.

The guards there kept me posted on the eight men upstairs, and their reports never failed to include something about Smith.

True to his word, he behaved perfectly. It became quickly apparent that he was no "tough guy" in the hoodlum sense of the word. But he was either rock-hard inside or he was putting on the best act we'd ever seen.

"He's a riot — a perpetual comic," one of the guards told me. "And so help me I think it's real. The guy just doesn't care."

"How are the others taking it?" I asked quickly. A little humour goes a long way on Death Row. Not many about to die like to laugh.

"Pretty good," the guard replied. "All but Hicks and Noelke. Hicks has made a few nasty cracks at Smith — nothing serious, yet. Noelke just broods."

I knew the two men. I didn't worry about Noelke. He was a queer, twisted, neurotic man who had slain his wife and child. Deeply introverted, he wouldn't be bothered

5

much by what went on around him.

But Heber Hicks was different. A wizened, bitter little man, he had plotted with three others to kill Captain Harry Miller, a retired Cincinnati fireman. His pals had already died in the prison's only triple execution. Hicks, with money and friends, had wangled several stays — the last one to May 6th.

He was fully capable of starting a bitter and troublesome feud. We liked to let the Death Row men out into their barred-off bullpen for at least a few hours each day to mingle with each other — under close scrutiny, of course — and to play cards or draughts.

But with a feud simmering, it could be disastrous. In a fight a man's brains could be bashed out against the concrete floor before guards could get inside the bullpen.

Yet I was reluctant to deprive the eight men of their small freedom of movement and association. I decided to keep a closer eye on Death Row and judge for myself whether Smith and Hicks might tangle. So I happened to be standing outside the bullpen gate the day it was all settled — without a blow.

I had come upstairs quietly, hearing a burst of laughter as I approached the Death Row gate. Smith had just finished a story. Then a cruel, bitter voice stifled the fading laughter, and I knew it was Hicks.

"You talk too much, Blabbermouth," he snarled.

I saw the gate guard reach for his key. I motioned him to wait and stood there, unnoticed and listening. Smith was playing draughts with Jimmy Swain, a happy-go-lucky young fellow who had killed a grocer. Smith looked up at Hicks, standing nearby, and I could almost see those grey eyes freezing to match his voice.

"Some of us," Smith said slowly, "aren't afraid of this place. We like it happy."

"Well I don't," Hicks replied — but there was a trace of whine in his voice.

"Then go crawl in your bunk and pull the blanket over your head," said Smith.

Hicks paused uncertainly. Then with tension nearly at breaking point, Bob Shaw, a lean, tall cop killer, drawled:

"Yeah, Hicks — be quiet! We like it this way."

Without another word, Hicks turned and went back into his cell. From that time on Smith was the king of Death Row.

As the days passed his good humour never soured. It was all the more amazing because he must have been bereft of all hope.

Every doomed man but Smith still had attorneys working or friends pleading for a commutation. But not Smith. He hadn't made a single legal move to avoid death, nor did he seem interested. A few days after May 6th, when Hicks was executed, I asked Smith why.

"It's not in the cards," he said. "Why prolong the agony?"

"Don't you care?"

"Not a bit!"

I searched his frank grey eyes for the lie that should have been there, and couldn't find it. I went away convinced that the Smith enigma wouldn't be solved until the final day — if at all.

Soon after that we had one of those Death Row dramas rarely found outside the movies. The day came for Jimmy Swain, the happy 18-year-old. When we took him from Death Row downstairs, Smith seemed genuinely saddened for the first time. He and Swain had ripened a natural friendship over the draughts board. Both played well. The guards told me that Swain nearly always won — but they suspected Smith wanted it that way because Swain got such a kick out of beating him.

The men were in their cells when we came to take Jimmy downstairs. Smith stuck his face up to the bars and shouted:

"Chin up, Jimmy boy!"

Swain turned and flashed him a big smile.

"And don't forget," Smith added, "ask St. Peter for a draughts board and get it all set up. I'm going to beat the hell out of you up there!"

"It'll be ready," Swain said, and then turned his face away so Smith couldn't see the tautness come into it.

I'll never forget that night. Jimmy Swain was very young and death to the very young is very hard. He had courage, though, and he spent those last hours like a man.

I stayed with him until an hour before the execution time. Then I left him to the chaplain and went back to my office.

With less than 20 minutes to go, my telephone rang. It was Warden Alfred Dowd, who had replaced Warden Kunkel only a short time before.

"Hold everything," Dowd said. "The governor just granted Swain a stay."

I put the phone down and walked to Swain's cell. He looked up as I appeared in the door and said weakly, "I'm ready, deputy!"

I shook my head, "No, Jimmy," I said softly. "I didn't come for you. You've got a stay."

He just stared at me in stunned disbelief. "Oh man, oh man," he murmured.

We didn't take Jimmy back upstairs until next morning. By then the whole prison, including Smith, knew what had happened. But Smith played it straight. When we brought Jimmy back to Death Row, Smith leaped off his bunk and grabbed the bars of his cell door.

"Wow!" he shouted. "A ghost! Get him outta here!"

Jimmy flashed him a big, happy smile. "Quit that stuff. Dee," he chuckled. "Whoever heard of a ghost as happy as me? Where's that draughts board? We got time for a few more games now!"

They didn't have long. Smith's days were running out. I wanted to get under his skin and see what he was really made of. But I knew it was useless to try until time had worked its ultimate corrosion.

Besides, I'd have all of the last day with him . . .

Not even a desperate personal aloneness seemed to crack Smith's hard shell. He had few visitors. His attorneys had long since been dismissed as no longer needed or wanted.

I watched him closely the last week. His manner didn't change. For the first time I began to suspect that Smith might go all the way without a trace of weakness. As I had done so many times, I wondered what had steered his life into the death chamber.

I discussed him with Chaplain Bob Hall who had visited him regularly.

"He doesn't joke about religion," the padre reflected, "but he doesn't seize it hungrily, either — like so many on Death Row. He's got a refreshing sort of faith — quiet, firm, matter-of-fact. He has a deep strength inside."

"He has that," I agreed. "Too bad it's wasted."

"It's a tragedy!"

On the morning of May 31st, when we came to take Smith downstairs, he said calm, almost jaunty goodbyes to the rest of the boys on Death Row, then paused in front of Jimmy Swain's cell. Jimmy stood at the cell door, his eyes downcast, his face glum. The little guy was losing a good friend and he knew it.

"Chin up, Jimmy boy," Smith said again. "I'll handle that draughts board deal with St. Peter."

Swain brightened a little and tried to help things. He said: "No sir! You'll come back in the morning like I did!"

Smith just shook his head, sobering for an instant. "I won't be back, Jimmy — but I'll be waiting for you. S'long."

Turning quickly away, he strode out of Death Row and down the stairs.

We sent Smith to the barber shop for his head shave. The prison doctor examined him. He was in perfect condition. By mid-morning he was in the death cell near my office, contemplating his left trouser leg which had been slit to above the knee so the electrode could be quickly fastened. He looked up as I stopped by his cell. His face was calm and his grey eyes were warmly friendly.

"Hello, deputy," he said eagerly. I could detect a

yearning for company in his voice.

"What will you have for dinner?" I asked.

Smith smiled wryly. "The hearty meal, eh?" Then he shrugged. "I don't much care. Chicken will do — with French fries, biscuits and gravy, a little corn."

"Coffee?"

"No," he chuckled. "It might keep me awake! I'll take milk — and peach pie á la mode."

"Smokes?"

"Yeah — cigarettes."

"Anything else?"

Smith started to shake his head, and then stopped. He peered at me a long moment and smiled. "You seem like a nice guy, deputy," he said. "I hate to eat alone — especially tonight. Will you join me?"

I said I would.

"And I'd like to write a few letters this afternoon," he went on. "Could I have paper and pen?"

"Certainly."

I left to pass his meal order along to the kitchen and send back writing materials. Even as I turned away Smith began to josh the watchful guard who would never leave the door of his cell that day.

I wondered what he would write. All prison mail is censored, including last letters. It was my job to scan Smith's, and I looked forward to it. Words penned in the shadow of death are invariably revealing and I knew very little yet about this man who was still laughing on his last day on earth.

It took him until mid-afternoon to finish three letters. Poorly educated, he struggled to say what he meant, rambled a lot and tripped over grammar. His handwriting was hard to read.

Despite these handicaps, he got a lot of the Smith I had come to know into the letters. I had an orderly turn his awful scrawl into clean typing.

He wrote the first letter to his father who lived in Michigan. This is what he said, precisely as he put it down:

"Dear Sir,

I again try to write you a letter. I am on the last stages of a fairly long trip — or — a short trip. You asked those folks who were up to see me to ask me something or other about a forgiveness. I know nothing about anything you might have done in order that you might ask such.

"Perhaps your mind is working one time again, or maybe you should take something for indigestion. Please stop overeating; it will raise particular hell with you.

"No doubt you have noticed the date. This letter was written some time before 4 p.m., a few hours before I was supposed to go to the chair. It sounds like a lot of time — ha, you should be around to count the minutes ... I'll be seeing you I hope."

I put down the letter and read the second — written to an aunt in Chicago. It was a mixture of the bouncy Smith who had been the life of Death Row, and of lurking bitterness.

"Dear Aunt,

This probably will be my last letter to you. I don't know. If anything happens, ha, she'll have to happen 'purty' soon, by cracky. However, that is what is worrying me. I will still show them how to die.

"There is one thing that has a funny ring. People who know what I am here for keep talking about my future. They are either fools or I will be departed by the time this reaches you ...

"Dad has been overeating again. He had a vision that the governor would commute my sentence to life and I would be out in a few years. I think you had better write and give the old boy a few instructions regarding his diet.

"The following is something I want you to remember and keep, it is simple and easy. This is it: Of killing, I am guilty, of murder, actual murder, I am not guilty.

"This note runs and jumps around like my mind is doing. I am rambling at large because I can't seem to think of anything of importance to say.

"I sure would like to write some of the experiences and

incidents I have had occur to me in the last three or four years. They would bring a million bucks, all put in fiction form. The time is now two p.m. I have less than twelve hours to go if things go like I figure they will.

"I have messed around all over the cockeyed country, and had a little fun, not too much, however. I think I could stand a little more: so it is like I said, I am going to take no chances on the next life."

The third letter was to a southern Indiana woman who had taken an interest in Smith's spiritual welfare:

"Dear Friend,

May your soul rest in peace and be not disappointed, for I have taken said red gentleman by the tail and kicked him hence and thither. For that matter, I have believed in our God and his Son all along; but I have broken, I think every commandment with the exception of one.

"However, it is like I said before, it is not my way to write entire religious scriptures to the people who have taken an interest in my welfare, spiritually or otherwise. I try to come as near as possible to saying what I mean when I write. I do not care for dandy words or fancy grammar unless there is an occasion for it. I have a grim sense of humour that is much too often taken as being serious. Like as before, I try to stick to ordinary stuff that people can read and understand because fine speeches is not becoming a fool; — me, I mean ...

"During the round of things I made a few wild charges against different parties here and there, some were correct, some were not. I would like to withdraw the charges I made against the American Legion in general, and cut it down to a few witnesses who slammed their souls into hell during the trial.

"That they lied has been proven beyond a reasonable doubt. Also that whether I was afraid of the chair has been proven too. It was because I may not be around when this reaches you. You people have scared me to death talking about hell and eternity and everlasting punishment.

"In a short time I will be knowing what great men are

wondering about.

"You might give Rev. B — my regards when you get around to it. Tell him and the rest of the people who were interested — THANKS! I'll be seeing them and not from a distance, I hope.

"The minister that has been up to see me has painted such a glowing picture of paradise that I sure would hate to miss it — not only miss it but run into a 'hell' of a lot of trouble below. I'll be seeing you."

I put the letters down, curious about Smith's perspective. He had killed, he said, but not murdered. Witnesses had "slammed their souls into hell."

Was there some doubt about his guilt? It seemed unlikely, but I made a mental note to draw him out.

At 6 p.m. two supper trays came over from the mess hall. I followed them into Smith's cell. As I sat down opposite him at a small table which had been brought into the cell, his face was strong and composed.

"Thank you for coming," he said, a faint trace of irony in his voice.

"I'm honoured," I replied, taking his cue.

He laughed, and we ate — mostly in silence. Smith ate casually, as though it was just another meal. I'm afraid I didn't, I picked at the tasteless food, silently damning a stomach that always knots up on execution nights. Smith noticed it after a while and said: "Buck up, deputy. This one won't be bad. I won't give you any trouble. I'll make it easy for you."

I shook my head slowly. "You can't. They're never easy."

"We can call the whole thing off," Smith suggested, the irony rich in his voice and eyes.

I smiled then. "It's okay with me — but I'm not the law."

"I know. It's the old eye for an eye. I kill a man so I must die."

It was a perfect opening for one of the things I wanted to learn from Smith. So I said gently: "You did kill Arlie

Foster, didn't you?"

"Yes," Smith replied readily, "but I didn't murder him. The fool reached for a gun. It was me or him ..."

So that was it! Smith, like so many possessed of criminal minds, was rationalising, drawing a fine line between killing and murder.

"And the witnesses who lied?" I asked gently. "They said you shot him in cold blood."

"Exactly! I didn't. It was him or me ..."

That was all I needed to know. The case was clear-cut and clean. Smith could never see it that way, of course. His mind had been twisted somewhere along the path of life. But I was more interested in knowing what went on in his mind than in trying to change it at this late hour. I shifted the subject.

"Ever since you came here," I told him honestly, "your good humour and don't-give-a-damn attitude has amazed everyone. Don't you really care about ... about what happens tonight?"

Smith forked up a last bit of peach pie and carefully topped it with a dab of ice cream. He put it in his mouth, added a final swallow of milk and gazed at me. It was a long moment, and he seemed to be groping for exact words. Finally he leaned back and said: "I won't lie to you. I care a lot about dying. I don't want to die. I hate to die. But I'm going to. There's nothing I can do to change that fact. So why weep over it?"

"That's fine — if you can manage it," I said softly.

"I can manage it," Smith replied. "I learned it as a kid."

I sensed that there was a story here and I probed for it. "What happened?"

"I was a harum-scarum kid, I guess — left pretty much to my own ways. I had a dog — a great dog, part collie, part shepherd. We were always together. One day the gang decided to hop freights. When I hopped on, Gimbo — that's the dog — got excited and ran alongside, jumping up at me. All of a sudden Gimbo made a jump and came down under the train's wheels!"

Even now, so many years later, that bitter childhood tragedy crept into Smith's voice as he talked.

"I jumped off the train and ran back," he went on. "I was already crying. A funny thing happened. A hobo hopped off the train too. I guess he'd seen what happened. He was a funny little man — small, hungry-looking and old. But he had the most piercing eyes I'd ever seen. He came up while I stood looking at Gimbo, cut in half and all bloody. He led me away and began to talk. I have never forgotten the gist of what he said. It went something like this:

'Your dog is dead, lad. It's over. It's done! You can never change the past! So why let it ruin the future?'

"He said a lot more. I was just a kid. It took me a long time to see what he meant. But I finally did see it. I learned from that day on never to look backwards, never to cry over spilt milk."

All of a sudden a lot about Smith was revealed. Here in a nutshell was the key to both his strength and his weakness. A man wasting no time brooding over the past is strongly equipped to face the future. But that philosophy also fertilizes latent irresponsibility. Man needs to brood over his wrongs or they'll be repeated.

Smith went on, proving both points as his life unfolded.

"After that I took things as they came. Our family had little. I managed one year at high school, then quit. I was sixteen, I wanted to work — but I was sixteen in 1932. There wasn't any work. So I took what I wanted — and didn't worry about it."

In Michigan, Smith got into a larceny jam. He did a short prison stretch.

"In prison I learned what a clumsy young idiot I'd been. I got a real education — how to hold a rod on a guy, how to plan a get-away, how to move from place to place quietly. I was smart, fast and strong and the cops were slow and dumb. Then that guy had to reach for a gun . . ."

"It always happens that way," I said slowly.

"I guess it does," Smith agreed. "I got away clean that

night. I was young and fit. I figured the cops would never get me. That was stupid. Someone had recognised me. I didn't know that. I drifted around a long time and almost forgot the killing. How could I know there was a 'stop' on my mug and prints all over the country?"

"Better men than you have made the same mistake," I consoled him.

We talked on into the night of little things. At 10 p.m. I left so that Chaplain Hall could spend the final two hours with Smith.

Back in my office I sat listening to the clock tick, wondering whether that strange, fleeting hobo had taught Smith a good lesson — or put him on the road to the electric chair.

Just before midnight I paid Smith a short, goodbye visit. His face was even more composed, and he smiled up at me from the bed on which he sat.

"Everything's fine," he said. Then with a quizzical smile, he added: "In fact, I feel better every passing minute."

I knew he spoke the truth. I had seen it happen many times before. The nearer strong men get to death, the calmer their minds are.

"You'll be all right," I assured him. Then I thought of little Jimmy Swain upstairs and added: "Don't forget that draughts board."

Smith smiled, grateful for the easy talk. "I won't," he said. "And I'll ask St. Peter if I can't come down and knock on your desk tomorrow to let you know everything is okay. You tell Jimmy!"

"I'll tell him."

A few moments later we executed John Dee Smith. Next day the newspaper stories said: "Unconcerned and uncaring, John Dee Smith died in the electric chair . . ."

I wondered if he could see them. I could never be sure. He didn't knock on my desk the next morning.

More Death Row experiences of former Deputy Warden L. C. Schmuhl appear on pages 97 and 245.

2

I WATCHED MY HUSBAND'S KILLER FRY

Clara Morris

"I felt nothing, only a dull, empty dumbness"

I AWOKE to hear someone pounding on my front door, pounding furiously as though trying to knock it down. Groping for my bedside lamp I switched it on and looked at the clock. It was after three on a bitter January morning.

The other twin bed, where my husband Raymond should have been sleeping, was empty. He had phoned earlier to say that he would be working late in the little drugstore we owned in Mena, Arkansas. The carbonator must be moved and he was doing the work himself to save money. He should have been home and in bed long before three o'clock.

Downstairs the impatient knocking continued. I fumbled my way to the door and opened it. A man stood there, warmly dressed against the icy wind.

"Where is your husband, Mrs. Morris?" His voice was gruff. Later I identified him as one of the two night policemen who patrol the streets of Mena, but at that moment I didn't know who he was. My voice trembled as I answered. "Why, he's working at the store tonight. But he should have come home before now. Has something happened?"

"Yes," he said. "There's been an accident at the store. I

think you'd better come at once. Better dress Johnny Ray and take him with you because you might have to be there some time. I'll go next door and get your parents."

That was all he would say. But I knew, with terrifying certainty, that something had happened to my Raymond.

My hands shook so badly I could hardly dress myself and our six-year-old son, Johnny Ray. The child was fast asleep and asked very few questions about being taken abruptly from his bed. In taking him with me to the store I was blindly obeying the well-meant suggestion of the policeman. If I had to go through the whole terrible night again, however, I would not take my child to see what he had to see that night. But now my nerves were on edge and I was not thinking too clearly.

The policeman hustled us into his car — my parents, who lived next door, myself and my small son. The policeman would tell us nothing, except to repeat that there had been "an accident." He drove rapidly. I held Johnny Ray tightly, his arms around my neck.

The car swung into an alley and stopped behind the Union Bank, next to our drugstore. We got out into the cold night. Lights were on in the store and a little group of men stood near the back door. As I approached the door I saw a hole in the glass, a splintered hole. I thought, it could have been made by a bullet.

I tried to push the door open. It went only so far and then stuck. I pushed harder and then one of the men present murmured something and helped me. The door gave a little and I slipped through. I stepped over the body of my husband.

I knew at once that he was dead. He was lying on his face in a vast pool of blood. Raymond was a big man, and healthy. I had never seen so much blood before in my life.

Stricken, I stood in the prescription room looking down at the body of the man I had loved, married, and given a son.

The screams of my mother and child brought me back to the living. "My God," screamed my mother. "It's

Raymond! He's been murdered!"

I took Johnny Ray into my arms and tried to comfort him. I knew that I must keep my head. I must stay on my feet and keep working. Through the babble of voices around me I heard someone say that the sheriff was on his way.

I went to the cash register and checked it. It had been shot open and all the money taken; a number of cheques littered the floor. About $72 was missing. Next I examined our small safe and found it had not been tampered with. Someone, probably someone who was drunk at the time or criminally insane, had murdered my husband for $72.

The criminal, or criminals had slashed at the pockets of Raymond's trousers. His watch and some change were gone. Vaguely I thought that whoever had done this must have been a stranger in Mena, or they would never have expected to find much money in our store. It had taken every cent we could scrape together to buy it and we were still heavily in debt. Now, as the first numbing shock wore off, I wanted more than anything else to know who shot my husband. I wanted to see them caught and punished.

One of the policemen said: "Whoever did this took your car too, Mrs. Morris. It was parked in front of the store. Could you give me the licence number?"

I gave him the number, answered some other questions, and then we went home in the cold grey of the dawn. How I could bear to return to our house, and to look at Raymond's empty bed, I don't know. Somewhere I found the strength. Our family doctor came and gave me a sedative, and mother tried as best she could to comfort me. The drug put me into a merciful sleep. Mother and I both remained in bed all day while neighbours took charge of Johnny Ray.

It was not until later that I knew of the manhunt which covered all of Arkansas and eastern Oklahoma. Throughout the states hundreds of policemen were on the lookout for the killer of my husband. I will tell it now as it came to me, through the words of friends and the police, and in the newspapers and over the radio.

Two policemen, Drew Powell and James Roberts, had discovered my husband's body in the early morning of January 24th, 1946. They were making their rounds when Roberts noticed that the back door of the drugstore was open.

The lock of the door had been opened from the inside and there was a bullet hole in the pane. Someone had obviously knocked out the glass, then reached in and unlocked the door. Raymond's crumpled body lay just inside. He had been shot twice, once through his neck, while the other bullet had struck at the base of his nose and penetrated his brain.

"It's Raymond Morris!" cried one of the officers. "He's dead."

The other policeman studied the bullet hole in the glass. "Looks like someone fired through the door first, then shot him again when they got inside."

Then the owner of a nearby filling station called the Mena police and complained that his premises had been broken into.

"Someone blew the door of the station open," he said. "Looks like they used a .38 and they knew how to shoot. They ripped things to pieces. Place looks like a cyclone hit it."

Chief of Police Gordon Cannon went to the filling station. He came to the conclusion that it had been raided before the robbery and murder at our drugstore, and suspected that the robbers had got nothing for their pains. The locks were secure on the petrol pumps and nothing seemed to be missing.

"Good," he thought. "The killer, or killers, will be short of gas for that stolen car and sooner or later they'll have to make a try for some, or start walking." He was positive that both crimes had been the work of the same criminals.

The bus station in Mena called and asked to speak to the officer in charge. When Sheriff Robert Hunter answered he heard a bus driver say: "I thought you people had better know about a black Chevrolet that's turned over out close to Y City. I didn't notice anyone around it."

A deputy sped to Y City, about 22 miles north of Mena, and called back to report that the car was ours. Now, at least, the police knew in which direction the murderer was heading.

While much of this was happening I was at home waiting for the sedative to take effect. I remember Mother saying: "They'll get them, Clara. Don't fret about that. They're sure to get them."

The state police phoned Mena to announce they were throwing up road blocks.

"We're putting up a block between Mansfield and Fort Smith," they said, "Nothing will get through us."

Then came a real break in the case. A few hours after the discovery of my husband's body, and still early in the morning, the owner of a Mena furniture store came hurrying to see the police. He reported finding the body of a man beneath his store. The premises were set on cement blocks and someone had apparently thrust the body of the man beneath the store in an effort to hide it.

Officers hurried to the spot to find that the man was not dead but only unconscious.

"Looks like he's been beaten over the head with a gun butt," said one of the police. "But I guess he'll live. Maybe when he comes out of it he can tell us something about who killed Raymond Morris."

This man, later identified as an ex-convict who lived near Mena and had been going straight, was taken to the local hospital and a guard stationed at his bedside. Doctors worked frantically to bring him back to consciousness so that the police could question him, but he was slow in responding to treatment.

Meanwhile the killers struck again. Sherman Caver, a butane gas dealer at Waldron, was the next victim. It was Caver who finally gave police the information that there were two fugitives, both young men and both armed.

He enountered them shortly after they wrecked our car.

Caver, a former state trooper, stopped his truck and picked up the two men. He asked them if they were hurt or in any trouble and at first they talked pleasantly enough. Then they rode awhile without saying much. Suddenly the older of the two, a handsome youth with hard eyes, pulled a revolver from his shirt front.

"This is it," he snarled. "Just keep driving and don't give us any trouble and you won't get hurt."

Presently he made Caver stop the truck and get out. They tied his hands behind him with his necktie and put him back in the truck. This time the older of the two gunmen drove. Soon they approached a tourist camp and the heavy truck loaded with 1,200 gallons of butane, skidded and went off the road into thick mud. There it stuck.

Caver told the police, "They left me in the mired truck and went up the road to the tourist camp. I heard them banging on a door and then I heard loud voices. They were threatening somebody, the way it sounded."

Delbert Blair was the unlucky fellow who answered the knocking. The pair stuck him up and took his money, a .38 automatic he did not get a chance to use, and his car. They made him get into the car with them and drove off towards the village of Ione.

Left alone, and thankful for it, Sherman Caver freed his hands and walked to a phone and called the state police. What he told them brought patrol cars converging on the neighbourhood from every direction.

By now, however, things were moving in Mena. Mother was called to the phone. It was the police. When she hung up she turned to me and said: "Well, now the police know who they're looking for. That man they found under the furniture store has regained consciousness and talked. His name is Arthur Smith and he's an ex-convict. He got drunk here in Mena yesterday afternoon with two acquaintances. Those two are the ones the police are after now.

"Smith says that when he was serving his prison term he

met a man named Eldon Chitwood. Yesterday afternoon Chitwood and another fellow, a kid by the name of E. J. Minor, came to Mena and propositioned him about committing a series of crimes. Chitwood wanted to start here and go to the west coast, making their living by robbery."

"I'm glad," I told mother, "that at last the police know who to look for. But is this Smith man sure that Chitwood and Minor killed Raymond?"

She nodded. "The police are sure of it. Smith claims that Chitwood beat him up and pushed him under the building when he wouldn't have any part of the crimes. They had been drinking all day and they were all drunk."

Mother went on to tell me what the police had said about Eldon Chitwood. Since he was 17 he had been constantly in trouble. Now he was 24 and wanted by the police as a parole violator. His family lived in Fort Smith, where he had served a term in a reformatory, but shortly after his release he was again arrested, convicted of robbery and kidnapping and sentenced to 21 years. Then he was released again on parole because he was a model prisoner.

I can't help thinking that if the parole board had been more careful my husband would be alive and by my side today.

"The other one, Minor, apparently has no criminal record," said mother. Later we were to learn that Minor was no man at all, but a 17-year-old who had allowed himself to be influenced by Chitwood.

The police now had Chitwood's description, his picture from the rogues' gallery, and his fingerprints.

After the two left Sherman Caver and abducted Delbert Blair they struck out down the road toward Ione, driving like madmen. Blair, who later escaped unhurt, said he had never seen such driving. "Only a miracle kept us all from being killed."

Soon Blair's car began to heat up. The radiator went dry and clouds of steam and smoke poured from the bonnet.

Chitwood, who was driving, turned off the main road and continued to push the car rapidly over a rough dirt road until he ran it into a ditch.

Leaving Blair, the two plunged into the heavy undergrowth bordering the road. Blair wiped sweat from his face and took his first deep breath in a long time, thankful that he was still alive. But he wasn't the last victim.

James Russell, who lived with his family on a lonely farm near Ione, was sleeping soundly when he was awakened by thundering knocks on his front door. Opening it, he found Chitwood and Minor. They had guns in their hands.

"You got a Ford out in front," Chitwood said. "Get your keys and come on. We're taking you and the car. And fill the radiator so we won't have any trouble!"

Frightened, but telling his wife not to worry, Russell obeyed. With him in the car they took off once more. Chitwood still drove wildly.

They had hardly turned onto the highway when the wail of a police siren sounded behind them. But Chitwood pushed the Ford to the limit and by taking wild chances he managed to pull away slightly from pursuing troopers.

Then he saw a police block ahead. He jammed on the brakes and the Ford slid crazily towards the ditch, fought back to concrete, then skidded and almost turned over.

Chitwood turned to James Russell as the car careered to a stop. "Hit the ground when you get out," he commanded. "There's going to be shooting. The cops are waiting up the road for us."

But there was no shooting. Russell did as he was told and crawled on his belly towards the police car that had come up behind. Officers swarmed everywhere and Chitwood changed his mind about shooting it out. He sneaked into the brush beside the road and got away.

The 17-year-old Minor, frozen with fear, sat in the car and waited for the police to take him. Two troopers, their guns at the ready, approached him cautiously.

"Come out with your hands up," one of them ordered. Minor obeyed and started walking towards the police car.

"Now halt," the troopers told him. "Who is in that car with you?"

"N-no one," quavered Minor. "Just me. Chitwood got away."

Bloodhounds were brought to the scene and went baying off through the woods after the killer.

I suppose Chitwood knew it was no use because on the evening of January 24th he gave himself up. Just about 16 hours after he had murdered my husband he walked into the jail at Van Buren and surrendered. He was unarmed, claiming he had tossed his gun into a creek. He said he was sorry for what he had done and that he knew it was no use trying to escape.

To say that I was elated or happy because Chitwood and Minor had been caught would not be true. For the boy, E. J. Minor, I could almost feel pity even though I knew he deserved all he would get. Where Eldon Chitwood was concerned I hardly thought at all, once the first spasm of hatred had passed. I knew he must die. I knew it was right that he should die. In society there must be laws and they must be enforced; otherwise neither person nor property will ever be safe.

During the first month after Chitwood's capture I worked hard at the drugstore and tried not to see the large brownish stain on the floor of the back room. Sometimes I felt almost at peace. Soon Chitwood would pay for his crime and I could begin the hard task of forgetting, of building a new life.

I was due for a shock, Chitwood began to fight for his life. He used every device the law allowed. It began to look as though he might get off with life imprisonment or even less.

Immediately after his surrender, on the advice of his lawyers, he pleaded not guilty by reason of insanity. He was given permission to employ a psychiatrist in his defence and was committed to the state hospital for observation. However, after 10 days Dr. A. C. Kolb of that institution said that Chitwood was sane under the law.

Another factor in Chitwood's fight to escape the electric chair was the state of feeling in the town of Mena. My friends and neighbours had rallied around me and offered me all their sympathy and help. It was largely through their efforts that I was able to keep going and to keep the drugstore open.

The murderer's lawyers, however, seized upon the seething indignation of the townspeople as an excuse to seek a change of venue. Chitwood, they said, could not obtain a fair trial in Mena. Their motion was overrruled.

Additional deputies were sworn in and remained on guard throughout the trial. One man who had been drinking was quickly removed when he stood up and yelled: "Let's get a rope!"

No doubt some of the people of Mena favoured a quicker and cruder form of justice for Chitwood, but I was glad that nothing of the sort took place. I didn't want it that way. I wanted justice done but I wanted it to be legal and fair. And so it was. Eldon Chitwood got more of a chance than ever he gave my husband. He didn't give Raymond one second in which to plead for his life, or to bid his loved ones goodbye.

So came the day, February 20th, 1946, when I sat in court and looked into the eyes of the murderer. Twist and squirm though he had, at last he was before the bar of justice. But of the two of us I am sure that I was the more nervous. Chitwood's eyes were hard and he was neatly dressed. Every strand of his dark brown hair was in place. He smoked cigarette after cigarette but his fingers did not tremble in the least.

The chief witness against him was his companion in crime. His words were enough to seal the accused man's fate in the mind of every juror.

Minor, looking like a boy who had never had his first shave, told the court: "Eldon didn't have to kill that man. He was drunk. We went around to the back of the drugstore and knocked on the door. The man came to the door but he wouldn't open it. He asked what we wanted.

We said for him to open the door.

"Again he asked us what we wanted. And a third time. Then Chitwood just backed up and shot him through the door. After we got inside he shot him again. Chitwood knocked out some glass and reached in and opened the door. We went in and shot open the cash register and Chitwood slashed at the dead man's pockets. He took his watch and some money and gave them to me."

The jury was out for only 50 minutes. They found Chitwood guilty and he was sentenced to death.

Two days later Minor went to trial. He refused to accept a prison sentence of 21 years, preferring to fight for complete acquittal, but this time the jury was out for only 13 minutes. The verdict was first-degree murder and he too was sentenced to be electrocuted, but this was later commuted to life imprisonment.

Mother and I decided that we wanted to see the act of justice carried out. We asked to be allowed to see the execution of Eldon Chitwood, but his appeal to the Supreme Court allowed him to cheat the executioner for a while and gave him new hope. And now an intensive campaign began, with me as the target, to beg clemency for the man who had so wantonly killed my husband.

I began to get letters from Chitwood. He begged for his life. He wrote that he was sorry, and that he had been drunk and hadn't known what he was doing at the time. He only wanted a chance to live and to spend the rest of his life in prison. These letters I did not answer. I had nothing to say to Raymond's murderer.

Soon relatives of Chitwood came from Van Buren to see me. They asked me to intercede and to ask for mercy for Chitwood. I told them I could do nothing. Next a minister who had known the murderer as a boy came to see me and pleaded for Chitwood's life. I gave him the same answer. But the telegrams and long distance calls continued through all the months until at last I was notified that mother and I had been granted permission to witness the execution. The Supreme Court had turned down Chitwood's appeal and he was to die on Friday morning, November 22nd, 1946. That was also the birthday of my son, who would be seven years old.

But until the very last, Governor Ben Laney was under heavy pressure from those who wanted Chitwood's sentence changed to life imprisonment. I sat down and wrote to the governor. Without hatred or bitterness I told him why I thought the death sentence should be carried out. Here is an excerpt from my letter:

"The reason I am pleading with you not to commute to life imprisonment the sentence of this murderer is so that in just a few years he will not orphan another boy or widow another woman. I am not asking for pity for my own broken home, but only for justice ..."

I do not know if my letter swayed the governor in his decision. In any case he refused clemency and on the evening of November 21st mother and I checked into the Marion Hotel in Little Rock.

Mother managed to catch a nap, but I found it impossible to sleep. I read in the Little Rock papers about Chitwood's last hours. One story said that he had found solace in religion and was quite ready to die. Although I wanted to see my husband's death avenged by the law, and that very moment was preparing to sit through a terrible ordeal to see it done, I hoped that Chitwood had indeed found his God. I hoped he was sincere in what he said.

Mother and I checked out of the hotel at 3.30 in the morning. We had toast and coffee and then a policeman came for us and we drove out of Little Rock towards Tucker Farm. It was deathly cold. Even through our thick fur coats we felt the cold, but more, I think, from nervousness. I wondered what thoughts were passing through the mind of Eldon Chitwood as he sat in his lone cell and watched the seconds tick away.

We reached the Farm and were admitted by a guard. In the dim murk of early morning the buildings of the penal farm, painted a drab grey, were like clumsy ghosts. We went to the superintendent's office and were glad to find a huge fire blazing in a pot-bellied stove. Around the fire a group of men were trying to keep warm. Most of them were newspapermen and they wanted to ask me questions. I answered as best I could and found that, strangely enough, my attack of the shakes had worn off.

Soon we left the office in a group and went to the death house. It was nothing more than a small shack. It was very cold, with no fire and only bare planks to sit on. At the far end of the room, beyond a curtain which could be pulled across to hide it, was the electric chair.

I had my first look at the electric chair, the state's instrument of justice. It was a plain, light oak-coloured chair with leather straps and electrodes. I understood that the curtain would be drawn while the prisoner was led in and strapped to the chair. About this time I began to feel a little sick but it soon passed. Mother sat close to me, holding my hand and saying very little.

A young newspaperman spoke to me.

"Are you nervous, Mrs. Morris? You look rather pale?"

"I was," I told him, "but I'm all right now."

He smiled. "Wish I could say the same. I'm as jumpy as a cat."

He went on to tell me about the meal Chitwood had eaten the night before. It had been a good one, he said, with steak, pie and ice cream. While we were talking a man pulled the curtain across the room, screening the electric chair. We heard them bringing Eldon Chitwood in.

They pulled the curtain back. The death cap was already on Chitwood's head. I wondered if his eyes were still hard, if he was still smiling as he had at the trial.

A young man tested the straps on the chair. There was a pail of water sitting by the chair and I knew they must have put water on the electrodes. For a moment there was absolute silence, then the young fellow went to the wall and pulled a switch. Water sizzled as the current struck Chitwood's body.

His head jerked back and his chest leapt forward straining against the straps. His hands knotted into fists and he turned bright red. He gurgled in his throat. After a few seconds the power was turned off and a prison doctor examined him.

The doctor shook his head. "This man is not dead."

Again the current was turned on. Chitwood, who had been lolling against the straps which kept him in the chair, stiffened and his head arched back. When the electricity was shut off this time the doctor pronounced him dead.

I looked at mother. Eldon Chitwood was dead. I felt nothing, only a dull, empty numbness. We went out into the cold, clean morning air.

On the way back to Little Rock we were silent. As we drove the sun came up and warmed the landscape. I remembered that it was Johnny Ray's birthday and that his father had promised him an electric train as soon as they became available. I would look for one.

3

AN ENGLISHMAN GOES TO THE CHAIR

Richard Devon

"A bunch of sick people ... acting like I was an animal, a sheep being prepared for the slaughter"

HIS GUILT was in little doubt. Nicholas Lee Ingram had committed a particularly brutal murder. What was disputed was the conduct of his trial, the means of his execution and whether he should die. In the media the American way of death for convicted killers found itself on trial.

The case against the 31-year-old British-born killer had been horrific. On June 3rd, 1983, 55-year-old John Sawyer and his wife Mary were at the dinner table in their log cabin on Blackjack Mountain, near Atlanta, when there was a knock at the door.

Going to answer it, Mary found herself confronted by Ingram, then 19. Brandishing a long-barrelled pistol, he forced his way in, ordering the couple: "Get back in the house or I'll blow your heads off."

After taking $60 from the husband he marched the Sawyers to some woods nearby. There he tied them to a tree and stuffed a piece of shirt into their mouths to keep them quiet.

Any doubt they might have had about his intentions was swiftly dispelled. "I like to torture men while their women watch," he told them. "It will take two or three days for your bodies to be found, and if any of your family finds any evidence to convict me, the most I'll ever get is thirty years. And I'll come back and get them."

The couple then endured two hours of torment from their drug-crazed torturer before he decided the time had come for their execution.

His first shot killed John Sawyer, but as the husband slumped against his bonds his weight pulled his wife down, causing the next shot to do no more than gash Mary Sawyer's head. She too slumped, pretending to be dead as she heard what she later described as "a popping sound" and realised "it was the air going out of my husband's body."

Twelve years later she sat at home awaiting the final sequel with her family and second husband. On Death Row for most of that time, Ingram was at last to be executed. He was to become the 434th person despatched in "Old Sparky," the Georgia electric chair which dates from 1924.

Appeal after appeal against the death sentence had been rejected. Ingram's lawyers had pressed unsuccessfully for a new trial. They claimed that unknown to his attorneys at the time, Ingram had been placed on a potent anti-psychotic drug and was under its influence throughout his court appearance.

He was also "the victim of a mean-spirited and vicious family environment," said his lawyers. His English mother had married an American serviceman stationed at Laken-heath, in Suffolk. The couple split up and their child Nicholas was devastated and eventually went to pieces altogether.

The fairness of his trial was also clouded by another factor. Ingram had not acted alone when John Sawyer was robbed and murdered. He'd had an accomplice who testified against him. An accomplice who was never prosecuted ...

But the last-ditch efforts of Ingram's defence team

succeeded only in prolonging his death-cell agony for a day or two. He had become the victim of a legal system which imposes its own form of mental torture, an ordeal more protracted though less intense than the horrific last hours John Sawyer had suffered.

But while Sawyer's final hours must have been filled with sheer terror, Ingram's were a mixture of fear and anger as he was buoyed up with hope one moment, plunged into despair the next as a 24-hour reprieve was succeeded by a 72-hour stay of execution which was then declared void.

During that time what was at first assumed to be Ingram's last meeting with his divorced parents turned out to be the penultimate one. He was to see them again, but on the next occasion his head had been shaved for his briefly postponed execution. It was no way to see one's parents for the very last time, and he was hopping mad about it.

So it wasn't a cowed and penitent prisoner who was finally escorted to the electric chair at Georgia's euphemistically named Diagnostic and Classification Center at Jackson on the evening of April 7th, 1995. It was a man who felt he'd been messed around enough, a sullen, bitter and defiant Ingram who'd refused his last meal.

Earlier, in a sworn affidavit, he had complained that his head and right leg had been shaved in preparation for the attachment of electrodes nearly 30 minutes after his 24-hour reprieve had been announced.

"Apparently at 5.55 p.m. my case was stayed," he said, "but nobody told me. They began seriously to prepare me for execution. It was devoid of humanity, a bunch of sick people who apparently volunteered for the job, acting like I was an animal, a sheep being prepared for slaughter."

His last request to his lawyer was to make known his "utter contempt for this whole system of killing people." And his final gesture as he sat in the electric chair was to spit at the warden.

But just as John Sawyer had died quietly, having little

option with the scrap of shirt stuffed in his mouth, so did Nick Ingram leave the world in a silence broken only by the slap of his back against the electric chair as his body gave a tremendous jolt in response to the first charge of 2,000 volts.

His fists tightly clenched, he then received a seven-second shock of 1,000 volts, followed by 208 volts for the rest of his two-minute execution.

Five minutes then elapsed in silence before two doctors examined the prisoner, pronounced him dead at 9.15 p.m., and his body was removed for blood and urine tests to ensure he hadn't faked death by taking a powerful sedative.

He had been entitled to nominate five witnesses for his execution, but he'd chosen just two: a former girl friend and his British lawyer Clive Stafford Smith, now distraught and in tears. Describing the electrocution as "barbaric," the lawyer said Ingram had "wanted to look forward to another life so he could look for something better because what had happened in this life had been so sad."

John Sawyer's widow saw things differently: "We begged for mercy and were given none. He was judge, jury and executioner, all in a matter of minutes."

She had hoped to see a change in Nick Ingram as he faced death, but on learning of his behaviour in the execution chamber she felt there had been none. His lawyer, however, revealed that Ingram had written a letter to her and her family, but he did not disclose what it said.

Nick Ingram was now dead, but his manner of passing wouldn't lie down. It reopened the debate about capital punishment. Was it necessary? Was it barbaric? Was there a better way? The whole process came under scrutiny as seldom before. To that extent Ingram had achieved something.

And for Mrs. Sawyer the execution had brought her peace of mind. "For years the spectre of this case has hung over me, but at last, I can now get on with my life."

4

HORROR IN THE COUGHING BOX

Brian Marriner

"... As his body seemed to relax, his head suddenly rose eerily ..."

WITH GRIM humour, convicts at San Quentin Prison north of San Francisco, California, call it the "coughing box." This macabre play on words says it all: it both makes human beings cough and acts as a coffin.

"It" is a green octagonal gas chamber, a steel vault with eight sides and glass windows for invited witnesses to watch the condemned person die. The only entrance is a rubber-sealed heavy steel door with a large locking wheel like something from a submarine. Inside the gas chamber are two chairs — in case of a "double event" — with thick leather straps to hold the thrashing body still.

San Quentin's gas chamber had stood idle for 25 years, even since the last execution in California on April 12th, 1967, and the state — which prides itself on being the most liberal in the Union — finally abandoned the death penalty in 1972, following a Supreme Court ruling that the death penalty was unconstitutional because it was a "cruel and unusual punishment".

However, in 1978 the voters in California approved the reintroduction of the death penalty, two years after the Supreme Court changed its mind and allowed individual states to resume executions.

In April, 1992, the gas chamber was overhauled, its chairs dusted ready for a new occupant: Robert Alton Harris, 39, sentenced to death in 1978 for the brutal murders of two 16-year-old boys. At dawn on Tuesday, April 21st, 1992, Harris was gassed to death. He was originally due to die at one minute past midnight, but a stay of execution was granted by a judge two hours prior to that. When this stay was duly overturned, Harris was taken to the gas chamber and strapped in at 3.30 a.m., but at the last second a telephone call provided a last minute stay of execution.

Harris — prepared to die and having said his last goodbyes — was removed from the death chamber and taken back to a cell until state prosecution officials could get the stay overturned. The temporary respite gained him an extra couple of hours of life, but it must have put him through unimaginable mental torture.

There can be no doubt that the execution of Harris was both repugnant and obscene; but before studying the officially sanctioned killing of this man, it is as well to examine in some detail the murders for which he was convicted and sentenced to death. They were far more obscene and horrific than his execution, but even so the state is *supposed* to be civilized and deliberate, its actions moderated by law and decency.

Harris was a callous psychopath who acted like an animal. For the state to lower itself to his standard of conduct is for society itself to become a psychopath. Set on death and revenge.

It began when Harris — still on parole from a jail sentence for manslaughter committed in 1975 — decided to rob a bank. He had served two and a half years in prison and was released in 1978 at the age of 25 despite warnings to the parole board from the Imperial County sheriff's department that he was "in need of psychiatric attention." It was alleged that in prison he had organised the gang rape of another prisoner.

Harris settled in San Diego, but soon grew restless. On Independence Day, 1978, he drove over to see his family in Visalia. The idea was for him to join in a family picnic. He prowled around, talking to his younger brother Daniel, then 18. He spoke to him about his plans to rob a bank, and the younger Harris was keen to take part. They stole guns from a neighbour, returned to San Diego, and put in some target practice.

Having studied the lay-out of the bank, the brothers set about stealing a car as their getaway vehicle. They drove to a hamburger restaurant in San Diego, knowing that the car park was usually full. The date was July 5th, 1978, just five months and 26 days since Robert Harris had been released from prison.

As they were attempting to hot-wire a car, two young students drove into the car park. John Mayeski and Michael Baker, both 16, planned to spend the day fishing and had stopped off to buy some hamburgers. When they got back into their car with their food, Harris walked over to them, pulled out a gun and pointed it at the head of the driver. Slipping into the back seat, he kidnapped the boys, ordering them to drive to a nearby reservoir. Once there, he ordered them out of the car, explaining that he intended to use their vehicle to rob a bank. The boys shrugged, instantly agreeing to report their Ford Galaxy as stolen.

Robert Harris told them to walk away, and they did so, but as they did Harris shot John in the back, and when Michael tried to run, he was gunned down with four shots after Harris had chased after him. Michael was alive when Harris got to him, and the lad pleaded for his life. Harris, however, cut him short. "Quit snivelling and die like a man," he sneered, just before shooting him in the head. He then walked back to where John lay and added the *coup de grâce* with a bullet to the brain. The grinning killer then calmly ate the boy's hamburgers!

Later that day Harris and his brother robbed a bank of three thousand dollars, but they were caught a couple of hours later after a witness had followed them and alerted the police. By a grim irony, the officer who arrested Harris was Steven Baker, father of Michael, who was unaware that Harris had earlier executed his son. Indeed, he had no idea at that time that his son was even dead.

In the court proceedings that followed Daniel Harris turned state's evidence against his brother in return for a six-year sentence. Of course, Robert Harris was sentenced to death.

The court which tried Harris — and the various appeal courts — knew of his past record; had studied the biography of the man prepared by the defence; and recognised the dossier as being that of a man destined to die strapped in an execution chamber somewhere. It makes interesting reading and may help answer the question about whether murderers are born, like a bad seed, or are turned into killers by their environment. Whichever way you interpret it, Robert Harris did not have a good start in life.

He was born prematurely in an army hospital at Fort Bragg, North Carolina, on January 15th, 1953, because his father — a drunken soldier named Kenneth Harris — had kicked his alcoholic wife in the stomach, sending her into labour. Sergeant Kenneth Harris was a strange, brooding man. He had won both a Silver Star and a Purple Heart in the Second World War, but he was not a soldier for peacetime. There were rumours that he suffered from shellshock.

His wife Evelyn was one of 11 children from a poor Cherokee Indian family in Oklahoma. She took her first drink at the age of eight, and never stopped drinking thereafter. As a teenager she picked cotton to pay for her booze. In adulthood she became a wild and vicious drunk.

Robert was the fifth of her nine children, and appeared backward. A loner from the start, he spent hours talking to himself or imaginary friends, saying that he had visits from mystical Indians and flying saucers.

Defence experts claimed that Harris was born suffering brain damage through foetal alcohol syndrome — the absorption of alcohol through the mother's blood. His father hated him. Kenneth Harris was convinced Robert was conceived while his wife was having an affair, and he reserved his special abuse for the boy.

Sergeant Harris was discharged from the army in October, 1962, taking the family to live at a farm labour camp outside the town of Visalia, California. By Christmas of that year their eldest daughter Barbara was arrested for theft. Once in Juvenile Hall, she revealed that her father had been sexually abusing his daughters for years.

Robert Harris was 10 when his father was sent to Atascadero State Hospital for 18 months as a sex-offender. Shortly afterwards Robert came to the attention of the law over the killing of cats, although he claimed to be an innocent bystander.

In December, 1964, Kenneth Harris became unusually violent and his wife sent for the police. He was sent to prison and the family began living as migrants, travelling to pick crops for farmers and living where they could. Meanwhile, Robert was having his own trouble with the police. At the age of 13 he was caught stealing a car.

In May, 1967, Evelyn Harris and six of her children moved into a small flat in Sacramento, California, living on social security. One day she and her boy friend and the four youngest children simply drove off, leaving Robert, now 14, to fend for himself.

Robert went to live in Oklahoma with his married sister Barbara for a time, but although she had enrolled him in a school, he was expelled after just one day. After one bitter quarrel he ran away, stealing a car and driving to Florida, where he was arrested. He spent the next four years in state reformatories where he frequently attempted suicide by slashing his wrists. He was diagnosed as being schizophrenic, and counsellors predicted that he would spend the rest of his life behind bars. In effect, he had been condemned while still in his early teens ...

When he reached the age of 19 Robert had to be released, the authorities having no power to retain him as a ward of the court. He was given 50 dollars and a bus ticket to Chula Vista, California, where his father lived. He got a job as a welder and married, fathering a son in due course. But by 1975 any rehabilitation was over. He was drinking heavily and living on social security.

Then in a drunken rage one night he picked a row with neighbour James Wheeler. After beating him with his fists Harris sprayed lighter fluid on him and set fire to him. Wheeler died as a result of his burns and Harris pleaded guilty to manslaughter, serving two and a half years in prison — from where he was released to kill two young boys ...

That is the bare bones of Robert Alton Harris's story. There is nothing memorable about him, nothing that deserves a few pages of newsprint — except that he was the first man to be executed in California for many years, the first in a long line of men and women sitting on San Quentin's Death Row.

He marks the moment when a liberal state took the same route taken much earlier by a number of "red-neck" Southern states — the easy route to solving their problems — the short walk to a death chamber.

There are 328 prisoners currently sitting on San Quentin's Death Row alone; 2,547 men and 40 women in the entire American nation. If they were to be executed at the rate of one a day it would take seven years — taking us almost to the turn of the century. It is a daunting thought. But before examining the arguments and controversy surrounding the death penalty — and already knowing something of the man through his brief biography — let us see how Robert Alton Harris met his death at the hands of the state.

He was set to die in 1990, but was saved by an appeal barely 12 hours before his scheduled execution. Then in April, 1992, as his hour of execution approached once more, the Civil Liberties Union got a District Court judge to order a 10-day stay of execution, arguing that gassing was a "cruel and unusual punishment."

Prosecutors responded with frantic efforts to get a Sunday hearing before three appeal judges to overturn the order. They were even prepared to apply for an alternative method of execution — shooting, the electric chair or lethal injection if all else failed — and they succeeded in getting the District Court's order quashed.

By April 20th, crowds had gathered outside the prison awaiting the execution. They kept a ghoulish vigil, chanting protests and singing hymns. There were clashes between pro and anti-capital punishment factions, hot-dog vendors were kept busy, as were ice-cream sellers; many local residents rented rooms in their houses to TV crews, and hotels advertised "special execution rates" for guests. One TV station wanted to broadcast the execution live. The only quiet place was on Death Row itself, where the inmates waited in uneasy silence for the outcome.

Harris had been scheduled to die at one minute past midnight on April 22nd. He ordered his last meal of fried chicken and two pizzas, cola and jelly beans. It was the end of 13 years, one month and seven days battling against his sentence of death, which had resulted in four stays of execution.

Many prominent people had been persuaded to seek clemency for him. Mother Theresa had phoned the state governor, having met Harris during a 1987 visit to San Quentin; other celebrities — including Jesse Jackson — had written letters begging for clemency. But polls showed that 80 per cent of Californian voters backed the death penalty. It would have been political suicide for the Governor, Pete Wilson, to have saved Harris.

At 8.15 p.m. Harris ate his last meal. Then, with less than two hours to go, 10 of the 28 judges on the 9th Circuit Court of Appeals ordered a stay of execution, followed shortly afterwards by a second stay. The time for Harris's execution passed. Then, soon after 2.30 a.m., the Supreme Court overturned the stays. An hour later Harris walked to the gas chamber.

Despite a Supreme Court ruling in 1976 allowing executions, at the time Harris was put to death only 168 had been carried out by 18 states. But by the summer of 1999 more than 550 executions had taken place. However, with the death penalty then on the law books in 36 states, opponents of capital punishment feared that the California decision could act as a trigger. Linda Hunt of the American Civil Liberties Union said: "There is something different about an execution in California. It tells the rest of the country it is all right to open the floodgates and accelerate the marches to the death chambers."

Fifteen minutes before he was due to die, Harris changed into his execution clothing: new denim trousers and a blue prison shirt. A heart monitor was attached to his chest to pinpoint the exact time of death and he was led from the "death watch cell" next to the gas chamber itself and into the room containing the chamber. A group of witnesses stood watching as he joked with guards, winked at witnesses and put on a brave face. The 49 witnesses included the prison warden, chaplain, lawyers and journalists, the relatives of Harris's victims and his own invited relatives.

Police officer Steve Baker was there with his wife and daughter. Also present was Harris's older brother Randy and a couple of his friends. Basically, the witnesses comprised two groups: those who were there to see "revenge" done, the others to let Harris know that someone still loved him.

Harris walked erect into the gas chamber, which is six feet in diameter and eight feet in height and has five windows for the witnesses to view the execution. This was to be the 195th execution in that pitiless steel box since it was built in 1938. The last man gassed there — Aaron Charles Mitchell — had to be dragged screaming to the chair. He took 12 minutes to die. Harris, however, walked the 13 steps from his cell to the chamber unassisted, a guard lightly holding one arm. He then sat passively in the chair as guards strapped him in. The mechanism which would release cyanide pellets into a container holding a mixture of water and sulphuric acid was ready. The resulting gas, smelling of rotten eggs, takes eight to 12 minutes to kill a human being.

At 3.51 a.m., just as the cyanide pellet was about to drop into the bowl of acid, the telephone rang. It was a last-minute stay of execution, the fourth of the night. One witness, a woman, lowered her head and murmured: "Oh, my God."

For 10 minutes Harris sat in the chair looking puzzled, staring around him. Once he mouthed the words: "Let's pull it" — meaning the lever which drops the cyanide pellets into the acid. At 4.01 a.m. three guards unstrapped him and took him back to the death watch cell, where he watched TV and smoked his last cigarettes.

Prosecution officials made frantic attempts to get the stay overturned, because their death warrant was due to expire at midnight that day, and it could take anywhere up to 40 days to get another one. They were successful, the stay was overturned. To ensure that Harris died on the appointed day, the Supreme Court — by a majority 7 to 2 decision — took the unusual step of ordering that no more stays should be issued except by the Supreme Court.

Two hours later Harris walked back into the gas chamber, this time looking grim, almost sad. "He seemed to be making a great effort to die well," said one witness.

Harris had been advised by his executioners to take deep breaths to ensure a speedy end. When Barbara "Babs" Graham entered the gas chamber in June, 1955, and was told it was best to take deep breaths, she retorted, "How the hell would you know?"

Harris was strapped in the chair, the stethoscope taped to his chest, then the air-tight door closed. The cyanide pellets dropped into the diluted sulphuric acid reservoir beneath the chair and the death chamber quickly filled with cyanide gas.

Harris took a number of deep breaths, and for several

minutes he gasped and twitched convulsively. Prison officials estimated that he took *11 minutes* to die. The pellets had dropped at 6.10 a.m. and he was pronounced dead at 6.21. Witnesses gave estimates varying between two and seven minutes for the time he took to pass into unconsciousness.

Michelle Locke, a reporter with Associated Press, said: "It seemed as if he was trying to inhale the gas and get it over with. He seemed to want to die his way, to have some sort of control."

Police officer Steve Baker, whose son Harris had murdered, stood with his arms folded less than six feet from the gas chamber, staring intently at the condemned man. "Justice was served," he said afterwards.

But other reporters present described the execution as a disgusting spectacle. TV reporter Michael Tuck gave a graphic account. He watched Harris gurgle and gasp for life as the cyanide gas choked the life out of him. "He looked at his family when he was brought in and mouthed the words, 'I'm all right.' Then he winked at a guard. We heard he had broken down and cried to a guard shortly before he was tied to the chair with leather straps, but there was no sign of that on his face.

"He looked calm and composed — resigned to his fate as the fumes filled the chamber. His head twitched from side to side and he breathed frantically, gasping for air — breathing the way a woman in labour might breathe. He began drooling and after a few seconds his head fell forward on his chest.

"I knew I was watching a man die in front of my eyes, but it felt like a dream. I had to insulate myself from what was going on. I think he was unconscious within a couple of minutes, but if you asked me, I would say that that was not a clean, humane way to die."

This was how reporter Dan Morain described what he saw:

"Harris gave the thumbs-up sign ... the pellets dropped and the colourless gas seeped in and Harris inhaled four or five times. His head snapped back and then dropped as he strained against the straps. After a minute his hands appeared relaxed. His mouth was wide open and his face flushed, then turned almost purple.

"Whether he was in pain, unconscious or numb, he seemed oblivious two minutes into his execution. But as his body seemed to relax, his head suddenly rose eerily . . . Three minutes later there was a cough and a convulsion. Harris's balding head was visible as was his tightly-banded pony tail."

The reporter concluded that 15 minutes after the pellets fell a prison spokesman announced: "Warden Vasquez declares condemned inmate Harris, B-66883, dead."

The actual cause of death from cyanide gassing is known as hypoxia — the cutting-off of oxygen to the brain. During the gassing process itself, Harris's eyes would bulge and his skin turn a purple colour. After death, an exhaust fan was switched on to draw the poison fumes from the chamber, while his corpse was sprayed with ammonia to neutralise the gas. Then, the last stage of what is laid down as "Procedure 769," orderlies wearing gas masks and rubber gloves entered the death chamber to ruffle Harris's hair to remove any trapped cyanide fumes. Then they unstrapped him and removed his corpse.

The prison warden, Mr. Daniel Vasquez, said that Harris's last words to him were: "You can be a king or a street-sweeper, but everyone dances with the Grim Reaper."

The entire event was meticulously recorded by a video camera, so ordered by a federal judge who had tried to block the execution on the grounds that it was a "cruel and unusual punishment." The resulting film was intended for study by judges who had to determine if gassing was the right way to execute people in the 1990's. If they decided that it was not, then California could have resorted to the electric chair, firing squad or lethal injection. In fact California banned the gas chamber in 1994 and opted for death by lethal injection.

At the moment of Harris's death, a local radio disc jockey told his listeners he would play them "the last sounds Robert Harris ever heard" — he then popped an effervescent fizzy tablet into a glass of water. Noisy parties were seen to celebrate the execution, much as they had when Ted Bundy went to the chair in Florida. These were not the attitudes of a civilised, Christian nation, arguably the most powerful, most technologically advanced country in the world.

Robert Harris survived both his parents. His mother died of cancer in 1981, and in 1989 his father shot himself.

The relatives of the victims predictably had no pity in their hearts for Harris. The mother of Michael said: "I've no sympathy for Harris and I doubt that his Maker has either. He needed to die. My son and his best friend were innocents with the best years of their lives ahead of them when they were executed by this beast. This nation has illiterate and underfed children in its ghettos, people on welfare lines. The money that was spent keeping Harris alive would have been better spent on them."

All this is quite true — but it is not the whole truth. It ignores the public demand for revenge. It ignores the fact that America is the only major democracy moving *backwards* to the death penalty; all others having abandoned it long ago.

Some will say that America is a particularly violent nation and needs capital punishment, but statistics show that the threat of execution has never been a deterrent. Indeed, many killers have *demanded* the death penalty — Gary Gilmore was not unique in that, Carl Panzram having made the same demand decades before — and there is evidence that some killers commit murder as a form of suicide, lacking the courage to kill themselves but knowing that the state will do it for them.

Then there is the bizarre fact that such notorious killers as Charles Manson, Sirhan Sirhan and the Hillside Strangler were allowed to watch news of Harris's execution on their prison TVs. The first thing America does is to demonise their criminals because it makes it that much easier to kill them. But it has spared worse demons than Harris, making the application of the death penalty arbitrary and unfair.

The most unfair aspect of execution in America is that there is such a large span of years between sentence and execution. Harris waited almost 14 years on Death Row; Caryl Chessman waited 12 years, writing several best-selling books in the process. After such a long wait the man you execute is not the man who committed the crime. By contrast, in Britain the period between sentence and execution was usually just weeks.

The worst thing about state executions is that as well as demonising the criminal, paradoxically they tend to mythologise the killer, giving him an undeserved status and fame, almost making him a hero.

So, even if the public cry out for revenge with all the fervour of Old Testament retribution — an eye for an eye — surely they must realise that Harris died far more quickly and in greater comfort than his victims? Death came too quickly for what he did. It would have been far more cruel — and civilised — to have let him rot behind bars for the rest of his life, feeling his soul shrivel as the years passed until he prayed for a quick death. Because life behind bars — and I mean life — is far worse than any death penalty.

Harris was failed by his parents, who beat him and ignored him and showed him the power of the gun. Long experience and research has shown conclusively that abused children become abusers in turn. Harris was failed by the reformatories and prisons in which he was incarcerated, but in the end, even his own society failed him. It sank to his level ...

5

ON DEATH ROW WITH JESSE BISHOP

Joseph L. Koenig

"I'd rather they kill me and feed me to the maggots than spend the rest of my life in prison"

BECAUSE a light head often leads to a light wallet, the more successful Las Vegas casinos usually offer free drinks to their customers. Downtown, where the older hotels are, the complimentary cup is usually filled with punch or a watered highball. In the heart of the Strip, where the newer and gaudier gambling emporia beckon for the vacationing dollar in a pulsating sea of neon, the stakes are higher, the competition is stiffer and the come-on is likely to be a glass of champagne. The El Morocco, vying with the mammoth Stardust just across the street and just a bit too close for comfort to the famed Sahara, offers the bubbly to everyone who passes through the doors.

Although not much of a gambler, 22-year-old David Ballard from Baltimore, Maryland, chose the desert city as the site for his wedding. Ballard, who was just starting out in life and did not have the money for a fancy ceremony, was smart enough to perceive that Las Vegas was the ideal honeymoon spot for someone in his financial position. Free drinks and champagne, he knew, were only the tip of the iceberg. To keep the gamblers happy and spending their money freely, most of the big hotels offered gourmet meals at coffee shop prices, plus luxury Hollywood entertainment on a cheap ticket.

To make life as easy for prospective spouses as for gamblers, the city fathers had decreed that there be no waiting period for marriage licences. These are available in Las Vegas 24 hours a day, seven days a week.

When Ballard and his fiancee arrived in Nevada on December 20th, 1977, they checked out the giveaways offered by the best hotels and then settled for the El Morocco. Within an hour of becoming spliced, the happy couple were honeymooning in the casino, toasting one another in free champagne and keeping an eye on the action at the blackjack tables. Both were so engrossed with the cards that they did not see the slender man wearing a bushy wig push a gun through the bars of the cashier's cage until the thoroughly frightened woman cashier suddenly screamed out.

"What's the matter?" the pit boss demanded. He was in his spot behind a row of well-thronged blackjack tables.

"We're being robbed!" the woman yelled back from inside her cage.

It was only then that the pit boss noticed the man in the bushy wig. Failing to see the weapon in his hand, he made a dash for the cashier's cage.

"Look out! He's got a gun!" a change girl cried out from her vantage point at a booth only eight feet away from the stranger.

Her words fell on deaf ears. The pit boss was already on top of the robber and grappling with him for his weapon. As the two men fell to the floor, the gun went off and the pit boss, seriously wounded, relinquished his grip on the stranger. David Ballard, racing towards the pair to assist the casino employee, stopped dead in his tracks at the sound of the gun being fired.

Ballard turned round and was actually retreating from the scene of the fight when he was spotted by the gunman. Although the young newlywed was no longer a threat to him, the bandit levelled his weapon and fired. Ballard, too, crumpled to the floor, a bullet lodged deep in his back.

As the casino erupted in pandemonium, the stranger in the bushy wig scooped up a few bills that the cashier had dropped on the floor in the confusion. Then the gunman was racing out of the door, sprinting to a waiting car and careering down the street.

A passerby on the pavement drew his own sidearm and squeezed off a shot at the fleeing gunman. His bullet was wide of its mark, though, striking the speeding car on the passenger's side and shattering the window.

Back at the casino, the first ambulance attendant to arrive on the scene determined that both David Ballard and the wounded pit boss were in bad shape. Because it seemed possible that one or both victims might die, the investigation was promptly handed to both homicide and robbery details. Homicide Detective Herb Barrett and Robbery Detective George Helm responded to the call at the El Morocco within minutes of the gunman's escape.

In his haste to flee the scene of the shootings, the gunman had left behind his wig. While Helm examined this valuable piece of evidence, Barrett began interviewing witnesses. The homicide prober was not greatly surprised to receive widely varying descriptions of the robber. He was much more intrigued to learn that a window had been shot out of the getaway car.

As word of the shootings spread throughout the Strip, a pit boss at the Frontier Hotel, across the street and a third of a mile away from the El Morocco, was coming off his shift. The news of the robbery had made a deep impression on him and he mulled the facts over in his head. When he stepped outside the Frontier and saw parked at the kerb a brand-new car with a shattered front window, he was certain that the police would want to hear about it.

From his position in front of the Frontier, he could look down on the Strip to the El Morocco, where a number of police cars were clustered. He could even see the mobile crime lab. unit. Without wasting any more time, he hopped inside his own car and sped to the El Morocco.

When Barrett and Helm heard the pit boss's story, they drove back to the Frontier to check out the damaged car. In the glove compartment, they found papers indicating that the rented car had been leased that day to 44-year-old Jesse Bishop of an address in Garden Grove, California.

"Find out if this car has been reported stolen," Barrett said to Helm. "I'll check and see if we've got anything on this Bishop character. If the car hasn't been stolen, I'd say he was our man."

A check with the rental agency turned up no indication that the car had been reported stolen or missing. Staff there recalled that the man who had rented the vehicle seemed to fit the general description of the El Morocco gunman. A more definite identification was impossible at that time because of the poor quality of the information received at the casino. The bushy wig evidently had done its job, hiding much of the holdup man's face from potential witnesses.

From California authorities, Barrett learned that Jesse Bishop had spent 20 of the past 25 years of his life in various prisons and mental institutions. During that period, he had admitted to no fewer than 23 armed robberies. The reputed heroin addict was on parole from two life prison terms in California.

"He's our man, all right," Barrett told Helm as they reviewed the case.

It was growing dark by then and both investigators were about to head for home and a good night's sleep. They had been assured that uniformed officers would be given Bishop's photo and that they would comb the Strip till dawn for the suspect.

Back at headquarters the following morning, Helm found waiting for him on his desk the report of a car having been stolen from the Union Plaza Hotel garage shortly before daybreak. He also received reports on the holdups of a couple of convenience stores.

"It was a pretty slow night," he commented.

"Yeah — except for that bit of action at the El Morocco," Barrett reminded him. "Any word on how those shooting victims are doing?"

"All I know right now is that the pit boss is going to pull through," Helm said. "But don't count on the other kid making it.'

Shortly after midday, the detectives were contacted by a woman who told them that, after driving into a grocery store car park at mid-morning, she had been abducted by a gunman who jumped out of his own car and forced his way inside hers. Then he made her drive around the city.

"He didn't seem to want to go any particular place," she told the officers. "I drove him into North Las Vegas and then he spotted this post office jeep. He made me stop my car and we both got out. The jeep was parked in front of a house and the mailman was making a delivery. When he came back to his jeep, the man shoved me aside, pushed the mailman away and drove off in the jeep."

The detectives later spoke to the postal worker. He backed up the woman's story.

At the grocery car park where the woman had been abducted, police found that the gunman's car was the one reported stolen overnight from the Union Plaza garage. The description of the driver, as supplied by the two new witnesses, was a perfect fit for Jesse Bishop.

"Let's get some men into the North Las Vegas area," Herb Barrett suggested. "We'll have them concentrate on the spot where he took the jeep. Maybe someone else saw it."

Before either detective could leave headquarters, word reached them that the post office jeep had been found abandoned by a patrol car crew less than half a mile from where it was stolen.

Just a few minutes later, at about 2 p.m. Wednesday, December 21st, Las Vegas detectives invaded the area to question local residents about the vehicle and its elusive driver. They came away from those talks with nothing of value, however.

While police hunted for Jesse Bishop throughout the city that afternoon, executives of the local United Parcel Service were quite concerned about one of their drivers. The man had failed to return his truck to his garage at the end of the shift. And neither had he phoned in to explain his absence. Worried that something serious had happened to the usually reliable worker, his employers reported him missing to the police. His whereabouts remained a mystery until 6 o'clock, when he suddenly turned up at police headquarters in Boulder City, a sleepy community some 20 miles from Las Vegas, with an incredible story.

The driver told Boulder City police that he had been abducted in his own truck by a man who he had seen earlier in the afternoon driving erratically in a post office jeep. The man had produced a gun and demanded to be driven about, though he apparently had no particular destination in mind.

"I knew who he was when he said he blew away a guy that tried to be a hero in the El Morocco casino the night before," the driver said. "I read the newspapers and I listen to the news on TV. I told him that, as long as he had the gun, the truck was going to go wherever he wanted to."

The driver told police that the gunman appeared to be highly paranoid and believed that every passing car was an unmarked police vehicle. It was the driver's opinion that his captor was convinced he was going to die in a police shootout some time that night and was eager for darkness, so that he would be able to see the flash of fire from police guns and know where to shoot back.

"I took him out to Hoover Dam (formerly Boulder Dam), at his request," the driver said. "When it got dark, he told me to slow down. Then he jumped out and disappeared into the brush."

Detectives Barrett and Helm were still at their desks when the report from Boulder City authorities reached them.

"If he thinks there's going to be a shootout, he probably won't leave the area," Barrett reasoned. "He'll probably stay right there to make his last stand. I don't think we'll have to worry about him slipping away from us any more."

Early that Wednesday evening, a group of uniformed officers, as well as two SWAT teams, were dispatched to the area where the driver had dropped off the gunman. The scene — rugged desert terrain near Hoover Dam — was close to the slow-moving waters of the Colorado River, which serves as the Arizona-Nevada Border. All that night and into the morning, the Las Vegas lawmen hunted their quarry, but without uncovering so much as a clue to his whereabouts. Their luck changed abruptly, however, at about 7.30 a.m. on Thursday.

The desert sun was still low on the horizon when the lawmen found Jesse Bishop sleeping under a caravan parked in an alley between Birch and Arizona Streets in Boulder City. Although the suspect was armed, he surrendered peacefully when officers ordered him out from under the caravan. Returned to Las Vegas, he was lodged in the Clark County jail on charges of robbery, kidnapping, car theft and attempted murder.

But on New Year's Eve, when David Ballard finally succumbed to his wounds at a Las Vegas hospital, one of the attempted murder counts against Bishop was to be upped to murder.

Prosecution of Jesse Bishop on the charges lodged against him became the responsibility of Deputy District Attorneys Mel Harmon and Steve Gregory. They made it plain right away that they would seek the death penalty for the prisoner, should they achieve a conviction. Bishop, oddly enough, seemed eager to co-operate with them, for he pleaded guilty to all the charges against him, including the first-degree murder count. As a result, there would be no jury to hear the penalty phase of a trial. Instead, a three-judge panel would listen to evidence and then make the final ruling as to the prisoner's fate.

Under the provision of Nevada's capital murder statute,

the three-judge panel would be made up of one local district judge and two from outside the jurisdiction. The jurists selected for the February 10th, 1978, penalty hearing were Paul Goldman of Las Vegas, Merlin Hoyt of Ely and William Foreman of Reno.

Among the witnesses the judges listened to during day-long testimony were the cashier and change girl from the El Morocco, the wounded pit boss and Bishop's kidnapped victims. Prosecutors Harmon and Gregory were careful not to call to the witness-stand the young woman who had become David Ballard's widow after less than an hour of marriage.

"We've got more than enough evidence, without bothering her," Harmon had commented to Gregory as they prepared their case.

Bishop, who had sacked his public defenders, represented himself at the hearing. He called no witnesses of his own and did very little cross-examining of the prosecution witnesses. In his final argument, Bishop did not ask that his life be spared, but instead told the judges that society had made him what he was.

"A poor man never has a chance," he insisted.

After overnight deliberations, the judges ruled that Jesse Bishop would have to die for his crimes. Bishop, who had entered his guilty plea because he did not want to tie up the case in appeals courts for years, accepted the verdict by announcing that he would not fight it. At a brief news conference, he made it clear that he had no death wish and was not eager to die in the Nevada gas chamber.

"It's just something I have to accept," he told reporters from the jury box in Judge Goldman's courtroom.

"Do you have any remorse over killing the bride-groom?" a reporter asked.

"I'm not weeping or moaning over it," Bishop replied. "I'm sorry it had to happen, but he shouldn't have got involved. That should have been a police matter."

"Do you think the death penalty is an effective deterrent to crime?" another newsman asked.

"Did it stop *me*?" Bishop retorted.

Before leaving the courtroom, Bishop stood and thanked Judge Goldman for the courtesies the court had extended to him.

"I know you did what you had to do," he told the jurist.

The court services officer who had brought him to the courtroom from the Clark County jail on the third floor of the courthouse also came in for Bishop's thanks.

"He told me he appreciated that I treated him like a man — not an animal," the officer said. "I was just doing my job. If they don't give me any trouble, then I don't give *them* any trouble. He's a good prisoner, that's all."

Sentenced to be put to death on August 27th, 1979, Bishop told newsmen that he would go willingly to the gas chamber to "get it done and over with."

"I'd rather they kill me and feed me to the maggots than spend the rest of my life in prison," he said. "If you plan on being a robber, you have to accept this as an occupational hazard."

The setting of Bishop's date with death dictated an unusual amount of work for Nevada Director of Prisons Charles Wolff Jr. Wolff told reporters that, after trying to determine whether or not the sentence actually would be carried out, he had come to the conclusion that it would not. Nevertheless, he said, he would continue with the preparations, which included testing the chamber, obtaining cyanide pellets, selecting three prison guards to take part in the pellet-dropping, drawing up a list of witnesses and moving the maximum-security prison psychiatrist's office from the death chamber viewing-room.

Wolff added that although the American Civil Liberties Union was planning to fight the execution, the condemned man's family had agreed that "in no way will they appeal or initiate appeals on his behalf which would delay the execution."

He added: "If history repeats itself, the ACLU will be successful on the first stay of execution. but, otherwise, we're going along with preparations on how to handle things in the event it does occur."

"Can Bishop actually force his own execution?" a reporter asked.

"Well, the court is the only one that can issue an order and set a date for execution," Wolff said. "The inmate can only stop the appeals process, but the court has to issue the order for execution, as has occurred in this case."

Bishop, he added, "seems very determined that no one will interfere with it."

Wolff noted that the last gas chamber execution had taken place in August, 1961. Since then, the gas chamber had been used as a storage area and office. In 24 years of prison work, Wolff added, he had never supervised an execution.

On Tuesday, August 21st, with his execution date less than a week away, Bishop told reporters that he had recently passed a psychiatric examination giving him the "green light" to the gas chamber and was prepared to fight lawyers trying to halt his execution.

A federal judge, he noted, had fixed a hearing in Las Vegas for Thursday, August 23rd, on a public defender's petition to block his trip to the gas chamber and he insisted that he would be there to protest it. A prison spokesman confirmed that Bishop would be flown from the maximum-security prison in Carson City, where he was being held, to Las Vegas for the hearing.

Acting Superintendent of Prisons Howard Pyle told reporters that Bishop's spirits and appetite remained good. He reported that the condemned man was smoking cigarettes and eating big meals — such as Monday's lunch of corned beef hash and oysters. In addition, he said, Bishop was taking "light tranquillisers."

This hasn't changed me mentally," Bishop said. "I don't really give a damn about their gas chamber. I can think of things I'd rather do ... but the point is, I can accept this, too."

Although admitting that he would prefer a life prison term, Bishop added that he did not see how he could win a commutation of his death sentence and that he felt it would be more cruel to stay his execution than to allow it to proceed on schedule. Insisting that he was "guilty beyond all doubt," he maintained that he would not ask the Nevada Pardons Board to commute his sentence, because "I won't beg — and that'd be begging."

On Thursday, the federal judge in Las Vegas refused to halt Bishop's execution. And on Friday, the U.S. Court of Appeals for the Ninth Circuit in San Francisco, California, also refused to grant a delay. At once, attorneys representing Bishop filed an appeal with the U.S. Supreme Court, but there was no indication as to when the high court would act.

That evening, in an interview with reporters at the prison in Carson City, Bishop said that he had already made his final request to the warden — for his girl friend and a bottle of bourbon.

"The treatment is good — better than I expected," he said. "But I wanted my old lady and a bottle of Jack Daniels. They turned me down. That hurt me. I've got a pretty woman. When they take my woman and my dope away from me, it's pretty hard to enjoy myself."

"Are you afraid of being strapped in the chair in the gas chamber?" a reporter asked.

"I've never met fear," Bishop bragged. "I don't know what it is."

The following day, to almost no one's surprise, Bishop's date with death was postponed when a stay was issued by Associate Justice William H. Rehnquist of the U.S. Supreme Court.

"I expected something like this," was all Bishop would say to newsmen. "I expect the stay will be ruled unconstitutional."

Ed Taylor, Nevada's deputy attorney-general, predicted that the stay of execution would eventually be set aside. Bishop, he said, would then be flown to Las Vegas, where a court would reset his execution date.

Bishop's public defenders, reporters said, were contending that, before their client could be executed, a court must make a formal finding of mental competency. The last such finding was in January, 1978. Although Bishop had been examined recently by a psychiatrist retained by the state of Nevada, he had refused to see specialists representing the public defenders.

According to the ACLU, a prison official had said that, for "the last two weeks, Bishop has been living on enough tranquilliser to knock you or me out." However, after a three-hour hearing, the pardons board rejected a plea by the ACLU for a commutation of Bishop's sentence.

In issuing his stay of execution, Judge Rehnquist had instructed lawyers to file papers responding to six questions concerning whether a court should determine Bishop's present mental competency to waive his rights to appeal — and whether the lawyers who had sought the stay were entitled to be heard in the case.

The stay of execution didn't last long, however. Bishop was again sentenced to die, this time on October 22nd, 1979. When he asked for a one-week delay to take care of legal matters, it was denied by the judge. Bishop commented: "So be it."

At one minute after midnight on Monday, October 22nd, 1979, Jesse Bishop went to his death in the gas chamber at Carson City. As anti-capital punishment groups marched in silent protest outside the prison walls, Bishop spurned last-minute offers to file an appeal against the sentence. State Prison Director Charles Wolff said that Jesse Bishop was "tough" and "self-controlled" to the end.

Earlier, the condemned man had consumed the proverbial "hearty meal" — a filet mignon dinner, but without the bottle of wine he had requested.

6
TWO AND A HALF POUNDS OF ARSENIC

Jack Heise

A convention of coroners unearths a multiple murderer

They were Coroners Alvin Querhammer from McHenry County, Illinois, and Robert Babcox from neighbouring Lake County.

They had just attended a seminar in which the speakers stressed the importance of post-mortem examinations. A toxicologist had pointed out that arsenic is one of the easiest poisons to administer and one of the most difficult to detect. It is tasteless and can be put into most foods. The symptoms, depending upon the amount given, simulate a variety of illnesses.

With a large dose, the cause of death may appear to be sudden heart failure. Smaller dosages, given over a period of time, can take on the appearance of a number of diseases, depending upon which organ is most severely affected.

If arsenic creates the most damage in the lungs, it may appear to be arteriosclerosis. Damage to the bone structure produces symptoms of crippling arthritis. The organs most often affected first are the liver and kidneys.

"Without a post-mortem and tissue samples being tested by a toxicologist, there are no positive means to determine whether arsenic is present," the speaker said.

"It is one of the big reasons why, even with what may appear to be natural deaths, there should be an autopsy."

On the other hand, the speaker pointed out, arsenic is a substance that remains in the tissues, fingernails and hair of a victim and its presence can be detected for a long period after death — unless, of course, the victim is cremated.

As usual the seminar was followed by shop talk. Querhammer and Babcox were discussing the lecture given by the toxicologist.

"Have you ever had cases in which you thought an autopsy should have been performed, but wasn't?" Querhammer asked.

"I think we *all* have," Babcox replied. "In fact, I almost called you last autumn about a woman who died in McHenry."

"Called me for what?" Querhammer asked.

"You probably weren't aware of it, because the woman in McHenry died before my one in Waukegan. Do you recall a woman by the name of Mrs. Mary Lambert?"

Querhammer readily remembered the name. Mary Lambert had been a very wealthy widow. At 89 she had lived alone in a plush apartment. Querhammer couldn't recall the date [it was August 6th, 1980] that she had died in the McHenry hospital.

"As I recall, it was a bit sudden," Querhammer said. "She had been in good health for her age. But she went to visit some relatives and suddenly took ill. Because the death occurred in hospital and neither the attending physician or family requested it, there was no autopsy. But why were you going to call me about her?"

Babcox explained that, less than two weeks after Mrs. Lambert died in McHenry, her daughter Marion Mueller died in Waukegan. Mrs. Mueller, 69, had also been a wealthy widow. But, as in the case of Mrs. Lambert, neither the attending physician or family requested an autopsy, so the coroner's office had been involved only to the extent of recording the death.

"But I heard about her mother dying and they'd both been visiting Mrs. Mueller's daughter in Spring Grove prior to the time they suddenly took ill," Babcox said. "I wondered at the time if there might be some connection between the deaths — maybe food poisoning or something like that. And I was going to call you about it, but then other things came up."

Querhammer told his colleague that he wasn't aware that Mrs. Lambert's daughter had died within such a short time of her mother. He asked about the daughter and about the granddaughter the two women had been visiting in Spring Grove.

"As I recall, the name was Albanese," Babcox replied. "I had planned on calling them to see if anyone else had become ill. But then other things came along and it sort of slipped my mind until now. Yes, the name *was* Albanese."

"Albanese!" Querhammer exclaimed. "I wonder if we may be on to something ..."

He explained that the Albaneses were a well-known family in McHenry County. Michael Albanese had founded the Allied Die Casting Corporation which manufactured award trophies that sold worldwide. Their plant in McHenry employed a large number of people.

Querhammer went on to say that shortly before he left McHenry to attend the convention Michael Albanese had died on May 16th.

"I knew Mike Albanese pretty well," Querhammer said. "He was getting along in age — sixty-nine, I think. Yet until six months ago he was a healthy, active man. Then something hit him. He became crippled, then bedridden — and I heard that in his final days they had to feed him with a tube."

Querhammer said that his interest in the death was that, while physicians thought Albanese had stomach cancer, he wondered if his demise might have been caused by some chemical used in the casting of trophies.

"The reason I thought about it was that his younger son, Mike Junior, seems to be afflicted with the same thing,"

Querhammer said. "I saw him only a short time ago and he was on crutches and thin as a rake, just the way his father went."

"Neither the family nor the physician requested an autopsy?" Babcox asked.

"No," said Querhammer.

Legally he couldn't have a post-mortem performed without the permission of the family, or specific evidence to indicate that death had not been from natural causes. He said that since only Albanese and his son had been stricken by the strange malady, he had intended to wait and see if others working in the trophy-manufacturing plant became ill as the result of some chemical being used.

The two coroners discussed this series of events that might just be coincidental. But it did seem strange that the two wealthy widows had died suddenly after visiting the Albanese family in Spring Grove, the elder Albanese had been taken ill and died, and his son was now similarly afflicted. The coroners agreed to check more closely on the cases when they returned from the convention.

As a result, they learned that the large estate of Mrs. Lambert had been willed to her daughter. But when the daughter died it had passed to Mrs. Mueller's daughter Virginia, the wife of Charles Albanese.

The senior Albanese had two sons, 44-year-old Charles and Michael Jr, aged 34. Following the death of their father, Charles had become president of the company and Mike Jr. secretary-treasurer. There were rumours that the two brothers didn't get along, although they were making a success of the prosperous business created by their father.

The two coroners went to State Attorney Floro with the information they had gathered. They pointed out that someone might be attempting to wipe out the Albaneses in order to gain control of the family business and fortune.

"That's a pretty serious accusation," Floro commented. He was aware that Charles Albanese appeared to be the only member of the family in good health. He was a highly respected businessman, lived in a $200,000 home complete with swimming-pool, drove expensive cars and holidayed in Europe.

"If it happens to be true, it's also a pretty serious situation," Querhammer pointed out.

Babcox added: "We aren't pointing the finger of suspicion at Charles Albanese. He might even be next on the hit list."

"Which would bring it down to Albanese's wife," Floro sighed.

"Not necessarily," Babcox told him. "It could be another relative, or possibly anyone. We haven't any idea, if this *is* a deadly plot, just how far it goes."

"What do you plan to do about it?" Floro asked.

The coroners suggested that the bodies of Mrs. Lambert, Mrs. Mueller and Albanese be disinterred, post-mortems performed and tissue samples sent to a toxicologist. But Floro pointed out that this would be impossible unless relatives agreed, or there was sufficient evidence to indicate that the deaths had occurred from other than natural causes whereby a court order could be obtained.

"It takes more than just a suspicion that foul play may be involved to get a court order," Floro said. Then he suggested that he assign his top investigator, Robert Hrodey, to check on the information the coroners had uncovered.

Hrodey began by questioning the physicians and hospital attendants who had cared for Mrs. Lambert. He learned that she had been admitted to hospital suffering from stomach cramps, diarrhoea and vomiting. It had been suspected that she was suffering from food poisoning.

A check had been made with her granddaughter, whom she and her daughter had been visiting. The doctors learned that she had been there only overnight and had become violently ill when she returned to her apartment in McHenry in the morning.

The granddaughter recalled that the evening meal had

been Polish sausage and sauerkraut. It had been served from a common platter and no other member of the family had been affected. Mrs. Lambert had consumed oatmeal, toast and coffee for breakfast. She hadn't eaten again before she became ill.

The information appeared to eliminate food poisoning. Mrs. Lambert was in the hospital for two days before she died. The cause of her death had not been diagnosed. Because of her age, however, it was felt that she might have become ill from over-eating the rich and spicy Polish sausage and the gaseous sauerkraut, which in turn caused her to have a heart failure.

The physicians and attendants at the hospital were unaware that 12 days later her daughter was admitted to hospital in Waukegan and died there.

Hrodey went to Waukegan to question doctors at the hospital where Mrs. Mueller died. What he learned was a virtual duplication of the information he had gleaned at the hospital in McHenry.

Hospital personnel recalled that Mrs. Mueller had been very sick when brought in. It was known that she had been shocked and deeply grieved by the death of her mother. The symptoms indicated possible food poisoning. When the 69-year-old woman succumbed, her death had been attributed to kidney failure.

Returning to McHenry, Hrodey checked with the physician who had attended Michael Albanese. The doctor was frank in saying that he did not know what had caused the death of his patient.

"For his age, up until six months before he died, he was a strong, healthy man," the physician said. "When he first came to me he complained of feeling tired, listless and his bones ached. I told him it was probably because he was working too hard and suggested he take it easy for a while and let his sons run the business. I wanted him to go away for a while on vacation, but Mike wouldn't hear of it. His business was his life and he felt he had to be there to run it."

Whatever had afflicted Albanese, it became progressively worse. Joints in his fingers, arms and legs became swollen and stiff to the point that he could scarcely walk or hold any kind of utensil. It was thought at first that he might be crippled by arthritis.

The doctor said he suspected that Albanese might have been poisoned by some chemical used in his factory. A check was made. Nothing was found that could be blamed for his condition, and no one else at the plant seemed to be affected.

When Albanese became so ill that he had to be kept in bed and finally taken to hospital, where he was fed through a tube, the diagnosis had been possible stomach cancer. At the request of his family, however, there had been no autopsy.

Asked if the symptoms displayed by Albanese could have been caused by arsenic poisoning, the physician said that it was possible. However, it hadn't occurred to him at the time because Albanese had no access to arsenic. It wasn't used in his manufacturing plant.

Hrodey took the information he had gathered to State's Attorney Floro. The three deaths and the illness of Mike Jr, with symptoms almost identical to those that claimed his father's life, appeared to be suspicious. Yet there was no real evidence of foul play.

"All I can say is that Chuck, the older brother, is in good health and enjoying the money he got from the deaths of his wife's mother and grandmother," Hrodey reported.

He had discovered that prior to the deaths of Marion Mueller and Mary Lambert, it was known that Charles Albanese was in financial trouble. The family business was successful, but he was apparently living beyond his means. Virginia was his third wife and he was also supporting his two previous wives and their children.

Hrodey added that the couple had sold the apartment owned by Virginia's grandmother. It brought in enough to pay off most of their debts and finance a trip to Europe.

Floro frowned as he listened to Hrodey's report. "You

know what you are implying," he said. "But would a man, even in dire financial shape, poison his own father and brother?"

Hrodey shrugged. "I'm not saying he did," he replied. "I've just given you the facts. But there's one way we can find out for sure."

Hrodey suggested that they go to the physician treating Mike Jr. with their suspicion that his patient was being slowly poisoned. The doctor could send fingernail clippings, hair and fluid samples to a toxicologist to determine if arsenic was present.

Floro agreed. If it were found that Mike Jr. had arsenic in his system, the next step would be to obtain a court order to have the bodies of the senior Mr. Albanese, Mrs. Mueller and Mrs. Lambert exhumed. But even if arsenic were found in the bodies, the authorities would still be a long way from having a case in which anyone could be charged.

"It's one thing to suspect murder, but an entirely different thing to prove it," Floro told his investigator. "The number one thing for you right now is to find out where arsenic was available. And then we have to see if we can put it into someone's hand. Meanwhile I'll contact Mike Junior's doctor."

When the physician attending Mike Jr. was informed of the suspicion that his patient might be suffering from arsenic poisoning he was sceptical. He said he had not been able to diagnose his patient's illness, although Mike Jr. was complaining of feeling nauseous, having a burning sensation in his stomach and that his joints were stiffening so much that he had to walk with a cane. While these were symptoms of arsenic poisoning, the doctor found it difficult to believe that it could be deliberate. "If we *do* find arsenic poisoning," he told Floro, "it may have come from some accidental source — particularly if it contributed to the death of his father."

Nevertheless, the doctor obtained specimens from Mike Jr. These were sent to the Illinois Department of Public

Health where toxicologists found excessive amounts of arsenic in the samples they tested. They believed that the poison had been ingested in small amounts over a period.

The report was sufficient evidence for Floro to obtain a court order to have the bodies of Michael Albanese Sr, Mrs. Mueller and Mrs. Lambert exhumed for examination. Meanwhile investigation of the Albanese family revealed that the senior Albanese had left the bulk of his estate to his widow. The estate was estimated to be well over $300,000, plus a $200,000 life insurance policy.

"The widow is in good health," Floro told Hrodey. "So if Charles is our suspect, what would he have to gain from his father's death?"

Hrodey thought he had an answer to that. He had learned that Mike Jr. had talked to an attorney about obtaining a warrant to charge his brother with grand theft. Chuck had been secretly selling scrap metal from the manufacturing plant and receiving payment by cheques made out to him, instead of the company. There was also talk that Chuck had sold some of the company's products below cost to certain distributors, who paid him in cash.

"The way I hear it, that's been going on for quite a while," Hrodey said. "Maybe while his father was alive even — because I hear he kicked Chuck out of the company for a time. It may not sound like a big deal, but it could amount to thousands over a period of time."

"O.K., so we may have a motive," Floro said. "But where did the arsenic come from? How was it given to the victims? Those are the things I'll have to prove in court."

Hrodey shook his head. He had checked every possible source for arsenic in McHenry County, without being able to trace any to Charles Albanese. And as arsenic was used in numerous commercial processes and by farmers to kill rodents, it could have been obtained almost anywhere.

"As to how it may have been administered," Hrodey said, "they've got coffee in the executive offices at the plant and people often eat lunch there. Charleyboy could have slipped a little arsenic into some food if he wanted to get rid of his father and brother. And his wife's relatives both visited his home and had dinner before they took sick and died."

"That's speculation," Floro grunted. "What I need to prosecute a case is proof. We've got to find the source of the arsenic and then put it into the hands of the killer. Without that it wouldn't be worthwhile to even file a charge."

Floro received the complete report on the autopsies within the next day or so. It had been determined that Michael Albanese Sr. had 37 times the normal amount of arsenic in his kidneys. An examination of his fingernails indicated that he had ingested arsenic over several months in small doses. The fingernail test reveals the length of time arsenic has been in a body because fingernails have gradual growth. The tips of the nails show the early signs of arsenic and the build-up as it is retained in the system.

As for Mrs. Mueller, she had 300 times the normal amount of arsenic in her body. The toxicologists said she had probably ingested a large dose just before death. Mrs. Lambert had also ingested a large amount of arsenic shortly before she died.

On November 20th, 1981, Hrodey entered Floro's office. "I hope you've got something good for me," Floro greeted the investigator. "We're in a bind — and we're going to have to do something in a hurry."

Floro explained that he had just heard that Charles Albanese, his wife and his mother were leaving for a vacation in Jamaica. "Now if something should happen to the old lady in Jamaica, we're going to have a tough time following through on an investigation there," Floro said.

"And the way I heard it, they're leaving by plane from O'Hare Airport tomorrow morning."

Hrodey waited until Floro had finished and then a big smile came over his face. Floro, noting it, said: "I hope that grin means you've come up with something."

"How would you like two and a half pounds of arsenic in a couple of plastic butter containers and a baby-food jar placed right in the hot little hands of Charleyboy?" Hrodey replied.

"You got it?" Floro exclaimed.

"I got it," Hrodey said. "And I guess you'd best file those charges before Chuck takes off on his vacation."

Hrodey explained that after checking all the commercial sources where Charles Albanese might have obtained arsenic and coming up with nothing, he next checked companies with whom Albanese's firm did business who might have access to the poison. He eventually found a metal-finishing company in Wisconsin that used arsenic in its manufacturing process and bought scrap metal from Albanese.

When he visited the plant and interviewed the owner, the man recalled that Charles Albanese had asked to buy some arsenic from him in order to kill off some rodents around his home. He said he had given Albanese two and a half pounds of arsenic, which he had put into empty plastic butter containers and a baby-food jar.

"He can place the date and will testify," Hrodey said. "It was about three weeks before Albanese's wife's relatives came to visit him and then went home to die."

Because of pre-trial publicity in McHenry, the trial for Charles Albanese, accused of poisoning his father, his wife's mother and grandmother, attempting to poison his brother and theft from the family company, was held in Bloomington. It took Floro a week to present the state's case. Witnesses included the physicians who had attended the victims.

The doctor who'd had Michael Albanese Sr. as a patient described his frustration in attempting to diagnose the illness. "He took sick and steadily went downhill," he said. "It was an unexplained thing. We suspected stomach cancer, but the test proved negative."

"While he was in hospital and under constant care, wouldn't the effect of arsenic have worn off?" Floro asked.

The doctor agreed that this was a reasonable assumption.

"Charles Albanese visited his father in the hospital often?"

"He was there, hovering over his father every day — often several times a day," the physician said.

"So he could have continued to put poison in his father's food, even while he was in the hospital?"

Floro next produced a biscuit jar which had come from a shelf in the office of the deceased Mr. Albanese. He then called a fingerprint expert who testified that he had found the print of Charles Albanese's left middle finger on the top of the jar and his right thumbprint near the bottom.

The next witness was a forensic scientist who said that an examination of the biscuit jar had revealed traces of arsenic. He also identified a thermos flask in which traces of arsenic were found. The thermos belonged to Mike Jr.

The state's star witness was Mike Jr. Now almost completely recovered from the effects of arsenic poisoning, he testified that he had learned of his brother selling scrap metal belonging to the company and keeping the proceeds. He said he'd also learned that his brother was selling company products below cost to certain distributors and keeping the payments. He testified that he had planned to charge his brother with grand theft.

From the witness-stand, Charles Albanese told the jurors that he had been framed. He claimed that it was his brother who had poisoned their father and then taken arsenic himself, in order to throw suspicion upon him.

"He wanted me out — and this was the only way he could get me out," Charles insisted. "It would have been too obvious if he had killed me too. With me out of the way, when my mother died he'd have the whole thing to himself."

Following the testimony of Charles Albanese, Floro produced a surprise witness who had been in jail with Albanese while the latter was awaiting trial. He testified that Albanese approached him to ask if he knew of anybody who could "take care of some people."

"Did he tell you who he wanted taken care of?" Floro

asked.

"He said he wanted his brother and some guy in business up in Wisconsin killed," the witness stated. "He told me there would be $10,000 up front and twice that much when the job was done."

"Did he contact you about anything else?" Floro asked.

The witness said that Albanese had asked him to write and mail four letters when he got out of jail. The letters were to be sent to Albanese's mother, uncle, wife and to the Albanese family business. The witness added that Albanese gave him a copy of what he was to write.

The letters stated that there was a conspiracy to frame Charles Albanese for the murder of his father. "Charles's brother Mike used me to kill those people and set up Charles," the unsigned letters claimed. They also related that Mike had taken poison to divert suspicion from himself. "Mike almost took too much in trying to make himself look like a victim."

The jurors were sent out to deliberate on May 18th, 1982. They returned seven hours later to find Charles Albanese guilty on all counts.

Following arguments in which the prosecution asked for the death penalty and the defence pleaded for imprisonment, Judge Cowlin sent the jurors back to deliberate the penalty. It took them just two and a half hours to agree that Charles Albanese should be put to death.

Following the completion of the appeals process, the final sequel to that coroners' convention took place in Illinois on Wednesday, September 20th, 1995, when Charles Albanese was executed by lethal injection.

7

DEATH OF A CLOWN

W. T. Brannon

"Mr. Gacy is not an evil man, though he has done some evil things"

WITHIN HOURS of committing some of his 33 murders, America's most notorious serial killer would dress up as Pogo the Clown and entertain children. But on Thursday, May 10th, 1994, it was somebody else's turn to play the clown ... at John Wayne Gacy's execution. Mockingly, revellers painted their faces and donned clowns' attire as they partied outside Stateville Prison, Illinois, awaiting the death of the 52-year-old homosexual building contractor who on Death Row had managed to stave off this day for 14 years.

"Kill the clown!" the crowd chanted. And then, with news of Gacy's death: "The clown is dead! Bring us the body!" There were jeers of "Turn that frown upside down — they've just fried the killer clown!"

There was even an element of clowning in the execution itself, because for the officials in charge it went embarrassingly wrong. Gacy took 18 minutes to die by lethal injection, double the time the process should have taken.

"Gacy is going to die twice!" screamed another prisoner as 42 witnesses filed into the building housing the death chamber. As things turned out, that inmate's warning wasn't far wrong.

Seating themselves on plastic chairs in the yellow-painted viewing room, the witnesses — reporters, prosecutors, Gacy's lawyers and police who caught the killer — faced a plate-glass screen separating them from the 10ft by 8ft death chamber.

At 12.38 a.m. the blue curtains across the window parted to reveal the mass murderer wearing a blue prison shirt and trousers, lying on a trolley. Straps secured his wrists, chest, hips and ankles, his vast belly protruding between them — his last meal had been Kentucky Fried Chicken, chips, strawberries and Diet Coke.

One of the witnesses later said: "It was freaky. Gacy was grinning and smiling and staring up at the ceiling. He turned to one of the guards, winked and said: 'You can kiss my ass.'"

Earlier he had claimed he was a victim of state murder. "Taking my life will not compensate for the loss of the others," he said.

Standing two feet away from him in the death chamber were Corrections Department Director Howard Peters and Prison Warden Salvidor Godinez. Attached to Gacy's right arm was an intravenous line which led to a silver-coloured metal box on the wall.

At 12.40 a.m. Godinez picked up a red telephone to tell the executioners to activate the first of the three injections. Gacy swallowed and closed his eyes, and a thump from the box on the wall indicated the release of an anaesthetic, sodium thiopentone, to render him unconscious.

"Gacy grunted, his belly heaved and then he lay still," reported a witness.

It was with the second shot, pancuronium bromide to stop Gacy breathing, that things went wrong. The tube clogged, and the curtains were hastily drawn across the viewing window while a new intravenous line was fitted.

Five minutes later the curtains parted again. The second shot and the third — potassium chloride to stop the heart — were administered. A chalk-white Gacy now lay motionless. The curtains closed, and at 12.58 a.m. a doctor pronounced Gacy dead.

Prison officials said he had not suffered because of the hitch during his execution and prosecutor William Kunkle commented: "He got a much easier death than any of his victims. It was an easier death than he deserved."

It had been Gacy's practice to torture his prey before finally strangling it.

In a floodlit field outside the prison there were cheers from the banner-waving death penalty supporters, estimated at 1,000. A small group demonstrating against the death penalty had the candles they were holding blown out.

Twenty-three relatives of Gacy's victims had watched a TV screen in a basement room at the prison, waiting to hear the execution had been carried out. In contrast to the scenes of jubilation outside, the atmosphere in that room was sombre. The reaction to the execution was one of relief, mingled with tears.

"Everybody has lost today," said one victim's brother. "We lost our relative. His family lost their father. He lost his life. There's a lot of losing going around."

The father of Gacy's last victim told reporters: "We've been waiting fourteen years for this. In the back of our minds was the thought that this guy could sneak out of prison under some technicality."

A woman who lost a brother said: "I'm glad it's over, but I don't have anybody left. My brother is gone and it was all this that really killed my parents."

Neither those relatives nor Gacy's own family — he had two daughters from one of his two failed marriages — had been permitted to join witnesses in the viewing room. It was feared there might be a clash between the two sides, but in the event none of Gacy's relatives turned up.

For six years he had pursued his horrific career, and he would doubtless have gone on to kill even more than his 33 known victims but for police investigation of the disappearance of 15-year-old Robert Piest, a Des Plaines schoolboy.

It was on December 11th, 1978, that Robert's mother went to a local chemist's shop to pick him up from his evening job.

It was Mrs. Piest's birthday, and the family were waiting until Robert got home before cutting the cake at the party.

When Mrs. Piest saw her son at the shop, however, he asked her to wait a few minutes as he wanted to see a man about a construction job he'd been offered — a job that would pay a lot more than he was presently earning.

That was the last she was to see of Robert alive. Later that night a worried Mrs. Piest phoned the police to report his disappearance.

The following morning Inspector Kozenczak questioned Robert's school friends, and then went to the chemist's shop where he worked.

The pharmacist said that the last he'd seen of the boy was the night before, when Robert's mother had arrived to collect him at about 9 o'clock. He remembered that she'd waited in the shop while her son went on an errand. Then, a few minutes later, she'd left. The pharmacist had assumed she'd joined Robert outside.

Kozenczak noticed that the chemist shop appeared to have been renovated.

Yes, the pharmacist said, the interior had been remodelled and the work had been completed only recently.

Was there anything unusual about the work? Well, the pharmacist said, practically all the workers had been teenage boys or young men. The contractor had been in the shop several times while his boys were at work. On several occasions he had been seen talking to Robert Piest. The pharmacist gave the contractor's name as John Wayne Gacy, and said he was apparently trying to lure Robert away from his chemist's job. The pharmacist believed that the contractor had offered the boy much more than he was currently being paid.

Was Robert skilled in repair work? The pharmacist didn't know, but he assumed that he might be. Otherwise, why should the contractor offer a larger salary? Unless . . . Kozenczak shuddered at the alternative. He continued questioning the pharmacist and learned that Gacy's office was at his home on Summerdale Avenue in Norwood Township, a Chicago suburb.

He phoned the contractor and asked him to come to police headquarters for a chat. Gacy said he would come in early the next morning.

Several of Robert's friends knew about his impending employment by Gacy, as he had told them about the job offer. He was to see the owner of PDM once more before he accepted and left his position at the shop. Presumably, he had gone to see about the job on the night he disappeared.

His friends told investigators that "PDM" stood for Painting, Decorating and Maintenance. Most of the firm's work was remodelling — and most of the workers were teenage boys.

The following morning John Wayne Gacy Jr., 36, chubby, well dressed with dark hair, a moustache and a jaunty step, appeared at Des Plaines police headquarters. He denied knowing what had happened to Robert Piest, but he agreed to meet the officers again at his home at 4 o'clock that afternoon. And he was waiting outside when the police arrived.

The officers looked around the two-bedroom, yellow brick ranch-style house, but the only thing of special interest they found was a receipt for a roll of film to be developed. They kept the receipt, with Gacy's permission.

From Gacy's house the police drove to the Piest home. Shown the receipt, the Piests said that the name on it was that of a girl whom Robert knew. He had volunteered to take the film to have it developed and had been given the receipt. He'd also offered to pick up the developed film and give the pictures to the girl. So how did the receipt come to be in Gacy's house?

Detectives now began keeping the contractor under surveillance.

Meanwhile, Chicago police were asked for help and missing-persons' reports for the past several months were checked — especially those involving teenage boys.

Chicago police turned up some background information about Gacy. Born in Chicago on March 17th, 1942, he had enrolled at a business college after leaving high school. Having completed the business course, he moved to Springfield, the Illinois state capital, where he took a job in a shoe shop. In 1963 he met the young woman who became his wife the following year.

Police traced the mother of his two children. The couple had divorced in 1969, but the woman said Gacy had been a good father. She also said he was "a likeable salesman, who could charm it right out of you."

But, she added, he was "always trying to build himself up" and "occasionally did crazy things." She cited one instance when he was driving to work and joined the mourners in a funeral procession. A policeman saw him cut into the procession and ticketed him for a traffic violation.

In 1966 Gacy's father-in-law hired him as manager of the fried chicken restaurants for which he held the franchises. They were in Waterloo, Iowa, so Gacy moved his family there.

When investigators contacted people in Waterloo who had known Gacy, they were told that he was extremely popular. He liked to attend parties and to be the centre of attention. He also worked long hours, taking care of his father-in-law's fried chicken outlets.

In 1967, however, the district attorney's office in Waterloo began receiving reports that Gacy was not the jolly good fellow he seemed. One report stated that teenage boys employed at the fried chicken restaurants were often invited to parties given by Gacy, who served them whisky and encouraged them to engage in sexual activities.

"It wasn't just one incident," said Assistant District Attorney David Dutton, who was assigned to the case. "It was going on for a few months before it came to our attention."

So Dutton carried on a discreet investigation that eventually revealed Gacy as a classic Jekyll-and-Hyde character.

One boy testified that Gacy gave him whisky, then proposed a pool game in which the loser would perform a sex act. The teenager refused, so Gacy forced him into a bedroom at knifepoint, chained his arms and legs — and began choking him. When the boy went limp, Gacy stopped and unchained him.

In 1968 Gacy was convicted of sodomy and sentenced to serve 10 years in the Iowa state reformatory. His friends were stunned. "We couldn't believe it," said one fellow-businessman.

"Gacy did all sorts of charitable acts — sending buckets of fried chicken to the boys' club, doing Christmas shopping for underprivileged children — and was always ready to do a favour for a friend."

Gacy himself insisted that he was being framed — and many people believed him. "He was a model prisoner, a good worker, but you had to watch him — he wanted to be the boss," said Gacy's supervisor at the reformatory.

"He was quite a businessman," said another official. "He seemed to be a regular guy — not queer at all. I think all he really wanted was for everybody to like him."

Only 18 months after he entered the reformatory he was released on parole, but he was arrested again in Chicago in 1971 for picking up a teenager at the bus station, taking the boy to his apartment and trying to force him to engage in a sex act. A date for trial was set, but the case was dismissed when the boy failed to show up.

Gacy then bought the yellow brick house in Norwood Township. Shortly afterwards, in 1972, his parole term was completed, and not long after that he met an attractive young woman.

"He swept me off my feet," she said later. Married before, she was the mother of two girls. After she and Gacy were wed, his new bride and her girls moved into Gacy's home. She also moved in her furniture.

In 1975, around the time his second marriage broke up, Gacy started his own business — PDM Contractors. After the divorce in 1976 he continued to operate out of his home.

The contracting business prospered and Gacy hired dozens of teenagers and young men. Police found one man of 28 who told of going to Gacy's house to see about a job. He claimed that Gacy made a sexual advance and, when he tried to break loose, the man became very angry, screaming that he had a gun and it would be easy enough to kill him and dispose of the body.

The young man claimed that Gacy told him: "As a matter of fact, I have already killed some people." He said he didn't believe Gacy at the time.

Meanwhile, Chicago police were continuing their sifting of missing-persons reports.

On December 21st, Des Plaines investigators obtained a search warrant for Gacy's house and the property surrounding it.

After he admitted them, Gacy was accused of holding Robert Piest against his will. The police threatened to tear up the floor if Gacy didn't tell them where they could find the boy. Gacy denied that Piest was anywhere near the house.

But detectives found a trap-door that led to a crawlspace under the floor. As they bent down to work their way inside, they encountered the cadavers of three teenage boys — and various parts of other bodies!

The local medical examiner, Dr. Robert J. Stein, was notified at his home before the officers made any further move. Although it was now almost 10 p.m., he lost little time in getting to the scene.

There he pulled on some overalls and was shown the door leading to the crawlspace. "I opened the door and, my God, there was the odour of death!" he recalled later.

Letting himself down through the trap-door, he

dropped onto the wet, soft earth of the crawlspace. He turned on a torch and immediately saw what he recognised as human bones. First there were the skeletal remains of two human arms.

Stein came back up into the house and had the whole place sealed and roped off. Guards were posted all around the house and other buildings on the property. Then the pathologist drove home.

But he was back the next morning with some fresh overalls. He ordered the removal of the floor of the house — and then officers began finding the bodies. The first three were quickly removed for autopsies.

Bodies and bones were not the only things found in that crawlspace. There were various kinds of jewellery, items of clothing and loops of rope around the necks of the three bodies removed that day. All these might be of use in determining the cause of death, identifying the victims — and possibly helping to convict their killer.

The medical examiner had several dental specialists at his disposal and he hoped that dental charts filed with the missing-persons' reports would identify the victims. At the time he didn't know how many there would be.

That day, December 22nd, 1978, Gacy was questioned at considerable length. And he began to talk ...

From the time he became an adult, John Wayne Gacy Jr. had sought to gain the status of a big-shot in the business world. Yet his queer sexual urges had undermined that ambition. Asked by police if he was homosexual, he admitted that he was — despite his two marriages and his fathering of two children.

He revealed that during the past three years he had killed 32 teenagers and young men, after forcing them to have abnormal sexual relations with him against their will. Of these, 27 had been buried on his property — one under the concrete floor of his garage — while five others, including Robert Piest, were disposed of in other ways. So what had he done with Robert's body? He said he had tossed it into the Des Plaines River, a short distance south of Joliet.

Asked where the others might be found, Gacy said he would draw the detectives a picture. He drew a neat diagram of his property, marking the spot where he'd buried each of the 27. Most of them were in the crawlspace, four feet under the house.

After he gave the names of six of his victims, he was shown two pictures from the missing-person files. He said he didn't know *their* names, although they were among his victims.

On Wednesday, December 27th, using the diagram on which Gacy had marked the burial places of 27 of his victims, the investigators searched each spot.

What appeared to be trenches had been dug in the crawlspace, as though they had been prepared in advance. This was confirmed when a teenage boy approached a detective at the scene and told him that Gacy had hired him to dig trenches two feet deep in the crawlspace.

Most of the bodies had been covered with lime to make them deteriorate more rapidly. Some were no more than skeletal remains, others were bones that had come apart from the skeletons. Most of the skulls were intact.

By the end of December 27th, eight more bodies had been found.

Meanwhile, the medical examiner and his associates — having completed some of the autopsies — had found that the cause of death in most cases had been strangulation — some victims had been strangled manually, some by choking with ropes tied tightly around their necks.

An investigator said it appeared that the first victims were buried in concrete — one in the garage floor and two covered in cement in the crawlspace. But for some reason Gacy apparently gave up cement and decided to have trenches dug.

"When he ran out of trenches in the crawlspace," said the investigator, "he really got reckless. He began dumping bodies in the river — he says there were five of them, including the Piest kid — despite the fact that someone could have seen him."

The search went on for several weeks, but it was not until March 16th, 1979 that the 29th body was found in the crawlspace.

On April 3rd work began on the demolition of Gacy's house. This was completed seven days later, and with only the driveway left, the digging went on — resulting in the finding of body No. 30. More digging followed, and two more bodies were uncovered, bringing the total to 32.

Meanwhile, the men dragging the Des Plaines River worked doggedly on. They came to the intersection with the Illinois River, near Morris. And there they found body No. 33. Using pictures, X-ray and dental charts, the body was identified as that of Robert Piest, the boy whose disappearance on December 11th had started the greatest search for bodies ever carried out in the Chicago area.

Assistant State Attorney William Kunkle said that he planned to try Gacy first for the murder of Robert Piest. During that first trial, Kunkle said, the prosecution would try to introduce evidence from the 32 other sex murders for which Gacy was indicted.

One of Gacy's attorneys objected, and legal arguments followed.

Gacy was now in the prison hospital after complaining of chest pains. His health wasn't improved by the legal bickering. "I just wish they'd get the hell on with it!" he told an acquaintance who visited him.

Thirteen months after his arrest, it was a slimmer, smarter John Wayne Gacy who took his seat at the defence table for the last of the preliminary hearings prior to his trial.

His hair was neatly combed, he was clean-shaven and he appeared relaxed, sometimes even jovial. His suit was a new three-piece grey tweed.

But when his trial began on February 6th, 1980, it was with a sombre expression that he strode across the room to the defence table. Instead of smiling and waving at the spectators as he had at previous hearings, he ignored the packed courtroom. He sat down with his lawyers and stared straight ahead, his gaze fixed constantly on Judge Louis B. Garippo.

Assistant Prosecutor Robert C. Egan began his address to the jury with these words: "I want you to picture, if you will, a young boy, 15 years old ..."

He went on to tell the story of the last night on earth of Robert Piest — last of the 33 to be slain.

"Robert Piest was frightened to tears," Egan told the jurors. "He was whimpering. Gacy said, 'Don't cry. I'm going to show you one more trick'." According to Egan, Gacy called it the rope trick. Gacy had taken the teenager to the bedroom, where Piest was handcuffed and then seated in a chair. Egan said that Gacy stepped behind the youth, put a rope around his neck, tied two knots in the rope and slipped a stick between the two knots. Then he twisted the sticks, drawing the knots tighter until the boy stopped breathing.

Egan told the court that at this point the phone rang. It was a business associate who wanted to know why Gacy had missed an important meeting. Gacy talked to him for a short time, then hung up.

"Then he left Piest on the floor, right there in the bedroom," Egan continued. "He spent the night in a bed in that same room. When Gacy got up at six o'clock the next morning, he moved Robert's body to the attic."

Then, on the night of December 12th, Egan told the jurors, Gacy put the boy's body in his car and drove to the Des Plaines River. "He threw him over the bridge like a sack of potatoes."

Egan described how, after Piest had left his mother in the chemist's and popped out to see Gacy about a job, the contractor had motioned him to get in his car. Egan quoted their conversation:

Gacy: How much time do you have?

Robert: About thirty minutes.

Gacy: Let's take a ride ... Are you liberal?

Robert: Yes.

Gacy: Are you liberal about sex with a man?

Robert: No, I wouldn't do that.

After Gacy told Robert that he would have to fill out a job application, they went to the contractor's home. Gacy led the boy to a bedroom, where Robert was told that he was not qualified for construction work. "Do you want to make twenty bucks fast?" Egan quoted Gacy.

The boy, now thoroughly frightened, refused when Gacy told him that the money would be for having sex with him. "I'm a clown," Gacy was quoted as saying. "Let me show you some magic tricks."

It was then that Gacy handcuffed Piest to the chair, stepped behind it — and strangled him.

Having given details of the last of the 33 murders, Egan turned to the other 32. "He started his rampage in 1972. And it took him six years — until December 11th, 1978," Egan told the jurors. The killings started, Egan said, when Gacy "went to see what he could pick up at the Greyhound bus station."

The first victim — the only one stabbed to death — has never been identified, although Gacy has admitted murdering him. "He killed people like he was swatting flies," Egan told the jury. "These murders were planned, mechanical and premeditated."

Egan said that when investigators asked Gacy why he'd had one of his young employees dig trenches in the crawlspace under his home, Gacy had replied: "Because I wanted to have graves available." Gacy also said of Gregory Godzik, who worked part-time for him: "When Greg worked at my house, he dug his own grave."

Explaining the murders to investigators, Gacy said: "They always asked for more money, or threatened to expose me. So I had to kill them."

Many of his victims were upright high school teenagers and ambitious young men seeking jobs. Others, however, were young male prostitutes, picked up in Chicago. Like their female counterparts, they had their price. Gacy paid fees he considered too high for a while. Then, when the young men refused to perform for less, he became enraged and strangled them.

Only 22 of the 33 males Gacy was charged with killing, Egan said, had been identified. Of the 11 not identified, he told the jury: "All we know is that they were boys — and they ended up in John Gacy's graveyard."

Gacy's counsel, Robert Motta, was next to address the jury. He claimed that Gacy suffered from an "unconscious and uncontrollable mental illness" and could not be held responsible for his actions under Illinois's insanity law.

Under Illinois law, a person is not guilty by reason of insanity if he does not understand the criminality of his act, or cannot conform his conduct to the law. Motta said that the fact that the killings occurred "over and over and over again" showed a "profound and incredible obsession."

"He sleeps with corpses," Motta went on. "He lives in a house with bodies under it for years. He was incapable of forming an intent, because of his profound mental disease ... Mr. Gacy's intelligence and thought process were completely helpless against that consuming mental disease."

Motta told the jurors that Gacy would throw himself into his work at his construction business, as a political worker and as an amateur clown "to consume all his time — because he knew something was happening to him. And he just couldn't help it."

He added that psychiatrists who would testify for the prosecution that Gacy was not insane when the killings occurred had made a "most superficial diagnosis." On the other hand, the four defence psychiatrists he intended to summon were "free from bias and interest."

The first witness called by the prosecution was 51-year-old Marco Butkovitch, whose son John's skeletal remains had been dug up from under the garage after Gacy's arrest. Assistant Prosecutor Terry Sullivan asked the witness if he had ever met the defendant.

Butkovitch replied that he and Gacy had met several times to discuss business. "He seemed to be a good man and said that young John was going to be a good businessman," the father testified.

Mrs. Dolores Vance, whose 18-year-old son Darrell disappeared on April 6th, 1976, was next on the witness-stand. She insisted that her son had never been gone from home more than a day or a night at a time. When he failed to come home, she notified the police. "I walked blisters on my feet looking for him," she testified. And when Sullian showed her a picture of her son, she burst into tears.

Then Mrs. Bessier Stapleton told the jury that her 14-year-old son Samuel had worked nights in a pizza parlour. On May 13th, 1978, she continued, Sam left home, saying that he was going to visit his sister. "That's the last time I ever saw him," Mrs. Stapleton said.

Sullivan quietly walked to the witness-stand, an envelope in his hand. He opened it and poured out a chain bracelet.

"That's Sam's bracelet!" she exclaimed, starting to sob. Then she fainted.

Detective Sergeant Jim Pickell told of the search for Robert Piest. The day after Robert vanished Pickell had gone to Gacy's home.

Robert's body was actually in the attic when Pickell arrived, though the officer didn't know it. Gacy claimed that his uncle had just died and he had "more important things to do" than go to the police station. "Don't you have any respect for the dead?" he asked the detective.

Sullivan next called to the witness-stand a young student who testified about an ordeal that lasted for about six hours. During that time, he said, he lost consciousness almost a dozen times as Gacy played Russian roulette with him and tried to drown and strangle him. At times during the student's courtroom testimony, Gacy grinned at him, laughed silently and shook his head.

Asked if he saw Gacy in the courtroom, the student

replied: "Yes, I do. But I wish he wasn't here."

When Sullivan asked him to give details of the sexual attack, he burst into tears. After a few minutes, however, the young witness was able to continue.

Around midnight on December 30th, 1977, he said, he left the home of a friend and began walking to catch a bus home.

A man in what he at first thought was an unmarked police car put a spotlight on him and asked him for identification. The man — whom he later learned was Gacy — "took a gun and pointed it at me and said: 'Get in this car, or I'm going to blow you away' ..."

The student told how, now handcuffed, he was driven to Gacy's house, where he was led into the living-room and thrown on a couch.

"I still thought he was a police officer, but I couldn't figure out what was going on," the student testified. Then, he said, Gacy removed the handcuffs. "He told me to behave myself. If I tried anything he would kill me right there and then. He said the house was soundproofed and he was a police officer, so they would never question him if he just shot me.

In a hushed voice the student continued: "He raped me." After that he passed out, he said. When he awoke Gacy led him to the bathroom, where "he reached around my neck and pulled something around my neck and started twisting it."

The student then quoted Gacy as saying: "My, aren't we having fun tonight?"

"He pushed my head into the wall a couple of times," the young man testified. "He turned me and tripped me down onto the floor. Then he picked me up by whatever was around my neck. He stuck my head into the bath full of water. I was squirming and moving and holding my breath."

The witness said that when he woke up his clothes had been removed and he was lying on the bathroom floor. "He stuck my head under the water a second time and I could barely hold my breath. I started breathing water and I passed out again."

Later, the student said, Gacy sat on him and forced him to watch a homosexual pornographic movie. When it was over, the student testified, Gacy got a gun, propped him against a wall, then sat in a chair a few feet away and pointed the gun at him.

"We're going to play Russian roulette," Gacy said. "Aren't we playing fun games tonight?"

The student went on: "He pulled the trigger and nothing happened. He did it again and nothing happened." The young man said that Gacy spun the chamber of the gun 10 or 15 times, until he finally heard the sound of a gunshot.

"I realised it must have been a blank — because I was still alive. He told me that when he killed me it wasn't going to be the first time he'd killed somebody. He had killed girls before, but stopped doing that and started killing guys — because it was more interesting.

"I looked up and he was shaking. He reached out and grabbed my throat with his hands and just started choking me. I was twisting my head ... I passed out." When the student awoke his ankles were bound and he had been gagged.

He told the court that Gacy began to torture him sexually. "I started to get dizzy and I passed out. The pain was so bad and I was terrified. I said: 'Look, if you're gonna kill me, just kill me now and get it over with.' Gacy told me that my time was coming and to shut up."

Later Gacy told him: "You're going for your last ride. How does it feel to know that you're going to die?"

But Gacy eventually released him on the morning of December 31st, saying he would return to kill him. He also predicted that if the student went to the police they would not believe him. "And they didn't believe me," the witness added.

Anthony Antonucci, 20, a student at the University of Illinois, testified that he first met Gacy in 1975 when the contractor was decorating his family's apartment.

Gacy came to the apartment one night when he knew the parents were not at home. The young man, then 17, said that Gacy brought a bottle of wine and a projector and showed him some stag movies.

"We began wrestling around — armlocks and head-locks. All of a sudden I felt John putting handcuffs on my left wrist," Antonucci testified. "I tried to avoid him grasping my other arm, but he got it cuffed and knocked me to the floor. My hands were handcuffed behind my back."

He said that Gacy then began undressing him, but suddenly stopped and went into the kitchen. "While he was there I realised the right cuff wasn't too secure. I worked my way out of it. I could squeeze my hand out. I kept it underneath me. I stayed there, looking like I was still handcuffed," Antonucci said.

When Gacy came back, the witness told the court: "I grabbed both his legs and tackled him. I put the handcuffs on his wrist. I found the keys to the handcuffs ... and handcuffed him behind his back."

Gacy fell to the floor, where he stayed for about 10 minutes, until Antonucci uncuffed him and let him go home.

"I thought it was a joke most of the time," Antonucci told the jurors. "Yet there was a seriousness. There was no talking or laughing. It seemed kind of mechanical."

David Cram, 22, testified that he had worked for John Gacy on a construction job and later lived in Gacy's house for several months. He told of digging some trenches in the crawlspace under Gacy's house — Gacy told him to spread lime in the trenches "to sweeten the smell."

"He said the trenches were necessary so that plumbers would have space to lay some new piping," Cram testified.

On one occasion, Cram told the court: "I came into the house and Gacy had a clown suit on. It was my birthday. He said he would show me the handcuff trick. He handcuffed me, with my hands in front. The trick was that you needed the key.

"He grabbed me by the chain and swung me around. He said 'I'm going to rape you.' I kind of freaked out ... I ended up kicking him in the head." Then Gacy fell to the floor — and that was the end of the attack.

Police officers testified that from December 14th to December 21st they followed Gacy all over Chicago. Gacy — aware that he was being followed — frequently told the officers where he was going and how to get there, in case they got lost.

Detective Robert Schultz said that when he and a colleague, having obtained a search warrant, went into Gacy's house they had to move back a sliding door, apparently designed to suppress the odour in the hall. When he went into Gacy's bedroom, he said, the furnace came on and warm air began to rise from a vent. "I noticed a putrefying, rotting smell," Schultz testified.

"What did you associate that odour with?" Prosecutor Egan asked.

"I associated it with smells I'd encountered down at the county morgue," Schultz replied.

Partly because of this smell the officers were able to obtain a second warrant. And the first of the bodies was found in the crawlspace.

Detective David Hachmeister said that a few days before the arrest he and Schultz went into a restaurant and sat down at a table. Gacy sat down with them and they chatted while they ate.

"He indicated that he was a registered clown," Hachmeister testified. "He said that people don't look at a clown as being a person. On a number of occasions when he was marching in parades he would see a good-looking woman on the sidelines and he would sit in her lap. He said he could even grab her breasts and she would laugh it off.

"He told me, 'You know, Davie, clowns can get away with murder,'" Hachmeister testified. Just a few days later Gacy was arrested.

Responding to questions from Prosecutor Kunkle, Dr. Stein testified that to a layman persons who have been strangled until they've lost consciousness may appear dead. This raised the possibility that some of the victims might have been buried alive.

"Would it be any less a homicide if the victim died of asphyxia in his own grave?" Kunkle asked.

"It would be a homicide," Stein replied.

Stein stated that 13 of Gacy's victims had died of asphyxia, six of strangulation and one of multiple stab wounds. The bodies of 10 others were so badly decomposed that it was impossible to determine the cause of death. But he'd nevertheless ruled that the 30 bodies he examined were all homicide cases. The other three were examined by assistant pathologists.

Sheriff's Officer Greg Bedoe testified that Gacy had confessed to using the Bible in a ritual in which a boy died. He said that the boy had refused to have sex with Gacy, who then told the youth that he would show him the rope trick.

He had used a stick and rope, as described by the student victim who had survived. In this instance the rope was twisted twice by the stick. Then Gacy opened a Bible and read the 23rd Psalm. When he twisted the rope again, the boy convulsed and died.

Bedoe said Gacy told him that he had engaged in 1,500 sexual adventures, none of them free. The usual fee was $30, sometimes more.

Daniel Genty, an evidence technician who had been involved in the excavation of the corpses, said that at one point digging was halted because officials were afraid that gasses from the bodies would make the workers sick.

The search had yielded 26 bodies, and the 30-inch-high crawlspace was infested with "thin red worms." At one spot three bodies were stacked neatly, one upon another, while another was folded nearly in half. He said that when Gacy's house was demolished two more bodies were found — one under the patio, another under the dining-room.

The first witness for the defence was a neighbour of Gacy. "His house was our house, our house was his house," the mother of six testified. "I don't believe it yet," she said. "I can't fathom that anyone would do anything like that, least of all John Gacy."

On cross-examination by Assistant Prosecutor Sullivan, she said: "There's no way I'm going to say John is crazy. He is a very brilliant man." She went on to tell the jury about the John Gacy she and her family had known from the time he moved in next door in 1971 until 1978, when he was arrested.

"He isn't smiling now, but I have never seen John without a smile on his face before today. It was a very genuine smile. His whole face lit up. I felt the John we knew was a very nice person, very warm ... generous, considerate."

This prompted Gacy to smile.

Gacy's second wife — who divorced him after living with him for three and a half years — was next to testify for the defence. On cross-examination she said she had repeatedly complained about the smell in the house. "It was some time after we married that I noticed it. It was just getting stronger and stronger." But, she said, Gacy had told her not to do anything about it — that he would take care of it.

She said that they had been acquainted when they were children, but lost touch until about six months before they were married in 1972. "He told me he was bisexual. At first I didn't know what a bisexual was. I didn't make anything of it. It didn't make any difference to me."

In the beginning, she said, their sex life was good. "He was very gentle, very warm, and a brilliant man. He had a memory like an elephant. He was also a very good father to my girls. They called him Daddy, even before our marriage. And they still call him Daddy today."

On March 12th, Assistant Prosecutor Sullivan began his closing argument. Pointing at Gacy, he said: "You are the worst of all murderers. For your victims were the young, the naive, the unassuming. You are truly a predator. You have pilfered the most precious thing parents can give — human life."

Turning to the jury, Sullivan said: "Justice implores you to find John Gacy guilty of murder — murder in the worst degree."

Amirante asked the jury to put aside their anger and hatred when reaching their verdict.

"A man does not have to look like a bulging-eyed monster to be insane," he said. "Mr. Gacy is not an evil man, though he has done some evil things."

Amirante told the jurors that if they found Gacy guilty and gave him the electric chair, "You will never find out what makes a mind like this work." He pleaded that Gacy should be studied to prevent future mass murders.

But the jury were to spend a mere hour and 50 minutes before unanimously finding Gacy guilty of 33 counts of murder. Then they recommended the sentence of death, which was eventually carried out 14 years later.

Few could have predicted just how long it would take to winkle the multiple murderer out of Death Row and into the death chamber. Fewer still could have foreseen the late blossoming in prison of John Wayne Gacy as an artist, albeit one favouring skulls, grinning clowns and Adolf Hitler as his subjects.

In the hour preceding Gacy's execution more than 100 of his works were offered for sale by auction at a Chicago art gallery. Some, it was reported, were snapped up for $10,000. Others were valued at as much as $38,000. They were highly prized, said a gallery spokesman, because they were unique. And their value was likely to increase because John Wayne Gacy wouldn't be painting any more ...

8

LETTERS FROM A DEAD MAN

L. C. Schmuhl

"In the last hour nearly all doomed men draw upon a deep, hidden reservoir of strength. Nearly all of them die bravely"

IT HAD been a hot, sultry morning and now, past noon, the sun was really bearing down outside. Even my office, tucked in a cool brick building, was suffocating. I got up to stand a moment at the window, tasting the faint breeze that smelled vaguely of nearby Lake Michigan. A few grey figures shuffled past along the prison's Main Street. I saw one glance at my building, which also housed the death chamber — then turn quickly away. He and the other 2,000 convicts knew that this was the day. Their minds would be on my building until after midnight.

I felt sweat trickle down my back. Behind me the door opened and I turned. It was August 15th, 1939.

"He's been shaved," an orderly said. "He's in his cell."

"How is he?" I asked.

"Good. He's writing his menu."

I nodded, and the orderly went out. After a moment I followed, turning right outside the door and walking a few paces along a clean wide corridor flanked by cells.

At the end of the corridor a screen stood in front of a squat old black chair — all set up and waiting.

One cell door was open. A watchful guard was framed in

it. He tipped a finger to his cap and stood aside when I approached.

As I went in Adrian Miller looked up from a pad on which he was scribbling. I searched his odd, square-cut face a moment and was reassured. There was no hysteria in it.

"Hello, deputy," he said calmly. "I was just writing you a note — my dinner."

I nodded and dropped into a chair opposite his cot. He tore off a bit of paper and I read it:

"Hearts of celery with Thousand Island dressing; shrimp cocktail with one-half pound Roquefort cheese; lots of frog-legs fried in cracker crumbs and egg; medium rare Filet Mignon with crisp brown American fried potatoes and corn and peas; whole wheat bread with real butter; one-half bottle of claret wine; butterscotch pie and chocolate ice cream; two cups of good, strong real coffee with cream, no sugar; toothpicks; two Corona Belvedere cigars and Camel cigarettes."

I glanced at him, slightly surprised. There was certainly nothing wrong with his appetite. He read my mind.

"I've been fasting all day," he said. "This is one meal I want to enjoy."

"You certainly know how to order a good meal," I replied. "We don't get many epicures here!"

"I don't imagine."

"You've been around in your thirty-one years."

"A little," he replied.

"Want to talk about it?"

"Not yet. Later."

I shook my head, exasperated. For days I'd been trying to draw Miller out. I've always tried to gain the confidence of men I had to help execute — for both practical and compassionate reasons.

Men rarely lie in the face of death. As a last friend and final confidant I had often obtained bits of information that helped police clean up their case, or, equally important, reassured them that the man they had sent to death was truly guilty. That was the practical side — a part of my job as deputy warden of Indiana State Prison.

My personal interest in these men who came to ride the thunderbolt went much deeper. For them I had real pity and compassion. Always I yearned to know where in their lives they'd veered off onto the road to the electric chair.

Most of the men quickly sensed that my sympathy was genuine. In their loneliness they grasped it eagerly. But Miller was exasperatingly different. He had remained aloof, preoccupied, apparently uncaring.

Somewhere, of course, his mind was canted off at an angle. His case showed it. But it was a brilliant mind — especially in mathematics and engineering. I wanted to explore it. So far I had failed.

Who but Miller would while away Death Row hours studying higher calculus?

Now as I prepared to leave his cell I saw him reach again for the calculus text he'd been studying for the past three weeks. I tried once more to break through his taciturnity.

"Shouldn't you be trading that for a Bible soon?" I asked quietly.

Miller turned his unperturbed face to me and slowly shook his head. He said something strange — yet provoking:

"All the universe operates in a system of perfect mathematics. Perhaps I'll be nearer to God in this book than in the Bible."

"You aren't an atheist, surely?"

"No one but a fool is an atheist, deputy," Miller replied.

I shook my head and went out. Back in my office I passed along Miller's meal order. It would be prepared, as far as possible, exactly as he wished.

Then, still puzzling over this strange man who so soon would die, I reached for his file. Scanning through it, I ran across a letter he had written a few weeks earlier to Governor M. Clifford Townsend.

Not many men who come to Death Row write clearly and lucidly. Again Miller was an exception. I began to read. The letter was revealing and tantalising.

"Have you ever sat alone," Miller had asked the governor, "and thought that on such or such a date I am going to die; and known that nothing you could do would prevent it? Are you capable of imagining how a man in such circumstances would feel?

"God and the law have given you a great power, that of life and death. Have you in the use or disuse of this power been guided by the wishes of both givers?"

"I have earnestly prayed to God that He touch your heart that you may use this power in my favour, and while hoping that He may do so I am resigned to His will. I am not afraid of death, for I am sure to spend my eternity with God. The uncertainty and the waiting for death are the hardest to bear, death itself is nothing. While the thought of spending the rest of my life here is horrifying, there are compensations which would make it endurable, namely the practice of my religion and the study of chemistry, so I venture to ask you for a commutation of my sentence.

"My greatest penance is and will continue to be the thought that I have been the cause of much suffering and I would gladly give my life if it could be undone. However, the fact remains that my death would benefit no one and by living I might still do much good.

"If you investigate you will find several factors that should influence you in my favour. A few of them I will name; I have no criminal record, but have always been a responsible man, often in charge of other men.

"The universal prejudice against me at the time I was indicted and at the trial, even admittedly among the jurors, precluded absolute impartiality, and even then there were some who voted in my favour on the first two ballots.

"We in no manner tried to vilify the girl's reputation, although there was ample justification. Because the only penalty a guilty verdict could carry was death, mitigating circumstances would not have any effect. So why sling mud? I do not nor did I try to deny that I killed the girl, but there was no rape and I should not have been tried under such an indictment. Even if I must die, to be called a rapist is distasteful to me. So I have written my side of the story and it will not lack for publishers for it is to be offered free.

"The whole affair was the outcome of a quarrel, due partly to a threat the girl made and to jealousy. I lost my temper. I have been told unofficially that several jurymen have since remarked that I should have been convicted of nothing greater than second-degree murder. The police have what was presented as a confession. It is what they told me I did, not what I said. I told the prosecutor at the questioning that I was willing to sign anything he wanted, if only he would let me sleep.

"If you would, by any chance, show me mercy I would never give you cause to regret it. I want to live and study and perhaps make something of myself, even in prison.

"I know no further argument, beyond the words of Jesus: 'Blessed are the merciful for they shall obtain mercy.' If God or His words mean nothing to you, who am I to try? Regardless of what your decision may be I should like to know it soon. Please do not ignore this letter. That would be inhuman."

I put down the letter, even more exasperated. It was obviously a mixture of truth and deliberate exaggeration; of simple faith and cynical bitterness.

What was the true Miller, and what was the real truth of his crime? I yearned to know, and I realised that time was running out.

I glanced at my watch. It was nearly 3.30. Picking up the phone I dialled Warden Alfred Dowd's office.

"Anything from the governor?" I asked when the warden answered.

"Nothing. I don't expect anything. He's never intervened in an execution."

The sultry afternoon literally melted away. I remained at my desk, avoiding Miller, letting the final hours work their corrosion on his loneliness.

At 4.30 Chaplain Bob Hall came to spend an hour with Miller. On the way out he stopped at my office.

"The boy is fine," Chaplain Hall said. Miller was past 30, but the chaplain called them all "his boys." He shook his head, a little puzzled. "He has a religion all his own," he went on, "but his faith is firm. He'll be all right."

"Did he talk to you?" I asked.

The chaplain smiled wryly. "Not much. He's a strange one. Lives deep inside himself somewhere."

I nodded, slightly disappointed. Miller was still in his shell.

After the chaplain left, I visited Miller's cell a moment before going out for my own supper. He was busy writing.

"A last letter?" I asked.

He glanced up at me with an odd smile. "No," he said slowly, "it is a story. Maybe it is my story. I ... I want you to read it. Will you?"

"Of course," I said.

He scrawled a few more lines and handed me the paper — one sheet of lined prison stationery, penned on both sides. I glanced at it, but Miller said quickly:

"Not ... not here. Please read it carefully, alone. Then..."

He paused and I waited hopefully.

"Then," he continued with a wistful note, "I hope you'll come and talk to me. Will you?"

I kept a poker face to hide my eagerness and relief. "I'll see you after you have eaten," I said, and went away.

I hurried to my residence just outside the prison's high turreted walls and ate lightly. The food was tasteless.

As I ate I wondered how Miller was enjoying the gourmet's repast he had ordered. I needn't have worried.

After supper I found an easy chair and unfolded Miller's "story." In many ways it was cryptic — but in and between the lines vital parts of his strange life began to unfold.

He had entitled the piece "Recuerdo" and it reminded me that Miller had spent part of his life in South America, working as an engineer in mining camps.

"I am facing my last great trial which in a few minutes will be over," the story began.

"Thinking of you for the last time, I remember only the nice things I found in you. Perhaps it is well that you will never know of these thoughts, for from where I now go, none return."

This, I thought, was written for a woman.

"I am well known in the country and the newspapers are sure to carry a story about me. If you see it you may wonder what really is behind the story. You will never imagine that you, my dear, are behind it — unseen and unsuspected. You are in no way to blame, of course, but it all started because you were your own sweet self.

"Do you remember when I drove you and your sister from the power-house to the main camp in the truck? How embarrassed I was, and how we laughed over my torn trousers. I began to love you then. Later when I was transferred to the mining camp in which you lived, and visited frequently at your home, I came to love you blindly, as I had been taught to love the Mother of God when a boy.

"Do you remember how I rode eight hours on horseback from another camp, over the Andes, to spend Christmas with you, and what a nice Christmas it was? I can still see your calm blue eyes that looked so honestly and directly at me.

"I have tried hard to forget, but ... but even after years when I am alone your face comes before me, so frank and unclouded, showing your every emotion, sometimes serenely smiling, lit by some inward light, and again the flash of quick anger which lasted but a moment.

"I was happy in those days, how happy I never realised till now when everything is as ashes to me. Then came the day when I went to the far south to take a better job. You will never realise the anguish I experienced at parting from you.

"In the new camp I was too busy to think much, but I missed you so. And how I loved your letters and the hint of what happiness might be mine someday. Then came my vacation and my visit to your home. I left you sure that we would soon be married, although no words to that effect were spoken between us.

"After I returned to my job, how eagerly I awaited your letters, hoping that in them you might express some wish that I could gratify. And you did, frequently. I gloried in serving you, for I realised that your father's strictness sometimes made your home life unhappy. Therefore I never complained when your requests got bigger and bigger, and I never begrudged you the money that those gifts cost, even when they threw me into debt to pay for them.

"Then came those weeks of anxiety when you didn't answer my frantic letters, and then finally the letter from your mother saying that you had run off and got married. That day I died — not physically, of course, but in my soul. I took to drink for a while to forget, but that did not help. And so from bad to worse, finally I quit my job and became a despicable outcast, wandering from place to place, always tortured by thoughts of what might have been.

"Eventually I returned to my own country, with ambition dead and haunted by your face and your laugh. I was as near insane as a person can get without actually crossing the line of sanity. Followed change after change of sanity, girl after girl — but the ache in my heart never left me. I long for you even now.

"(Someone has come into my cell and reads an official paper. After he finishes I am led out.)

"Night after night in my loneliness my heart has called out to you, but you never answer, except in my dreams. I wish that ...

"A doctor, stethoscope in hand, steps to the chair holding the sagging body. He applies it to the now still breast, and after listening a moment, he turns to those waiting around and says, 'I pronounce this man dead.' Guards remove the slouched form and take it to the morgue.

"The electric current crashing through that body stilled

the last wish shaping in my thoughts. What would it have been had it been completed? The answer is hidden in eternity, from which none has been able to lift the veil.''

Those are Miller's precise words, as he penned them in death's shadow. I haven't changed a line of the "story" which I still have.

I let the paper fall to my lap and stared out of the open window, contemplating this strange man.

So a woman had guided Miller to the road to the chair — a different woman, obviously, than the one he had slain. It was an old, old story — yet always new: man betrayed by woman.

The letter shed light on the doomed man's hidden life, yet left new puzzles. I folded the letter and went back to the prison, more eager than ever to talk.

On the way I passed through a big cell block and paused at one of its tiered cells. A dark little man with flashing white teeth came up to the grilled door and smiled.

"Evening, deputy," he said.

"Good evening, Gomez. Do you speak Spanish?" I asked.

He grinned even more broadly. "Better than English, I bet," he said.

"What does 'recuerdo' mean?" I asked, thinking of the title of Miller's story. "Does it mean record, or the record?"

"Oh, no, señor," the prisoner said quickly. "It means remembrance, or memory."

I waited until Miller had almost finished his last meal. He was drinking his coffee and drawing on a good, fragrant Corona Belvedere when I walked past the watchful guard at the door and into his cell. He looked up and smiled.

"A wonderful meal," he said. "Thanks."

I glanced at what was left. He had eaten most of it. Only the salad had been neglected. Miller read my mind.

"Your chef can't make good dressing," he said. "He ruined the salad." He shrugged. "But it didn't matter. I had more than enough to eat."

He was sitting on his cot, and now he leaned his back against the wall and pulled on his knees. He drew deeply on the cigar and the blue smoke rose towards the grey ceiling.

For a moment he held the cigar at arm's length and peered at the fingers which held it. They trembled slightly.

"I guess I'm a little nervous and scared," he admitted.

"I have never seen one who wasn't," I said calmly and honestly.

There was gratitude in Miller's face and he said, "Thanks, Mr. Schmuhl. That helps." He drew again on the cigar. "How much time?"

We don't permit clocks or watches in the death cell. They are infinite torture during the final hours. Nor are we specific about time. So I replied. "Quite a bit — several hours."

That seemed to calm him. I waited through a long silence as he smoked and sipped his coffee. At last he asked, "Did you read my story?"

"Yes — but it was only a fragment of your life," I replied.

"It was a lovely fragment — for a while," he mused wryly. Then he added bitterly: "Like my life — cut short by a woman!"

It's strange, I thought. *They never blame themselves!*

"My life isn't much," Miller went on. "My family was poor. We had very little. I got through high school by working, and got a year at a little engineering college the same way. It was rough going. I got in a little jam — so I took off for South America."

"A girl?"

Miller lowered his eyes. "Does it matter now?" he muttered.

It mattered to me because it was a revealing clue to the man's character. In a small crisis he had run away.

But I let it go, and Miller continued:

"In South America I worked in mining camps. I had

enough education to be foreman — but that's all. It was a rough life, and there were no women ...

"Then I met the girl you read about. She was a dark, soft, warm señorita ..."

Miller's voice took on a husky tinge. His eyes were far away, and I could see that he was half telling, half reliving that period of his life. I pretended to listen carefully, but I was actually studying Miller's face. It was a mixture of strength and weakness.

His jaw was long, tough and square — but it sloped up to a tight, weak mouth. His eyes were wide-spaced and intelligent behind rimless spectacles bridging a big, ungainly nose between awkward, sloppy ears.

Only 31, he was already half bald, and it was that ugly baldness which draws a high forehead back into a straggly fringe of hair.

To most women Miller must have been a comic figure, and to ruthless women an easy conquest. But he wouldn't realise it. His vanity would lead him on.

I began to listen again.

"... I sent her money, presents, everything. It took all I could earn. When she asked for more I borrowed $100 from a friend. Then I got word that she had married someone else ..."

For a moment I glimpsed a terrible, white-hot anger and hatred in Miller's eyes. He calmed down and went on: "I quit my job and tried to find her. I never did. I began to drink and wander. I got lower and lower and I didn't care."

He looked up at me quizzically and asked: "Have you ever seen some of the cesspools of Panama?"

"No."

"They're the world's worst. I saw them all. It's a wonder I wasn't murdered for a few coins or rotted by disease. I guess I was lucky. After a year I came to my senses. I found work and saved enough for passage home. I was determined to forget and start a new life."

Back home he got a good start. An uncle gave him a

little money to attend business school in Fort Wayne, Indiana. He endured the loneliness and poverty for a few months, determined to complete his education.

I knew the facts of his case and as he approached them I listened intently.

"I met a girl at school — Alice May Girton. She was only eighteen, a clean, wholesome girl from a fine farm family. I began walking home with her. Later I got a room at her boarding-house so I could be near to her. She seemed to like me ..."

I looked at Miller's balding head, his odd face and big ears and wondered if this young girl had really loved him. More probably she had sensed his need for companionship and had been kind. Miller continued, and what he said confirmed my guess.

"But she kept going out with other boys from the school. I argued with her. It only made things worse ..."

Once again that terrible rage crept into Miller's eyes. It reminded me of a vague entry in his record. Once he had been arrested in San Diego, and sent to a mental hospital for examination. He had been adjudged sane, but ...

Miller was talking now almost in a monotone and he came finally to the night of October 13th, 1938.

"She had gone out that night with a young boy. I stayed in my room, restless and angry, waiting ... and waiting ... and waiting. It was almost two a.m. before I heard her come in and go to her room. I waited for a few minutes and then tiptoed out of my room to her door and knocked.

"She wouldn't let me in. I told her I'd raise a row and wake the landlady. She opened the door finally and I pushed in. She wore a pretty, wrap-around dressing gown tied loosely at the waist and she looked so frail and scared and lovely that I calmed down.

"We talked awhile. She begged me to leave. I told her I would if she'd promise not to go out with other men again. When she wouldn't promise I got mad again and grabbed her shoulders and shook her..."

Miller paused and rubbed his thumb and index finger

over his eyes as though they ached.

Then in a voice so low I could barely hear he continued: "When I shook her the gown fell away. She stood there, terrified ... and stark naked! Something exploded inside me."

"What happened?" I asked softly.

"I ... I don't remember ..."

I looked at Miller closely. A memory gap is an old, old alibi. In this case it may have been true. Sometimes the mind smothers a memory too hideous to contemplate — a sort of protective cloak.

"What do you remember?" I asked.

"It was later ... a few minutes or an hour. I don't know. I just remember her face staring up at me from the bed. I remember her throat tied with a piece of clothing ... She was dead and I knew I had to get out of there. I went back to my room.

"I knew I was in an awful jam. I started to pack some things to get away. Then I did a little thinking. If I left they'd know I killed her. If I stayed and outsmarted the police I might get away with it."

So Miller stayed. Next morning he left for school at the usual time. It was noon before the landlady discovered the girl's body. Police swarmed in. They questioned everybody — Miller included.

"I told them I had been in my room all night and had heard nothing unusual," Miller said wearily. "I was sure they couldn't prove any differently. I'd be under suspicion awhile, but if I played it smart they'd never get proof. I wasn't even worried when they went around taking fingernail scrapings from everyone in the boarding-house.

"They came and got me the next day and took me to headquarters. They'd found traces of the girl's skin and flesh in my fingernail scrapings.

"I tried desperately to lie. Every time I did they trapped me. It got worse and worse ... a nightmare. Finally there was only one way out. I told them the whole story ..."

"You mean the police forced you to confess?"

"No, no! Nothing like that! They didn't abuse me. It was simply their questions — boring every minute closer and closer to the truth until I couldn't lie any more. They knew I killed her, and they knew their job. I had to tell them the truth in the end or go crazy."

After that Miller had been promptly tried. He was charged with rape and murder. In Indiana that calls for a mandatory death sentence. The jury deliberated only a short time and found him guilty. The crime had been heinous, and not one to encourage mercy, Judge Harry Gilgeman pronounced the death sentence and Miller came to us.

Time was running out and Miller's story had left only one tiny gap. I asked him: "Did you rape the girl?"

He squirmed and lowered his eyes. "Honestly, I don't remember ... It's all a blank. They examined her and said I did. But I don't remember ..."

I didn't press the point. It didn't really matter. The case was closed without any vital doubts. Soon it would be completely ended.

A guard put his head in the door. "Telephone, deputy," he said.

I got up. As I did, wild hope flared in Miller's taut face. I shook my head quickly and said, "No, Miller — it won't be that. Don't let useless hope upset you now."

I walked the few steps to my office and picked up the phone. It was Warden Dowd.

"The governor's office called. There'll be no stay," he said. "How is he?"

"He'll be all right, sir," I replied. "We've been talking. I think he feels better."

"Fine. I'll be over in a little bit."

I put the phone back slowly and glanced at the clock on my desk. It was 11.30. Miller had 40 minutes left. I picked up the phone again and dialled Chaplain Hall, who was waiting for my call.

"You'd better come over now," I said. "He'll be wanting you during the last hour."

I went back to Miller's cell and told him calmly that there was no possibility of a stay. He took it well, nodding quietly. He was smoking a cigarette, and now he examined the fingers that held it. There was no visible tremor.

"That's odd, isn't it?" he mused aloud. "Now that it's certain I'm no longer nervous or afraid."

It wasn't odd. I had seen it happen many times. Somehow when hope is gone so is fear. In the last hour nearly all doomed men draw upon a deep, hidden reservoir of strength. Nearly all of them die bravely. In nearly 40 executions, I've never seen a man carried to the chair. "You'll be all right, son," I told Miller. "The chaplain is here now. I'll be in to say goodbye."

"Thanks, deputy," Miller said. "You've been a good friend."

The chaplain came in and I walked slowly back to my office to wait and to ponder the things Miller had told me. I wondered how much was pure truth, how much understandable exaggeration, how much deceit.

It was a clean case as Death Row cases go — no doubts, no loose ends, no question of guilt. I never like to express opinions about capital punishment. It was the law in Indiana, and my job was to fulfil it when so directed.

Presently the warden came in and the official execution party began to assemble. I went to Miller's cell. He looked up quickly and I shook my head.

"No — just goodbye. You have a few minutes."

"Goodbye — and thanks," he murmured, a ghost of a smile on his tight lips.

He was praying with the chaplain when I turned away.

Indiana's executions aren't the movie variety. The law forbids anyone but official executioners and official witnesses. Not even newspapermen are allowed, and there is no long, dramatic death march. The death cell is only about 15 steps from the chair. The execution crew is efficient. Everything is mercifully swift.

At 12.02 the death mask was fitted over Miller's face in his cell. It muffled his prayers slightly. Precisely at 12.03

two guards went to his cell. Each touched an elbow gently, steering him out of the cell and along the quick, short "last mile." He walked strongly.

It took only 80 seconds from the time Miller left his cell until he was strapped in the chair. The guards stepped back. I gave the straps and electrodes a final scrutiny, and then signalled.

Miller's fingers curled out on the end of the chair arm. A wisp of smoke appeared at the top of his head. I glanced away, tightening my stomach, and looked at my watch. It was 12.05 on Wednesday, August 16th, 1939.

Seven minutes later the undertakers were carrying away the body. As they went out I gazed a long moment at the stilled figure, wondering: did a woman put Adrian Miller on the road to the chair, or did he put himself there? I reread Miller's letters, but years later, I still couldn't decide!

9

"BURN, BUNDY, BURN"

Charles Cleveland

"As each crime passed he grew desensitised. He couldn't feel any more"

THE FLORIDA neighbourhood where Ted Bundy was to claim his last victims certainly appeared peaceful enough. If somewhat shabby now, it was a comfortable shabbiness, familiar to most old Southern college towns. The former gentry who once called it home had departed, but its broad streets, shaded by ancient oaks, remain.

Many of the old mansions still stand, their white columns or wide verandahs set back on generous lawns. Their elegance, however, has departed with the aristocrats who built them. Most have been divided up into boarding houses, small apartments, or taken over by the fraternities and sororities of Florida State University.

One would not have imagined that such was the setting for violence.

On September 29th, 1970, a female medical student was found dead in her bed in her flat on West LaFayette Street. Her nightgown had been hiked up around her head and she had been beaten to death with a blunt instrument.

Then, one evening in May, 1975, an art student living on St. Augustine Street took her Irish setter for a walk and disappeared. Both she and the dog were found dead on

May 17th, the dog on the back seat of a car, the partly disrobed body of its mistress in the boot. She had been shot four times with a .22 pistol.

Not far from where the art student's car had been discovered in Apalachicola National Forest, another student was found on May 1st, 1977. She had been beaten senseless and dragged to a campus car park.

The woman survived, recovered and returned to her parents' home in the Midwest. But "she couldn't remember a thing; it was a case of total amnesia," announced the police.

While the young girl lay struggling for life in a Tallahassee hospital, one of her closest college friends and sorority sister, Margaret Bowman from St. Petersburg, Florida, visited her frequently.

Margaret Bowman was so upset emotionally that she couldn't attend classes for several weeks. I know it upset her terribly. They were very close," said a university professor who taught both women.

The battered student did not return to Florida for the autumn and winter terms in 1977-78, but Margaret Bowman did. She moved into the Chi Omega sorority house (a sorority house in the US is basically a female dormitory; the male equivalent is a fraternity house) which is a short distance from where her friend had been attacked, and just a few blocks from the West LaFayette and St. Augustine Street addresses where the two earlier victims had lived.

Built in the early 70s, the sorority house is a comparative newcomer among the stately but decaying homes of an earlier era. A brick and white painted building, in the winter of 1978, it housed about 40 female students.

Twenty-one-year-old Margaret Bowman was studying fashion merchandising, and had been elected to the student senate. The daughter of an Air Force officer, she was born in Honolulu. She also worked part-time at The Colony, a clothes shop to help pay for her studies.

The room next door to Margaret's was occupied by

another St. Petersburg student, 20-year-old Lisa Levy. Lisa also worked part-time at The Colony, as well as the Army/Navy surplus store to help pay for her education, and she was also studying fashion merchandising.

The room across the hall from the two St. Petersburg girls was shared by Karen Chandler, a fashion design student, and petite Kathy Kleiner from Miami. Karen had taken the previous year's sex assault on her sorority house sister almost as hard as Margaret Bowman, and worried endlessly about the safety of the girls living at the house.

On Saturday night, January 14th, 1978, most of the girls were out on dates. They straggled back in ones and twos, some of them not getting home until early Sunday morning, January 15th. Generally, they entered by the back door, which had a push button combination lock that was supposed to be kept fastened after midnight.

Karen Chandler was one of the early ones in. She'd had dinner with her parents and got back to her room about 10.30 p.m. After watching TV for a while she went to sleep about midnight. Kathy Kleiner was already in bed. She had been to a wedding earlier in the day and retired by 11.30 p.m.

Lisa Levy made it an early evening too. After a nightcap with another student at a bar next door, the two girls returned to the house at about 10.30 p.m.

Lisa went to bed. The other girl sat up talking to Margaret Bowman until about 2.45 a.m. She remembered noting the time on her digital clock as she got into bed.

Student Nita Neary from Altamonte Springs got back from a party at 3.00 a.m. and found the rear door ajar. Even more strange, the hall lights upstairs had been turned off.

Nita changed into her night clothes and went to the bathroom, which as in most dormitories, was shared and opened into the common hallway. While she was brushing her teeth she heard the closed bathroom door squeak.

"It only does that when someone walks by," she later explained. "But when I came out, there was no one there." Nita then went into the living-room to turn off the lights. As she did so she heard a thump and footsteps from the floor above. The footsteps then hurried down the stairs.

Nita turned towards the foyer, then paused. A man was standing by the door. His left hand was under the door knob; in his right hand he grasped a club, holding it in the centre so both ends protruded from his fist.

"It looked like a log because of the texture. It was rough, like tree bark. I thought it was either a burglar or one of the girls had got up enough courage to sneak a guy up."

"The man appeared "frozen." As she was standing in the now darkened living-room "three or four yards" away he was motionless. For a matter of seconds the silent tableau held, then the man disappeared through the door.

"I don't think he saw me," Nita later told the police. His face had been turned the whole time, his profile to her. But as an art student she had been trained to observe. She had seen a white man wearing light trousers and a dark coat. A knitted ski cap covered most of his face. He had a sharp triangular nose, thin but prominent.

Concerned, Nita ran upstairs to wake her roommate and alert her to the possible burglary. The roommate grabbed her umbrella from a cupboard, and thus armed, the two girls ventured back down to check the front door. It was locked. They peered out of the window. The front garden and street were deserted. Still concerned, however, they went back upstairs to wake the sorority president.

Down the hallway, they saw Karen Chandler stagger out of her room, bent over, her head in her hands as if she were ill. They ran to help her and saw that blood covered her face and hands.

Through the open dormitory door they saw Kathy Kleiner sitting up in bed, "moaning and groaning".

The police arrived at 3.23 a.m. and were admitted by Nita and her roommate. The first thing Officer Oscar Brannon asked for was a description of the intruder, which the student provided. White male, young, five-foot-eight,

12 stone, slender build, clean shaven, prominent nose, knitted cap and carrying a large stick with a dark cloth or stocking around it. Officer Brannon repeated the description to headquarters.

Officer Ray Crew then called down from upstairs that they had a body.

Margaret Bowman had been found lying face down on her bed, her yellow nightie hiked up, her arms twisted around and turned palms up on her back.

"Around her neck was a tightly wound stocking. Her body, head, bed, walls and floor were splattered with blood. Her panties lay on the floor by the bed."

Trailed by the housemother, the officers began a room by room search. Crew entered room number 8 and discovered a figure lying covered up on the bed.

"That's Lisa Levy," murmured the housemother from the doorway. Crew reached down and pulled away the bed covers to reveal Lisa's battered and bloody head.

On the beds of both victims, on the pillows and in their hair were fragments of tree bark. Police found similar fragments by the front door.

By this time an emergency rescue team had arrived. They took over from the girl who was holding a plastic cup under Kathy's chin to catch her blood. She was still sitting up in bed, moaning and incoherent when the rescue men eased her into an ambulance. Karen Chandler was now unconscious.

The emergency team leader pointed out a puncture wound near Lisa's right nipple. To the police it looked like a bite mark. Her nipple had almost been severed.

There was a similar mark on Lisa's left buttock, and on Margaret's thigh was an abrasion similar to a rope burn.

Margaret Bowman was pronounced dead at the scene. Lisa Levy died in the ambulance on the way to hospital. Mercifully Kathy and Karen would recover and never fully remember what happened that night.

Meanwhile, at an apartment block just a short distance away, two girls who occupied one of the flats came home at about 2.00 a.m. Entering they made loud catty remarks about the volume of their neighbour's TV, hoping to be overheard. It was a bone of contention between the two roommates and the girl from Virginia, a ballet student named Cheryl Thomas, the single occupant of the other room. The volume was lowered and the roommates went to sleep.

At about 4.30 a.m. one of the girls was awakened by loud thumping noises coming from Cheryl's room.

"We then heard Cheryl. She wasn't crying, she was whimpering. I called a guy I was going out with and asked him what I should do. He told me to phone Cheryl's room to see if she was all right."

The two roommates called Cheryl on the phone. "We let it ring five times. As soon as the phone started ringing I heard real wild noises, like running, and I could hear Cheryl both crying and laughing. She didn't answer the phone so I thought something was wrong."

Consequently, they called the police. Twelve police cars were there in minutes, while the dispatcher kept the girls talking on the phone, urging them to stay calm and sit tight.

It was now about 4.40 a.m., just a little more than an hour after the first call from the Chi Omega house only a short distance away.

Officer Wilton Dozier found Cheryl Thomas crossways on her bed, a pair of tights entangled in the bedding. "She was in a semi-conscious state; she did not respond to any of our commands and there was blood all over her body and bed."

Cheryl did not recover consciousness for nearly a week, and as with Karen and Kathy she mercifully could not remember much about the attack. She had been severely battered, perhaps with a length of board she used during the summer to keep her window propped open.

She had lost the hearing in one ear, and what was tragically worse, damage to her inner ear threatened to permanently impair her sense of balance and end any thoughts of becoming a dancer. She also underwent brain surgery.

Reconstructing the crime, the police believed the intruder, who they assumed to be the same man who had invaded Chi Omega, had removed the screen on the door, bent back a curtain rod, and thrust himself into Cheryl's apartment. They also believed that the ringing telephone had no doubt saved her life.

By 5 a.m. all the Chi Omega girls had been finger-printed so their own fingerprints could be eliminated by technicians processing the house. All available police personnel were combing the neighbourhood. In the next few weeks 40 different police agencies would become involved in the manhunt.

"We have a deranged murderer on our hands, a crazy man," warned horrified officials of the 22,000 student campus. "We don't know where he is or what he will do next, but you must not go out by yourselves. You must not go out."

Fraternity students armed with bats volunteered as extra security guards for the residences. Many parents withdrew their daughters from the university, and students walked in groups to classrooms.

A few crumbs of information were gathered. Three of the girls, the two that were killed and the ballet dancer, had all been at Big Daddy's bar earlier on the evening of the attack. Other students who were also at the bistro spoke of a young man with a thin sharp nose who had stared at them offensively.

Meanwhile, an intensive search did not recover the murder weapon, but police thought it must have been an oak branch. There were many old trees in that neighbour-hood and a pile of such timber was stacked by the Chi Omega back door.

All of the girls had been savagely battered. In the opinion of Dr. Thomas Wood, Leon County medical examiner, the two who were slain were first clubbed unconscious. This theory was borne out by the lack of any signs of a struggle in their rooms.

Lisa Levy had strangulation marks on her neck and "suffered trauma to her anal and genital areas." Police had recovered a hair spray bottle from her floor on which lab. technicians found blood and faecal matter, leading the police to surmise her assailant had used this to sexually assault her. She had also been bitten on the breast and buttocks.

"But in all likelihood," said Dr. Wood, "she was first rendered unconscious by the blows to the head, then bitten, then penetrated by an object and finally strangled to death."

Dr. Wood theorised that the abrasion on Margaret Bowman's left thigh had been caused by the forcible removal of her panties, and she had been hit so hard on the head that her skull was depressed. She had then been strangled with the tights found knotted tightly around her neck.

The bite marks on Lisa's body were photographed and measured. The bite on her buttocks was surgically removed for preservation.

The tights found on the bed in Margaret Bowman's room had had one leg cut off, the other tied, and holes cut out for eyes. Lab. technicians found brown curly hairs inside.

The Chi Omega killer, according to the police reconstruction, walked through a recreation room after entering by the back door, which he found unlatched. He then mounted the stairs. At the top was a corridor with doors along both sides.

"He did in fact pass over several rooms before entering one. It is entirely possible he looked in on the others, but he was probably looking for a room with just one person in it," said one detective.

Working from Nita's description of the man whose profile she had glimpsed, a university professor of art drew a sketch which the police released widely.

When she was able to talk, Cheryl Thomas told the

police that she had returned home that night shortly before 2 a.m. She had heard the girls in the next room come in and loudly complain about her TV. After making herself a snack, she went to bed. Some time later she was awakened by a noise.

"During the night I heard a plant being knocked over, but I had a cat and I thought maybe it had knocked something over. So I went back to sleep."

She remembered nothing more until she woke up in the hospital several days later.

Despite many hours of overtime and frustration, the case had not advanced after a month when, 220 miles west of Tallahassee, Pensacola policeman Robert Lee, on routine road patrol, stopped an orange Volkswagen Beetle at about 1.30 a.m. on Wednesday, February 15th, 1978.

Something about the vehicle stirred Lee's suspicions. He radioed in to see if it was stolen, then stopped the driver near a restaurant asking for identification.

A young man got out and produced identification for a Florida University student. At that moment, the patrol car radio crackled back the information that the Beetle had been stolen from Tallahassee the previous Sunday.

Officer Lee ordered the young man to lie down on the ground, and he started to handcuff him. The policeman thought another person was hiding in the car and his attention was diverted. In a swift movement, his captive kicked the feet out from under the officer, hit him with the handcuffs dangling from one wrist, and ran off.

Scrambling to his feet, Lee drew his service revolver and gave chase, shooting and calling for his quarry to halt. The suspect eventually stopped and muttered, "I wish you would have killed me!" And as Officer Lee took his prisoner in, the young man commented, "This case ought to help you make sergeant."

Searching the orange 1972 Volkswagen, police found credit cards and other identity papers in 21 different names, most of them for students.

The suspect continued to insist on the identity originally

given to Officer Lee, but the real student was quickly located and told police he'd lost his identity papers some time over the Christmas holidays.

The following day, Pensacola detective Norman Chapman, puzzling over the riddle of all the credit cards, suddenly had an idea. The latest FBI "Most Wanted" list had been circulated just the previous Friday. Chapman studied a new name on it: Theodore Robert Bundy.

Chapman phoned the FBI. Agents arrived with wanted posters and fingerprints, and an identification was quickly made.

Acting FBI Director James Adams confirmed that Bundy was wanted for questioning in 36 sex assault murders in four Western states, dating back to 1969. He had escaped from prison in Colorado while awaiting trial on one in which he had been formally accused.

There was only one conviction, that for the 1974 kidnapping of a 17-year-old girl in Salt Lake City, Utah. Bundy received a one-to-15-year sentence. While in prison he was arrested for the 1975 sex-slaying of Carolyn Campbell, a Michigan nurse and sister of a Fort Lauderdale, Florida, police officer.

Her nude, badly bitten body had been found in a Colorado snow bank after she vanished on a skiing holiday. Petrol credit card receipts in Bundy's own name placed him in the immediate area at the time of the crime and were among the clues leading to his arrest.

On New Year's Eve, 1977, Bundy had squirmed through a ceiling light fixture hole and escaped from prison.

Several of the slayings involved bludgeoning, sexual battery and strangulation. Consequently, Detective Chapman contacted authorities in Tallahassee investigating the Chi Omega killings.

Among credit cards found in the orange Beetle Bundy was accused of stealing was one that might provide leads to another case provoking Florida headlines. Twelve-year-old Kimberly Leach had disappeared from her school on

February 9th. She was currently being sought all over northern Florida. Investigators in this case, as well as those involved in the Tallahassee slayings, questioned Bundy on Friday, February 17th.

At the same time detectives in Tallahassee examined the quarters Bundy had rented on January 7th in a boarding house only a short distance from Chi Omega.

This house was known as "The Oaks" because of the mammoth old tree in its front garden. Bundy's fellow-boarders were astonished that the young man they knew as "Chris Hagen" was a suspect in the monstrous student killings.

In a long, rambling all-night interrogation, only part of which was taped, Bundy talked of his personality and his "problem." In later testimony, Detective Chapman said that Bundy complained of "fantasies" taking over his life.

"He said to keep his fantasies going he had to do acts against society. He said he was a voyeur. He felt like a vampire because he could get by on three hours sleep a night while getting in his car and driving many miles."

Asked about the Chi Omega murders, "Bundy dropped his head, and in a very sincere tone with tears in his eyes, he told us, 'The evidence is there. Go find it,' " Chapman said.

While the tape was still running, Bundy spoke freely of his New Year's Eve escape. He made his way to the University of Michigan and rented a room at the YMCA. But because the Colorado victim was from Michigan, his name was in all the papers there. He then decided that he wanted to go to Florida and look up the colleges in the library catalogue.

He found that the University of Florida was in Gainesville, so he bought a map of the state. "Here's Gainesville in the middle of nowhere, and I wanted to be by the ocean for Christ's sake. Gainesville on the map didn't look right. Isn't it strange? Didn't look right. If it had been by Tampa Bay, I may have gone there. Who knows? And so I came to the catalogue for Florida State

University. All this is almost random in a way. Superstitious."

He bought a bus ticket to Tallahassee, "but I made a mistake in choosing Florida State University. It's not that big, the kind of major metropolitan campus I was looking for." Nevertheless, he started shopping around for suitable identification.

He wanted a recent graduate. "I figured I had a degree on my own, you know. Wouldn't be terribly deceitful of me to get the identity that had a degree." So he selected the one he was arrested under.

Resolutions to play it cool and careful faded, and in Tallahassee his "habit of wanting to acquire things" resurfaced.

"Little things, things to make life comfortable. I don't mean Cadillacs. I started to take short cuts, see. I stole things. Towels, you know, some cologne or a racquet ball or a pair of shorts. Like going to the supermarket and stuffing my bag full of cans of sardines. I'm not a very good job hunter, and uh, I kinda procrastinate. I was losing sight of my plans to just stick with it, get some identification, get a job, stay inconspicuous. Stealing a car was a shortcut . . . A stupid shortcut."

He stole a series of cars, but he did remember to wear leather gloves most of the time, thereby avoiding fingerprints.

Bundy side stepped questions about a stolen white van that Lake City witnesses had seen the 12-year-old schoolgirl enter. "I really can't talk about it," Bundy said. "We, we better not talk about it."

Pressed about the Chi Omega murders, he asked that the tape be turned off and the investigators not take notes. It was then that he rambled on about "uncontrollable fantasies" and "vampire feelings," police said, but he did not admit to any murders.

Bundy was ordered by the court to submit to blood and hair samples and teeth impressions. Although DNA fingerprinting had not been discovered, this forensic evidence was to prove crucial.

A Coral Gables dentist, who is also consultant to the Dade County medical examiner, found that transparent overlays of Bundy's teeth impressions "lined up exactly" and "fitted perfectly" onto a police photo close-up of the bite mark on Lisa Levy's buttock.

Bite marks, however, present problems. The soft, yielding, elastic nature of human tissue makes reproduction for comparison difficult. A video-computer technique developed in the NASA space programme allows moon photographs to be read for three-dimensional information. It also allows depth of bite marks to be determined by computer analysis.

The dentist found "30 points of positive comparison" between Bundy's teeth and the bite marks on the victim. It was a double bite, he said. Twice the lower teeth sunk into Lisa's flesh with tremendous force, holding the tissue, "while the upper teeth did the scraping. It is convincing beyond any discussion whatsoever. There is absolutely no way that this can be refuted," declared the dentist. "His teeth made those marks."

Investigators were convinced they had the right man. Prosecutors agreed. In July, 1978, a Leon County jury indicted Theodore Robert Bundy for the Chi Omega murders. The first act in what was to be a long Bundy drama in Florida was over.

It took almost a year of judicial manoeuvring, frequently prompting screaming headlines, before a jury in Miami, after seven hours of deliberation, found him guilty. The same jury recommended the death penalty.

On Tuesday, July 31st, 1979, Judge Edward Cowart formally sentenced Bundy to the electric chair. He imposed the sentence twice: once for Lisa Levy and once for Margaret Bowman.

Meanwhile, other Florida officers had been assembling evidence linking Bundy to the disappearance of 12-year-old Kimberly Leach, whose battered and ravished body had been found in an abandoned pig sty.

She was still missing when Bundy was arrested in Pensacola. The 21 credit cards in differing names found in the stolen car he was driving provided the first lead in the search for the girl, who went missing from Lake City Junior High School, about 100 miles east of Tallahassee.

Kimberly Diane Leach, a runner-up for school Valentine queen, had already picked out her party dress for the Saturday night Valentine dance on February 11th, 1978. Two days earlier was the last day she was seen alive, returning to her classroom to pick up her bag which she had left there during the first lesson that morning. A classmate told the police she had seen Kimberly getting into a white van.

Stolen credit cards found on Bundy were used in Jacksonville and a Lake City motel the day before Kimberly disappeared. The white van had been stolen near the Florida University campus and a man fitting Bundy's general description had signed into the Lake City Holiday Inn using one of the stolen credit cards.

Hundreds joined in the search for this missing youngster, but it would be 39 days after her disappearance that the grim hunt came to its grisly conclusion.

On the afternoon of Friday, April, 7th, Trooper K. Robinson, one of about 40 investigators making a second search of an area about 20 miles west of Lake City, lifted the sheet-metal covering an old lean-to that had formerly sheltered pigs. Stuffed under a mass of debris was a decomposing body clad in the jeans and T-shirt Kim had been wearing when last seen.

On July 20th, 1978, the Columbia County jury returned a sealed indictment in connection with the rape- murder of Kimberly Leach. The envelope was opened in Lake City on Monday, July 31st, just hours after Bundy had pleaded not guilty in the Chi Omega murders. Any trial would have to await the resolution of that earlier case.

But after several delays and the arranging of a defence motion for a change of venue, a jury was finally selected in

Orlando in January, 1980. The five-man, seven-woman jury deliberated for seven and a half hours before finding the 33-year-old former law student guilty. Bundy, already facing two death sentences in the sorority slayings, stood expressionless. As in the earlier Florida trial in Miami in July, 1979, he had acted as his own attorney.

A parade of police officers testified to finding fibres from Bundy's and Kimberly's clothing in the white van; bloodstains on the van carpet; semen on her panties; and two footprints made by Bundy's shoes.

Bundy, in a last minute plea for an acquittal, claimed to have been a victim of circumstances. While the jury was still out, his 32-year-old fianceé, his devoted supporter at both trials, bought four red roses and sent them back to her lover via a bailiff. When the verdict came in, she raced to phone him comforting words.

At the penalty phase of the trial she was the only witness for the defence, and begged for a life sentence, saying, "Ted forms a large part of my life."

However, the jury was not swayed and recommended the convicted killer be sent to the electric chair.

On Tuesday, February 12th, 1980, Judge Wallace Jopling formally imposed a third death sentence on Theodore Robert Bundy.

Bundy remained on Death Row for almost 10 years, and just putting him there had cost an immense effort.

However, on, January 24th, 1989, Bundy finally went to the electric chair. He was 42. He declined the traditional last meal and went to his death with a look of controlled anger. His appeals against his death sentence had cost American tax-payers over four million dollars.

The night before his execution, in an attempt to stave off the inevitable, Bundy tearfully confessed to many more murders with full horrific details. He said he blamed pornography for his sick obsessions.

A panel of 42 witnesses saw Bundy die at dawn, a one minute surge of 2,000 volts passing through his body. They reported that he had arched his back against the restraints and clenched his fists as the current hit him.

Outside the prison demonstrators cheered and set off fire-crackers. Many wore T-shirts bearing a picture of the electric chair with the words, "Burn, Bundy, Burn."

The deceptively wholesome looking man with the engaging smile and film-star looks was finally gone. He had confessed to murdering 23 women and young girls, but police suspected he had killed at least another 15.

At the end Bundy's cockiness deserted him as he spent his last few days helping detectives from Washington State, Utah and Colorado clear their books on unsolved sex killings. America's most infamous son had been written about in hundreds of newspaper and magazine articles, and in half a dozen best-selling books. A television film about him, *Deliberate Stranger*, was made starring Mark Harmon as Bundy. Many young American women still cherished romantic notions about Bundy, but there was nothing romantic about him.

Dr. James Dobson, a psychiatrist who saw him the night before his execution, said that only after the first killing had Bundy felt any remorse.

"But then the sex frenzy overcame him and he killed again, and as each crime passed, he grew desensitised. He could not feel any more ..."

Bundy himself felt embarrassed at his bloody career; at being what one judge called "the most competent serial killer in the USA today."

He refused to allow prison guards to overhear him confessing to detectives, and wrote the names of his victims on pieces of paper.

One detective said at the time, "From what he's told us I'd say he was the worst mass killer of all time. There's not been another man like him."

10

THE LADY COP AND THE SERIAL KILLER

Steven Barry

"Oh, my God, I'm looking at the man who did all those terrible things to those women"

RENÉE LANO was a police cadet when the first murder took place. At the time she was too busy mastering the nuts and bolts of police work to pay any attention to it. But just eight months later, when the case developed into the first serial killer saga in the history of Delaware, the attractive 23-year-old blonde would be asked to put her life on the line. Night after night Renée Lano would offer herself as a human decoy for a diabolical killer who was stalking and butchering young women.

It all began on Sunday, November 29th, 1987.

By 9.30 p.m. the temperature had dropped into the mid-40s, and it was drizzling as a young couple pulled into a lovers' lane behind the Old Baltimore Pike Industrial Park some 10 miles south of Wilmington. They were about to park when they saw a body lying on the ground. They left at once and phoned the Delaware State Police.

After nine years as a state trooper Joe Swiski had been assigned to the major crimes unit just two months earlier, and this was his first homicide investigation.

The corpse, still warm, was that of a young white

female, 5-foot-6 and 11 stone, who was nude except for a pair of turquoise sweatpants that had been pulled down around her calves. Her skull had been crushed, and blood was soaking her shoulder-length dark hair. Her entire body had been badly bruised. Strangulation marks ringed her throat. But what caught Swiski's attention most of all was the duct tape that was binding the victim's hands and feet, and the fact that one of her nipples had been torn from her body.

Investigators searched the crime scene all night but failed to uncover a single piece of evidence. Furthermore, they were unable to establish whether the murder had taken place where the body had been discovered or elsewhere.

Meanwhile, the body was taken away for an autopsy. Using fingerprint comparisons the pathologist identified the victim as 23-year-old Shirley Ellis and narrowed the cause of death to any one of three violent blows to the head — each of which had driven shards of bone into the woman's brain. He described the murder weapon as a blunt instrument, probably a hammer.

The next morning Swiski drove to Brookmont Farms, a housing estate about three miles from where the body had been found. There Shirley's parents told him that she had left the house around 6 p.m. on Sunday to visit a friend in a Wilmington hospital. They said she had left on foot and had been wearing turquoise sweatpants, a denim jacket with a pink hood, and white high-top sneakers.

That evening Swiski stopped at a convenience store on the main road — U.S. Route 40 — opposite the entrance to Brookmont Farms. A shop assistant said he remembered that Shirley Ellis had called at the store shortly after six o'clock on Sunday evening, bought a packet of cigarettes and one red rose, and left to hitch a ride towards Wilmington.

At the hospital Swiski interviewed Shirley's friend, who confirmed the victim's visit and said that Shirley left the hospital at 7.30.

That was as far as Swiski could trace the victim's last steps. From there, he theorised, Shirley must have hitched a ride home from the hospital and been picked up by a psychopath who tortured her, mutilated her, and then dumped her body. The whole episode had taken place in the two hours between 7.30, when Shirley had left the hospital, and 9.30, when the body was found.

Renée Lano completed her police training three months later in February, 1988 and became a rookie cop, responding to complaints and trying to resolve domestic disputes before they escalated into violence.

In the meantime no progress had been made in the Shirley Ellis homicide investigation. To Joe Swiski it was beginning to look as if his first murder case would remain unsolved.

Then at 6.30 a.m. on June 29th, 1988, construction workers found the second body.

"It looks like she was pushed out of a car," one of the workers told a police dispatcher, "and she's beat all to hell. The back of her head's crushed and her body's all covered with bruises."

Detective Jim Hedrick went to a building site three miles from where Shirley Ellis's body had been found and a mile from where she'd last been seen.

The nude body was that of a white female aged about 30. Duct tape bound her hands and feet, and her breasts had been mutilated. Hedrick, who had familiarised himself with the investigation of the Shirley Ellis case, recognised the similarities at a glance.

He shut down the building site and called for help. For most of the day police searched the dirt piles and excavations for clues. But, as in the case of Shirley Ellis, nothing was found.

That afternoon relatives identified the victim as Cathy DiMauro, 31 years old and the divorced mother of three small children. She had lived at the Greenfield Manor Apartments on U.S. 40, and had last been seen at home on the day before the building site workers discovered her body.

A pathologist listed the cause of death as a series of blows to the head administered by a hammer. He vacuumed the body and recovered nearly two dozen different types of fibres — most blue.

That night Hedrick called Swiski to compare notes. Both women were young and white. They lived near one another and both were frequent hitch-hikers on U.S. 40. They both died from hammer blows to the head, they'd both been tied hand and foot by duct tape, and both had suffered breast mutilations. As a result of that conversation the two investigators struck up a partnership.

They drove to the FBI offices in Washington and met Special Agent John Edward Douglas. Ten years earlier Douglas had helped design the FBI's Criminal Investigation Analysis Programme, under which criminologists analysed violent crimes, interviewed the perpetrators, and catalogued the psychological profiles of murderers. In the course of his work Special Agent Douglas had interviewed Charles Manson, Richard Speck, John Wayne Gacy, and David "Son of Sam" Berkowitz.

"When we first talked to the FBI," Hedrick would say later, "they told us we had the beginnings of a serial killer case. And they told us: serial killers don't stop killing. You will continue to get bodies until this individual is apprehended."

Special Agent Douglas explained that serial killers always slay three or more people, allowing a cooling-off period after each killing. Douglas said this method of operation differed from that of mass murderers, who kill four or more victims at a time, and from spree killers, who kill their victims without cooling-off periods until they're caught or commit suicide.

"There's a lot of fantasy involved," Douglas told the Delaware investigators, "and serial killers like to keep mementos from their kills. Above all serial killers are not stupid people; their IQ is generally between one hundred and one-forty-five."

For the next two weeks the FBI's Behavioral Science Unit analysed the data Hedrick and Swiski had given them. Then Agent Douglas phoned Delaware.

"The man you're looking for," he said, "is a white male between twenty-five and thirty-four. He lives near the sites of the killings, and he's employed as a carpenter, a mason, or an electrician."

Douglas also recommended the use of a decoy.

Both Shirley Ellis and Cathy DiMauro were known to have regularly hitch-hiked on the busy U.S. Route 40, on a stretch along which more than 60 arrests for prostitution had been made the previous year. While newspapers stopped short of calling Shirley Ellis and Cathy DiMauro hookers, the suspicion existed.

Swiski and Hedrick interviewed everyone involved with businesses along the strip. They parked outside porn shops, noted car numbers and traced customers. Inside the shops they looked at the "personal" ads on the boards and questioned the proprietors: are any of your customers acting in a nervous or suspicious manner? Any customers interested in bondage? Who's been asking where they could find hookers?

"The cops asked me if any weirdos have been coming in," one proprietor recalled. "Hey, in this business, what can I tell them? All my customers are weirdos."

Swiski and Hedrick interviewed dozens of men and eliminated all of them as suspects — except one: Billy Henderson. Just 72 hours before Cathy DiMauro's body had been found, witnesses had seen Henderson, who worked at a truck stop on Route 13, take DiMauro for a ride.

"I knew her by face, but not by name," Henderson told the detectives. "She was one of the prostitutes who congregated at the truck stop hustling the truckers. That night I drove her to a building site. We had sex and I dropped her off a little while later."

With no other suspects the detectives kept an eye on Billy Henderson. At the same time they put the FBI's decoy suggestion to Renée Lano. They wanted her to pose as a hooker and try to lure the killer into approaching her.

"I'm Catholic," she would say later, "and I had some real moral questions about doing this at first."

Lano had grown up in West Chester, Pennsylvania, in a tight-knit family with a brother and two sisters. When she was 16 her family moved to the Wilmington area.

"I was considered a tomboy," Renée recalled, "yet I was a cheer-leader. We moved at a crucial stage of my life — boys and cars — and I didn't really apply myself in school. If it weren't for cheer-leading, I might not have made it through school. But it gave me some focus."

Near the end of high school Renée got involved with the Police Explorers programme and found the regimentation of police work to her liking. After high school she worked as a cook during the day and took criminology courses at night. Then she applied to join the police.

Describing her role as a decoy, she said: "I would do my regular eight hours on the street, then come in and get into my shoulder-length brown wig and walk the highway. I usually wore jeans and a tank top — I'd put on a flannel shirt if it got cold — and I carried a handbag.

"They didn't tell me a lot about what was going on in the investigation. I was very new — still on probation — and didn't need to know most of the details. They didn't want to confuse me with too much information. About all I knew was that young women were being killed and blue fibres had been collected from one of the victims."

For Renée's safety she wore a concealed microphone and officers were stationed as close as possible in unmarked cars, watching her movements and monitoring her conversations. However, sometimes the microphone malfunctioned.

"It was very important to me to know that people I trusted were out there," she recalled. "Jim Hedrick, Joe Swiski and all of the officers who took turns watching me were very supportive, along with my whole family. In fact, my father called every day to make sure I was all right."

The decoy operation began at the end of July.

"At first we had five or six guys working on the case," Hedrick recalled. "We'd work all day investigating leads and then we'd go out with Renée until two or three in the morning. Then we'd come back in later that morning and start all over again."

"The hours were unreal," Swiski echoed.

Still the killings continued.

Margaret Finner was 27 years old and a supermarket cashier with two small children. On the night of August 22nd, while Renée was working one section of U.S. Route 40, Margaret Finner disappeared from another.

Swiski, Hedrick and Renée found out about this the next day when Finner's family reported her missing. Moving fast, Hedrick and Swiski located a barmaid who had seen Margaret standing in a motel car park the night before.

"A van pulled up," the barmaid said. "They talked for a while and she got in."

Hedrick asked her to describe the van.

"It was blue," the barmaid replied.

"What about the driver?"

"I couldn't see him," she said.

Nineteen days passed.

Shirley Ellis and Cathy DiMauro were dead, Margaret Finner was missing, and Renée Lano was still walking the highway every night, hoping to make a connection with the killer. Then, on the night of September 10th, the "Corridor Killer," as he would soon come to be called, claimed his fourth victim.

Earlier that evening 26-year-old Kathleen Meyer had an argument with her boy friend and left the house in a huff. The couple shared a home in Brookmont Farms, the estate where Shirley Ellis, the first victim, had lived. Family members reported Kathleen missing.

Although the bodies of Margaret Finner and Kathleen Meyer had not been found, the police assumed that the two young brunettes had become victims number three and four. They contacted Russell Vorpagel, a retired Behavioral Science Unit agent, for additional assistance.

"Your killer is akin to a wolf on the prowl," he told the investigators. "He kills just for the fun of it. Serial killers get pleasure from the pain, the dominance, and the crying of their victims. But the pleasurable effects of killing wear off more rapidly with each occurrence, and the killers become jaded.

"When lust killers act out their fantasies the first few times they are often so caught up in the killing that they don't think about what they are going to do with the bodies. The first few are dumped, just to get rid of them, or they may be left as a challenge to the police. Then, as a series of crimes becomes more established, the killer takes more care in disposing of the victims."

This was exactly what was happening. The time between the killings was growing shorter, and the killer was hiding the bodies.

By September 14th the investigators had conducted more than 500 interviews, but they did not have one suspect. Even Billy Henderson had been eliminated because he could not be tied to the disappearances of Shirley Ellis, Margaret Finner, or Kathleen Meyer.

In the seven weeks that Renée had been operating as a decoy she had been approached by more than 100 prospective clients.

"I was supposed to talk with them," she explained, "try to ascertain their names, their business, and why they were in the area. Most were interested in sexual acts, but at no point did I ever enter a vehicle."

None of her "clients" became suspects.

On the night of September 14th Renée was walking along the highway, close enough to the shopping centre to be partially illuminated in a yellowish light. At around 8.30 a blue van drove slowly past ... once ... twice ... a third time. It was a blue windowless Chevy.

"Jim," Renée said into her microphone, "if you can hear me, honk."

About 100 yards away a car horn beeped.

"This guy's been scoping me and it feels weird," she said, then gave Hedrick the van's number which he ran through the Bureau of Motor Vehicles computer. It was registered to a Steven Pennell, 30, who lived in the nearby Glasgow Pines mobile home park.

"My guys picked me up," Renée recalled. "We disappeared for a while to make it look like I was doing a trick. At that point we all huddled and decided to move me to some place where it was darker, hoping this guy would stop and try to pick me up."

At around 11.30 p.m. the officers dropped her further down the road. A few minutes passed.

"Here he is," she said into her microphone.

The van pulled onto the shoulder and the driver waved her over. As she approached the van from the passenger side she felt her heart pounding.

"Hi, I'm Jackie," Renée said. "What's your name?"

"Jim," the driver answered.

She looked into his eyes, trying to get a quick read.

"They were brown," she recalled, "and lifeless, as if he were looking right through me. It was like they were dead and everything about him was very different. He was big and hairy and very intimidating.

"Most of the other guys who tried to pick me up would really try to woo me into their cars — 'You're really gorgeous, baby, you're this, you're that, come on, let's go somewhere and party' — but not this man. He just sat there and stared at me and I kept babbling. I had to do most of the talking."

After a while Renée asked him if he wanted oral sex.

"Are you a cop?" he asked her.

"No, are you?" she shot right back at him.

"Get in," the driver told Lano.

Lano opened the sliding door in the middle of the van and looked inside. It was possible that if this were the killer he might be working with an accomplice.

"Turn the lights on," she said. "I want to see what your

van looks like."

He turned on the interior lights.

Renée looked inside but didn't see anyone hidden in the back.

"I saw this blue carpet," she recalled, and she remembered the blue fibres that had been found on Cathy DiMauro's corpse. "My heart really came up into my throat and I said to myself, 'Oh, my God, I'm looking at the man who did all those terrible things to those women.' No way did I want that done to me. So I kind of played the dumb, stoned routine."

"Get in," the driver said, more insistence in his tone this time.

"Your van is really sharp," she replied, and she started running her hand over the blue carpeting.

"Get in," he said for the third time.

At this point Renée began to feel threatened.

Jim Hedrick was sitting in his car 100 yards away, listening to the conversation.

"Don't get in, Renée!" he said out loud to himself. "Whatever you do, don't get into that van!"

"Look, I've got a bad headache," she told the driver, "from doing too much dope. We'll party next time."

She shut the van's door and walked away. But before she did she'd pulled several strands of carpeting from the floor of the van and hid them in the palm of her hand.

When the van drove away Hedrick followed.

A few minutes later the blue Chevy pulled onto the shoulder of the road and the driver propositioned a hooker. She got into the van with him and he drove away. When they stopped at a convenience store and bought a six-pack, Hedrick got a better look at the driver. He was tall and burly. He drove the hooker to a nearby motel, and the pair entered one of the units.

Hedrick parked and called for back-up.

An hour later the driver and the hooker left the motel room. He dropped her off on the highway and went home.

The next day the investigators sent the carpet fibres that

Renée had extracted from the van to the FBI lab. for analysis. They also ran a background check on Steven Pennell and learned he was married, the father of two young children, and was also helping bring up his wife's teenage daughter from a prior marriage. He worked as an electrician, and his arrest record showed only one misdemeanour. There was nothing that implied violence or sexual deviance.

"He's like the biggest teddy bear you'd ever want to meet," was the way one of Pennell's friends described him, "and he wouldn't hurt a fly. He was always talking about being a cop, and that was his sole goal in life. He applied, but when he took the physical he had a hard time doing the pull-ups. That was the only thing that kept him from being a cop."

Steven Pennell had left high school in 1976. His assistant principal remembered him as a good student and "a quiet kid who never got in trouble." Pennell later took criminology courses to prepare himself for a career in law enforcement. From all indications he appeared to be merely a husband who was cheating on his wife. But Renée Lano felt otherwise.

"Guys," she told her partners, "this is him. I'm telling you it's him."

As innocent as he looked on paper, Pennell matched five of the FBI's guidelines: he was white, he possessed above average intelligence, he was 30 years old, he worked as an electrician and he lived close to the crime scenes.

A surveillance was established. Detectives got on Pennell's trail in the morning and followed him to work. They stayed with him during the day, followed him home from work, and monitored his movements until he went to bed. Then the investigators terminated the surveillance until the next morning.

Two days passed without incident.

The third day, September 17th, was just like the first two. Nothing suspicious happened. When Pennell turned in for bed around 11 p.m. the detectives terminated the surveillance for the night and went home.

Shortly after midnight the suspect grew restless. He got dressed and went for a ride. A little while later Pennell pulled into a motel on U.S. 40, where a 20-year-old brunette was soliciting in the car park. Her name was Michelle Gordon. Born in England, she had moved to America with her family at the age of four, but her teenage years had been filled with one minor brush with the law after another.

"She's a suburban kid who got involved with drugs," said her lawyer.

In the early-morning hours of September 18th, 1988, Michelle Gordon got involved with more than drugs.

She got into the blue van and Pennell took her for a ride to a remote area a couple of miles away. He parked and asked Michelle if she liked bondage.

She told him that for the right price she liked just about anything.

They climbed into the back of the van and he wrapped duct tape around Michelle's hands and feet. He didn't bother gagging her. For one thing they were in the middle of nowhere. For another his van was sound-proof. Besides, he wanted to hear Michelle's screams.

As soon as he was in complete control Pennell sliced off Michelle's clothing with a knife, and cut fine lines up and down the fronts and backs of her legs with the tip of the blade. Pennell then rolled Michelle onto her belly and spanked her hard across the buttocks. He said dirty things to her. Then he took a pair of case-hardened steel pliers out of the toolbox he kept in the van.

Michelle Gordon must have screamed her lungs out as Pennell pinched her abdomen with the pliers and slowly worked his way towards her breasts, pinching here and squeezing there at his whim. One at a time Pennell twisted Michelle's nipples until streams of blood ran down her chest. Then he pulled each one off.

No one reported Michelle Gordon missing. As far as Swiski, Hedrick and Renée Lano knew, nothing had changed and the surveillance on Steven Pennell was leading nowhere.

Two days later, on September 20th, boaters discovered Michelle Gordon's nude body floating close to the west bank of the Chesapeake and Delaware Canal. By the time police officers arrived the body had washed onto the rocks, face down, less than a mile from the Summit Bridge.

Nearly 100 lawmen searched the area for evidence. This time they found something: fresh tyre-tread impressions in the dirt road that ran alongside the canal in close proximity to Michelle Gordon's corpse. Plaster casts were made.

At 4.30 that afternoon detectives followed Steven Pennell to a tyre firm, where he dropped off his van to have four new tyres fitted. Later Detective Hedrick returned with a search warrant and seized all the used tyres in the storage bin. Out of 30 discarded tyres he found the three 15-inch Firestone Supremes that had been removed from Pennell's van — Pennell had kept the fourth for a spare. Hedrick sent the tyres and the plaster casts of the tread imprints to the FBI lab for comparison.

Meanwhile, a pathologist had determined that the injuries and mutilations suffered by Michelle Gordon were consistent with those inflicted upon Shirley Ellis and Cathy DiMauro. The main difference between the three corpses was that Gordon had been in the habit of shaving her pubic hair and the others hadn't.

The next morning, September 23rd, Lano had a court appearance. After court she returned to the squad room.

"Renée," one of the investigators said to her, "did you hear the news about the fibres?"

From the tone of his voice it sounded like bad news. Renée's heart began to sink.

"It was a match," the straight-faced detective continued.

"What do you mean?" she asked confused.

"The FBI says whoever got the fibres deserves a medal."

The fibres which had been vacuumed from Cathy

DiMauro's corpse matched the fibres that Renée had plucked from Steven Pennell's van. They were trilobal polyester fibres produced by the DuPont Company and distributed to six carpet manufacturers in Georgia. Specifically, they matched imperial blue "Captivate" carpeting, Style 46, manufactured by the World Carpet Company in Dalton.

Detective Swiski flew to Georgia. He traced the fibres from the manufacturer to a carpet retailer in Wilmington to the customer who bought the carpeting and installed it in Pennell's van. There was now no doubt in the detectives' minds that Steven Pennell was the serial killer, but they still decided that they lacked sufficient evidence to make an arrest. This seems incredible, surely after the murder of Michelle Gordon and the carpet fibre match there was plenty of evidence to bring Pennell in for questioning. But no, a round-the-clock surveillance was established.

A week passed with no developments. Then on September 30th police officers stopped Pennell for a traffic violation as he was driving through Wilmington. While officers escorted him to court, evidence technicians examined his van.

"As I recall," one of the technicians would later say, "we were able to stretch it out to about an hour, but we were constantly being pressed to hurry. We had a search warrant, but we didn't want the suspect to know he was under surveillance. So, after the search, we had to restore the van as it appeared when we first entered." This again must be open to question. Why did they not make an arrest?

The technicians seized carpet fibres and pieces of upholstery. On the carpet they found bloodstains and several hairs. Newspaper articles about the murders of Shirley Ellis and Cathy DiMauro were on the van's dashboard. The investigators sent the evidence to the FBI lab for testing and awaited the results.

A month later, at last, it was time to move. Officers

searched Pennell's home and van. In the process they seized several hammers, sets of pliers, rolls of duct tape and pornographic videotapes and magazines. The titles of the videos were *Our Secret Spanking Sessions, Domination and Submission: Masters and Their Slaves Spill Their Sleazy Secrets,* and *The Taming of Rebecca,* which included a scene showing one man ordering another to pierce a naked young woman's nipple with a safety pin. The rest of the movie showed a torture chamber where men experimented on young women who were enslaved, torturing them until they were all dead.

But Delaware State Police decided it was still not enough evidence to make an arrest.

On November 12th deer hunters stumbled across a badly decomposed body in reeds along the edge of the Chesapeake and Delaware Canal, less than two miles from where Michelle Gordon's body had been discovered. Although the corpse was unrecognisable it bore similar mutilations to those inflicted upon Shirley Ellis, Cathy DiMauro and Michelle Gordon.

Two days later the pathologist used dental charts to identify the remains as those of Margaret Finner.

On November 18th officers called off the search for the missing Kathleen Meyer, but the test results had started coming in. The discarded tyres matched the casts of the tread imprints. The pliers found in Pennell's van were consistent with the pincer marks made on the victims' abdomens and breasts. Pennell's hammer was consistent with the damage to the victims' skulls. Red fibres that had been vacuumed from Cathy DiMauro's body matched upholstery fabric from the van's bench seat. Cotton fibres found in the hinge of Pennell's pen-knife matched Shirley Ellis's turquoise sweatpants. And pubic hairs vacuumed from the back of the van matched those of Michelle Gordon.

"The tips of the pubic hairs had been cut," FBI Agent Paul Bennett explained, "and I can assure you, most individuals do not razor-cut the tips of their pubic hairs."

At 11.30 p.m. on November 29th, 1988 — a year after the killings began — police officers arrested Steven Pennell. Two days later a grand jury indicted him for three homicides: those of Shirley Ellis, Cathy DiMauro, and Michelle Gordon. Margaret Finner's body was too badly decomposed to enable the authorities to charge Pennell with her murder, and Kathleen Meyer's body had never been found.

The trial began nearly two years later, in October, 1990, and lasted two months.

On the 25th day Steven Pennell took the stand on his own behalf. He denied ever meeting Shirley Ellis but admitted knowing both Cathy DiMauro and Michelle Gordon. He told the court he had been experiencing marital problems and started cruising the highway looking for women.

"I was driving up U.S. Forty and I saw a lady hitch-hiking," he testified, referring to Cathy DiMauro. "I asked her if she needed a lift. She mentioned going to an area bar. That's when she informed me she was a prostitute.

"We decided to have intercourse and settled on twenty-five dollars. I pulled into the car park and we hopped in the back and undressed. I noticed she was on her period and I mentioned it to her. So we decided to have oral sex and she gave me back ten dollars."

Pennell said he saw Cathy DiMauro on the night she was murdered.

"I asked her if we could do intercourse," Pennell told the jury. "She said fine. So I parked behind a mobile home dealership and we hopped in back, undressed, and had intercourse."

After they finished, Pennell continued, DiMauro got out of the van and he drove home. A friend came over and the two of them drank a few beers and some daiquiris and they watched porno videos.

Pennell said he met Michelle Gordon on September 14th while she was walking along U.S. 40. He said he drove her to a convenience store, then to a motel. And, he told the jury, he met her again two nights later.

"She said she was a prostitute," Pennell said, "but she refused to have intercourse. Then I asked her about oral sex and she said fine. I parked outside a convenience store along the highway and paid her an extra five dollars to take off her clothes. Afterwards, she got dressed, hopped out, and said, 'Maybe I'll see you around some time.'"

When Pennell finished his testimony his defence attorney approached him.

"Look the jury in the eye," the lawyer told Pennell. "Did you kill Catherine DiMauro?"

"Absolutely not," Pennell replied, staring at the jury.

"Did you kill Michelle Gordon?"

"Absolutely not."

The jury deliberated for six days. Then they found Steven Pennell guilty of murdering Shirley Ellis and Cathy DiMauro, but not guilty of murdering Michelle Gordon. He was sentenced to life imprisonment.

Eleven months later, on October 30th, 1991, Pennell pleaded "no contest" to charges that he killed both Michelle Gordon and Kathleen Meyer. Although he maintained his innocence in all five deaths, he made the pleas on the condition that he would quickly be put to death.

"I do not wish to put my family through another trial," he told the judge. "This court has found me guilty, so I ask that the sentence be death. 'Whoso killeth any person, the murderer shall be put to death! Whoso sheddeth man's blood, by man shall his blood be shed!'"

Detective Renée Lano drove to the Delaware Correctional Centre on Saturday morning, March 14th, 1992. At nine o'clock she entered a brown, windowless trailer. She sat in a small white room with two large windows. On the other side of the glass was the death chamber.

Twenty minutes later attendants led in a bearded Steve Pennell. He was wearing a blue prison jumpsuit and two clergymen stood at his side.

The attendants strapped Pennell onto a padded metal table. A gold cross was pinned to his collar and a large woven cross of blue and white cloth was tucked into his left breast pocket.

Shortly after 9.30 intravenous tubes were inserted into his arms, and moments later his chest heaved once.

Steven Pennell was pronounced dead at 9.49 a.m. It was the first execution in Delaware since 1946.

Renée Lano received a unit citation for her work in bringing Steven Pennell to justice.

11

AN AWFUL SPECTACLE FAR WORSE THAN HANGING

Martin Lomax

The humble origin of the mighty electric chair ...

Everyone knows of the electric chair, but not so many know its invention was prompted by accidents. Fewer still are aware that its creation began with a bitter battle between two commercial giants, one of them determined to block it.

To understand how this came about you need to know a little of electricity's early history. The first electric lighting system, perfected by Thomas Edison, used low-tension direct current which required such heavy wires that it was very expensive. Then George Westinghouse developed a high-tension alternating current transformer system which cut costs so dramatically that it threatened the future of Edison's business.

About this time several people were killed by accidentally coming into contact with wires using Westinghouse's high-tension alternating current, and Edison's men exploited this mishap. They said it demonstrated the superiority of their own direct current transmission, which at that time did not develop enough power to be dangerous. There were even calls to ban the Westinghouse system

Nevertheless the comparative cheapness of Westinghouse's alternating current enabled it to gain ground steadily, the company minimising the system's dangers.

Edison's men made the most of their one argument — danger — by engaging Harold P. Brown, a young electrical engineer, to demonstrate publicly that alternating current was a killer. He did this by using a Westinghouse generator to slay horses, stray dogs and cats.

Members of the Legislature who witnessed this had the previous year watched the horribly bungled hanging of a woman. They realised that electricity offered a quick, sure way of execution, and in 1888 a New York State bill was introduced to abolish hanging. Henceforth execution would be accomplished "by causing to pass through the body of a convict a current of electricity of sufficient intensity to cause death."

The bill was vigorously opposed by Westinghouse: the company feared that the use of their alternating current system to put people to death would ruin their business. Prospective customers might be deterred by the knowledge that, cheap though it was, the Westinghouse way could kill them.

The majority of the Legislature, however, believed that electrocution was "a painless and instantaneous means of stopping the lives of condemned criminals."

Then something happened that gave everyone pause for thought. Doctors revived two men who had apparently been killed by coming into contact with wires carrying alternating current. Westinghouse executives were jubilant, for it seemed that this development would torpedo the bill. The proposed electric chair would be nothing but an embarrassment if its occupants started coming round after their "execution."

Brown claimed, however, that while a shock which merely stunned the heart might not kill, one that passed through the nervous system would invariably be fatal. The authorities were not entirely convinced, but they still wanted to introduce execution by electrocution. Consequently a new clause was added to the bill, requiring an autopsy immediately after execution to "prevent any possible chance of the subject ever returning to life." With that, the bill was quickly passed.

It was signed by Governor David B. Hill, who had a prisoner's agonising death on his conscience. He had refused clemency for the woman whose hanging had gone so horrifically wrong.

The prison authorities who now had to implement the new means of execution were at a loss how to go about it, so Brown offered his services and they were accepted.

First he needed a Westinghouse dynamo, but Westinghouse refused to sell the state one, also declining to supply other necessary apparatus. Brown therefore got a man in South America to order a Westinghouse generator, and when it arrived it was reshipped to Auburn Prison. There, under Brown's direction, Edwin F. Davis made and installed the first electric chair and became the state's first executioner.

Meanwhile William Kemmler of Buffalo had been convicted of murder and committed to Auburn Prison, where he awaited execution. He was duly electrocuted on Wednesday, August 6th, 1890. "Don't hurry," he told a guard fumbling with the straps. "We got plenty of time."

The mandatory autopsy followed, confirming Brown's promise that his chair would do the trick. Until that moment there were still doubters. After all, although several people had died from electrocution by accident, until Kemmler went to the chair nobody had been electrocuted on purpose.

Not that everything could be said to have gone without a hitch. Kemmler took nine minutes to die, a *New York Times* reporter describing the execution as "an awful spectacle, far worse than hanging."

Nevertheless two more chairs were made at Auburn and installed at Clinton and Sing Sing Prisons. The first man to go to Sing Sing's chair, on Tuesday, July 7th, 1891, was inapproppriately named Harris A. Smiler.

Over the years the technique of execution by electrocution was improved by electricians in collaboration with doctors. Tests carried out by representatives of Columbia University's College of Physicians and Surgeons established that a lethal current of one ampere acted on the brain in one 720th of a second. As this was more than 70 times faster than the human nervous system can register a sensation, the electrocuted prisoner could not possibly feel pain. Or so the experts said, and there was nobody around to contradict them.

The amount of electricity applied to the condemned man in the chair would illuminate 800 house-lights. A third of this was dissipated in the brain, where the temperature approached the boiling point of water.

The prisoner undergoing electrocution in Sing Sing's chair was given two shocks of 2,000 volts, followed by a shock of 500 volts sustained for 57 seconds. Electrocution then concluded with another shock of 2,000 volts before the current was switched off.

The voltage was lowered after the initial shocks to avoid burning the body and at the same time to hold paralysis of the heart, respiratory organs and brain at a standstill for the rest of the execution. The whole operation took two minutes, thanks to refinements introduced since Kemmler's electrocution.

Never again, at least in New York State, would witnesses suffer the spectacle of a hanging woman struggling in her death throes. And the chair's inventor Harold P. Brown was by now largely forgotten, although there were those who recalled that his early demonstrations with animals had not been a total success. One creature which failed to perish by electricity had been finally despatched by a blow on the head with a brick . . .

But more horror was to come at Auburn Prison — See opposite page.

12

ELECTROCUTED TWICE

George Courson

His legs shot forward, tearing the front of the chair from its moorings

IT WAS high noon. Over the shadow-flecked Auburn valley, in New York State, the July heat hung like an invisible pall.

Perched on the walls of Auburn Prison, shirt-sleeved guards sat beneath their cupolas, their backs turned to the green landscape. Their eyes were fixed on the bare exercise yard that stretched between the wall and the death house. But not even a mote of yellow dust stirred in the shimmering air.

Inside the death house Thomas J. Davis, prison executioner, made his final adjustments to the squat, broad-based chair that dominated the white-walled room by its sheer ugliness.

He placed an electric lamp on the seat, and clipped two wires to the arm rests. Then he stepped to the control panel at the side of the room and lifted the switch handle until its copper arms meshed with the metal jaws on the board. There was a whir and a hum and the lamp on the chair began to glow. He looked at the instrument panel, saw the voltmeter needle swing to 1,260 and hold steady. Only then did he turn to the stocky man in blue uniform who stood in the doorway.

"Everything's in order," he said quietly.

Without a word, Warden Stout turned and disappeared into the gloom of the corridor that led to the death cells. His footsteps were hollow on the stone floor.

His tread was measured, for the law was precise in its allotment of time to the condemned.

Ten yards away, William Taylor was sitting on his bunk. His white shirt was rolled up over his elbows, and his black trousers were slit up the sides like the seams of a Chinese dress. Despite his years of imprisonment he was thick-muscled and bull-necked.

He was going to die because he had decapitated a fellow-prisoner with a carving knife, after having previously struck down a guard with a hatchet in an attempt at escape. Now his lips were moving silently as he followed the chaplain in the prayers for the dying.

In the glare of the unshaded light that hung in the corridor, the warden's shadow lengthened towards the cell. The chaplain touched Taylor's arm. "Ready, my son?"

Taylor rose without a change in expression. His felt slippers shuffled softly on the stone. As he stepped into the corridor two keepers fell in alongside and turned him towards the back door. The chaplain followed, a prayer book in his hand.

The witnesses in the death chamber sat rigidly in their straight-backed chairs. As the clock hands pointed to 12.15 all eyes turned to the door. The warden entered, then the condemned man. The prisoner's face was pale, but he showed no emotion. He sat in the chair, and when the guards began to fix the electrodes to his legs he bent his head to observe what they were doing.

They worked swiftly. Within five minutes the preliminaries were completed. Warden Stout, standing behind the chair, nodded to the executioner. The latter meshed the switch points, sent the full charge of 1,260 volts hurtling through the line.

The condemned man reacted with a convulsion of his

entire frame, which suddenly arched forward, straining at the straps. The muscular pressure was so great that within a few seconds there was a crashing sound, and the witnesses saw his legs shoot forward and upward, tearing the entire front of the chair from its moorings.

Warden Stout looked anxiously to the executioner. The latter watched his voltmeter and saw the current flowing unchanged. For 52 seconds he kept the power on, and then cut it down by stages.

Had it not been for the restraining straps Taylor would have pitched forward on his face. As it was his head bent forward, and his skin was ashen beneath the mask.

The doctors now stepped forward. Dr. J. W. Brown was in charge, assisted by Doctors Conway, Mooney and Wright. They were about to make their usual examination for proof of death when there was a gasp from the man in the electric chair.

Scarcely able to believe their ears, the doctors looked at one another.

"Good Lord!" exclaimed the warden. "He's still alive."

Dr. Brown felt for a pulse, but could detect nothing.

Then came another gasp.

"Well?" asked the warden.

The doctor shrugged, and stepped back from the chair. "Tell the executioner to try again."

Davis shook his head. "Can't," he said. "Current's out. We'll have to wait until I can mend the chair."

Then Dr. Mooney felt a thready response in the condemned man's pulse. Next, the latter's chest began to heave and breathing commenced.

"Get a cot," ordered Dr. Brown.

Two guards ran into the cell area and came back with a wooden folding bed.

Taylor was unbound, stretched on the cot and removed to an adjoining room, which was customarily reserved for the autopsy following the execution.

William Taylor's pulse was now beating at the rate of 100 to the minute, and body movements were progressing so vigorously that he was starting to roll from side to side.

The warden and the physicians were in a quandary. By law they were now charged with restoring life long enough to allow the law to destroy life in its own fashion.

Dr. Brown thought that a sedative might be helpful, and Conway administered a morphine hypodermic into Taylor's arm. Fifteen minutes passed, with the only visible result that the condemned man was becoming increasingly more vigorous.

Finally Dr. Brown opened his black bag. His face was set in stern lines as he took out a gauze cone and saturated it with ether. He held it over Taylor's face. The latter, choking, opened his eyes. In a burst of energy he tried to give voice to his objections. The doctor's grip held firm, and Taylor's protests grew weaker until he passed into a state of anaesthesia.

Events now moved swiftly. The guards picked up the convict's limp frame and carried him to the chair, which by this time had been repaired. The electrodes were fixed, and for the second time the warden signalled the executioner. Contact was made, and for 40 seconds 1,260 volts were fed into the line.

This time the condemned man made no resistance. By two o'clock on that afternoon of Thursday, July 27th, 1893, all signs of life had vanished. Having been subjected to one of the rarest of rarities in the annals of crime — a double electrocution — William Taylor had paid his debt to society.

13
TENSIONS IN THE HOUSEHOLD

Ben Tilsley

A *massacre in Missouri*

THERE HAD BEEN a blizzard in north-west Missouri on December 10th, 1985, so it was decided not to open the schools at Lathrop the following day. Most of the pupils lived in the outlying rural areas surrounding the small town, travelling to school by bus.

One of them, Jason Sloan, lived several miles outside Lathrop with his parents and two older brothers. Jason was the baby of the family, indulged by everyone. He was Jeffrey's special pet.

Jeffrey, at 19, was the oldest of the three Sloan boys. He'd had trouble sleeping the night before, but he was dozing when his alarm clock went off at 5.30 a.m.

His mother and father, Judy and Paul Sloan, were sleeping in the bedroom across the hall.

Paul, awakened by the alarm, got up and called Jeffrey. Then he went into the kitchen and smoked a cigarette.

Jeffrey got up and began to dress for work with no particular enthusiasm. He was still tired from his sleepless night, and his job loading and unloading boxes at a local warehouse required a lot of energy. He considered skipping work that day.

As he walked through the living-room on his way to the kitchen he passed his two younger brothers. The boys had both bunked down in the living-room, since their bedrooms were not well heated. Jason, a lively nine-year-old, was curled up on a love-seat. Timothy, 18, was sleeping on a roll-away bed in the middle of the floor.

Jason awoke and began to watch television. Tim, who had got home from work around midnight, was sound asleep.

Paul finished his cigarette and went back to bed, where he slept again. Jason snuggled down into his blanket on the love-seat and nodded off too.

Jeffrey was fighting the urge to go back to bed, but a knocking at the door roused him from his stupor.

Two of his colleagues had stopped by on the way to work to see if he wanted a lift. He told them that his dad had said he could drive the truck to work. He would see them later.

Jeffrey just could not seem to get started, and he let himself doze off. He was roused again by the telephone. It was one of his friends, at work now, asking him if he was coming in. The work was piling up, and the boss was going to be very unhappy if Jeffrey did not show up.

He began to rush around, going over in his mind what he had to do before he could leave.

The truck didn't want to start and was stuck in the ice and snow. It took several minutes of hard work, but Jeffrey finally got the engine going. The Sloans' house fell silent as the four occupants slept on.

None of them heard the door open, nor did they hear the footsteps that crossed the hall and went into the bedroom occupied by the mother and father.

The roar of a gun shattered the silence. Paul, 44, was killed instantly by a bullet that entered his skull.

Judy, 38, woke with her ears ringing. She looked up and saw the gunman standing at the foot of the bed.

She had no time to speak. The gun roared again. The bullet pierced her right breast, travelled up into her throat and nicked the jugular vein. Judy rolled off the bed and fell into the small space between the bed and the wall. Blood was spurting into her mouth and she began to scream.

In the living-room Timmy was awakened by the two blasts. He was out of his bed and starting up when the killer entered the living-room.

"No! No!" He raised his arm in a futile attempt to deflect the bullet. It grazed his arm and entered the soft tissues of his cheek and mouth. He fell back on his bed, stunned but still alive.

Jason, sleeping on the couch, was roused by the sound of the three gunshots.

He looked up and saw the killer and the gun. Terrified, he flung himself back on his pillow, pulled his blanket over his face, and wrapped his arms around his head.

The killer placed the muzzle of the gun against the child's arm, near the wrist. The flesh of the arm was stripped by the gunpowder in the explosion. The bullet passed through the boy's arm, fracturing the small bones, and exited, leaving a smudge of black residue on the inner side of the arm.

Then it penetrated the child's skull and entered his brain. Jason died instantly.

Judy was still screaming.

The killer walked back down the hall, reloaded the gun and went into the bedroom. Judy still lay on the floor between the bed and the wall.

He pointed the gun at her head and pulled the trigger. Judy's screams stopped.

The killer heard a noise from the living-room. He turned and retraced his steps. As he entered the living-room he heard Tim going out through the back door. He ran after the boy, flung open the door and called to him. Timmy paused and turned. The gun roared again, and the bullet entered the boy's skull between his nose and eye sockets. He fell backwards, spreadeagled in the snow.

The Sloans' home was silent once more. A half-hour or so later the phone began to ring. It rang and rang, the bell shrilling through the silent house, but no one answered. Jeff, at work, dialled the number repeatedly, but no one responded.

Melissa Merritt was Jeff's girl friend. They had known each other for years, and although Melissa was only 15 their acquaintance had ripened into romance. It was of short standing, however. For a few weeks it had been limited to numerous phone calls, and they'd had their first real date only the weekend before.

On that weekend, however, they had spent almost every waking moment together. They'd talked on the phone during the brief intervals when they were separated.

It was only natural that when Jeffrey couldn't reach his parents on the phone he would think of Melissa. And besides, the Merritts lived less than a mile from the Sloans.

Mrs. Merritt answered the phone. It was 10.15 a.m. but Melissa was still sleeping.

Jeff explained that he had been trying to call his folks, but the phone seemed to be out of order or something, since no one answered. He asked Mrs. Merritt if she would call and see if she could get an answer.

Then he asked if he could talk to Melissa, who got up willingly enough to come to the phone. He told her that he wanted to let his father know that he had got to work all right and he hadn't had any trouble with the truck. "I know he's going to be worried if he doesn't hear from me," Jeff explained.

Melissa dressed and her mother tried the Sloans' number. She got no answer and assumed that the blizzard had probably damaged the phone lines. Since Jeffrey had seemed so concerned the pair decided to drive to the Sloans' house and relay Jeff's message in person.

It was after eleven by the time the two were on their way. Their Bronco, a four-wheel-drive vehicle, had no trouble on the icy roads.

Mrs. Merritt pulled into the driveway and Melissa hopped out. As she made her way to the front door she saw a small splash of blood in the snow but thought nothing of it. She knew the Sloans had a cat, and she thought that it had cut a paw or caught a mouse.

She knocked at the door several times and was perplexed when no one answered. She was just turning away when she heard a scream.

"Oh, Timmy! Timmy! Oh, God, Timmy!"

Mrs. Merritt was out of the Bronco, standing at the side of the house and staring into the back garden.

"Oh, don't come any closer!" she sobbed, but Melissa rushed past her mother. Then she stopped short in horror. Nothing she had ever encountered in her short life had prepared her for what she saw.

Timmy, dressed only in a pair of underpants, lay flat on his back in the snow. His torso, his arms, and even his legs were splattered with blood; a crimson pool stained the snow around his head.

Melissa now saw that a trail of blood led from the door to Tim's body. The small stain she had seen was only one of many.

Terrified, she and her mother ran to the car. They did not know if the killer had gone, or was perhaps still in the house, but they knew there was nothing they could do here.

Melissa's first thought was of the conversation she'd had with Jeffrey the night before.

She had been planning to go to see him, but he had called her first and told her that maybe she should not come over. He said that his family had been receiving death threats through phone calls and letters, and that a mysterious car had been parked across the road, watching their house.

Melissa was alarmed and asked Jeff if the letters had been saved. Jeff replied that his dad wasn't worried because he had a gun.

Jeffrey seemed depressed, and because of the threats the conversation between the two young people drifted to the idea of death.

Melissa knew that Jeff had an indentation in the back of his head — he had shown it to her and she had felt it with her fingers. It was a depressed fracture, sustained several years earlier. Although Jeff seemed healthy enough, he told her that he had only four years to live, that the skull fracture would kill him.

Melissa tried to cheer him up and called him back later that night to see if he and the family were all right.

When she saw Timmy dead in the snow all she could think was that the person who had been menacing the Sloans had made good his threat. She was thankful that Jeffrey had left for work when the killer came. Otherwise it might have been Jeff's body lying in the snow.

Mrs. Merritt made for the nearest phone to call the sheriff's department. She and Melissa also wanted to phone Jeff and break the news as gently as possible, but they didn't know the name of the firm where he worked. They finally located a friend who had Jeff's work number.

When Jeffrey came on the line Melissa tried to speak to him, but broke down sobbing. Mrs. Merritt took the phone. "There's been an accident, Jeff," she said. "You'd better come home."

Then it occurred to her that by the time Jeff could get home the place would be swarming with police. She didn't want Jeffrey walking unprepared into whatever had happened at that house.

"No, Jeff, don't go home. You come here first," she said. She didn't have the heart to break the news to him that Timmy was dead. That would be better done in person.

Jeffrey left work immediately. He jumped into his dad's truck and raced for home.

At 11.30, when the Highway Patrol message came over the radio, Troopers Richard Johnson, Eric Tilford and Corporal John Elliot were patrolling various sectors of the area some 15 miles from the Sloans' home. They arrived at the crime scene approximately 15 minutes later.

The officers stared at the body. They traced the trail of blood which led to the front door where they found bloodstains disappearing into the house.

Not sure of what awaited them inside, the officers

approached the house with caution.

As they entered the living-room they saw a couch covered by a sheet and a blanket. They pulled the blanket back and saw the body of a small boy. The pillow under his head was soaked with blood, and he appeared to be dead.

In the middle of the living-room floor was a roll-away bed with a bloodstained sheet and blanket. The television set was still on, providing a grotesque accompaniment to the officers' work.

As they stood in the hall outside the bedroom they could see the body of an older man lying on the bed. The pillow under the victim's head was soaked with blood. It seemed that he had been slain while sleeping.

There was no one in the bedroom across the hall. The officers would later discover that this was Jeffrey's bedroom.

The phone rang. Trooper Tilford answered. It was a beauty shop in Lathrop, calling to see why Judy had missed her hair appointment. The shocked officers didn't know where Judy was, but feared for her safety.

They continued their search down into the basement. Deputy Kincade, who had arrived with the sheriff, went down the steps. Nothing seemed amiss.

Trooper Johnson was on the telephone, beginning the co-ordination of the detective work. He also put out a "try to locate" order on Jeffrey Sloan.

Deputy Kincade began the task of photographing the three bodies the officers had found. He walked into the parents' bedroom to photograph the corpse of Paul Sloan. As he moved around the bed to get another angle he saw Judy Sloan lying face-down in a pool of congealing blood. It was obvious that she, like her husband and two sons, had been shot in the head.

The search revealed no sign of a break-in and no sign that an intruder had been in the house. Nothing seemed to be missing, and as there were no broken windows or doors the officers believed that the killer had been admitted by one of the Sloans.

Trooper Johnson was on the telephone when Jeffrey arrived at the front door. He had disregarded Mrs. Merritt's instructions and had come straight to the house. Corporal Elliot met him at the door and refused to let him enter.

"What's going on? Let me in!" demanded Jeffrey. "Mom! Mom!" he called. Standing at the doorway, he was unable to see into the bedroom, or even into the living-room where his little brother Jason lay dead.

Trying to calm him, the officers put him into the sheriff's car. Trooper Tilford was instructed to watch him. At about 12.30 Jeffrey was transferred from the sheriff's car to Corporal Elliot's patrol car and driven to the Clinton County courthouse.

Melissa and Mrs. Merritt waited at the neighbour's house for several hours, but Jeffrey never showed up. The next time Melissa saw Jeff she would have only one question to ask him: "Why? Why did you pick me to talk to?"

Jeffrey, while sitting in the sheriff's car, had kept asking, "What has happened to my family?" He also kept calling for his mother. Trooper Tilford, who stood beside the open door of the car, did not tell him the terrible facts. That was something he'd leave for his superiors.

Now, in the patrol car, Jeffrey sat in the front with Elliot. Trooper Johnson was in the back. As the trio rode along the country road Jeffrey suddenly pointed to a house they were passing. "That's where the S.O.B. lives who killed my family," he said bitterly.

So how did he know that his family had been killed? Johnson reached over Elliot's head and took a card from a clip on the sun-visor. The card listed a suspect's rights. Johnson read them out, asking if Jeffrey understood them.

"Yes," replied Jeffrey.

The troopers knew that in cases like this, in which whole families were assassinated, the prime suspect was usually the surviving member.

Tilford and other officers followed Elliot's patrol car to the courthouse. When they arrived Jeffrey was taken into the courthouse and fingerprinted by Tilford.

At about 1 p.m. Trooper Johnson sat down with Jeffrey, hoping that he could throw some light on what had happened.

"Jeffrey," Johnson began, "I'd just like you to tell me what's been going on in the last twenty-four hours."

Jeff, who now seemed calm and unemotional, described the last night the Sloan family spent together alive. "When I got home last night from work, my mom was fixing supper," he said. He told Johnson about the phone call he made to Melissa, that he'd told her not to come over because the family had been threatened.

He rambled on, telling of an evening spent playing cards with his little brother. He said that later that evening the phone rang, but the caller hung up when his father answered.

"That must have been your boy friend," Jeff quoted his father as saying to his mother.

"I don't have a boy friend any more," he said that his mother answered.

He also went on to tell Johnson that his mother had been playing around and had been having an affair with George Thompson, who lived near Lathrop. His father had found out and had argued with Thompson. Soon afterwards the family began receiving threats and had seen a car parked across the road, apparently watching the house.

Jeff said that he had sat up the whole night before, watching and waiting, because he was so frightened. When Johnson asked why he thought the killer had waited till he left for work he had no answer.

According to Jeffrey, the only person he knew of who might have harmed the Sloans was Thompson, the man who he said had made the death threats. Jeff also told Johnson that the reason his mother "fooled around" was that his father beat her and the two older boys.

Sergeant Robert Anderson arrived at the Clinton County courthouse to test Jeffrey's hands for powder residue. The officers knew that the firing of a handgun leaves a film of powder on the hands of the person holding the gun. They also knew that a thorough washing can remove this residue, and when Jeffrey told Anderson that he washed his hands with an industrial-strength cleaner that morning Anderson was not optimistic that the test would reveal anything.

He was right — the test would prove to be negative.

George Thompson, the man named by Jeff as his mother's lover, was interviewed. He convinced the investigators that he had nothing to do with the murders. He admitted that he'd had an affair with Judy. It had started 20 years earlier, was put on hold while the family lived in California for 16 years, and had resumed when the Sloans moved back to the area.

Thompson showed the officers a small school picture of Jason. He said that Judy had given it to him and had said, "Jason wants you to have this." He had carried it in his wallet ever since.

On the back of the picture was written, "We all love you, Jason, age six, grade one." The man's affection for the small boy was apparent.

He confirmed that Paul had beaten Judy and said that he had seen her with a black eye. She had also told him that her husband beat the two older boys.

Judy had left her family briefly some time before and had moved into a caravan rented for her by Thompson. He told the officers that he had talked to Paul during this time, and Paul had threatened him, but he had no desire to fight Judy's husband.

He knew nothing about any threats, and said that he talked to Judy a day or so before the killings and she seemed normal to him at that time. He added that she had a cancer and needed a hysterectomy, but she had decided against having the surgery.

The officers were beginning to form an idea of the

tensions in the Sloan household, but they had turned up no evidence that any outsider had intruded.

Sergeant Anderson walked into the room where Jeffrey sat. He slapped the small picture of little Jason on the table and said, "Look, that's Jason! He's dead, and he's not going to be back!"

Jeffrey showed no emotion as he looked at the picture of the little boy who had been his particular favourite.

Anderson lowered his voice. "Now, do you want to talk to Trooper Johnson?"

Jeffrey nodded and the other officers filed out of the room.

It was around 7 p.m. when Jeff began to talk.

About two hours later Sergeant Larry Stobbs went out with a group of officers. They parked along a rural road and began to beat the bushes.

With torches, stumbling through the snowy woods, they searched an area approximately a half to three-quarters of a mile along the road, and stretching back 150 feet from the tarmac. At around 11 p.m. they gave up and returned to the courthouse.

While the men were searching, Sergeant Miles Parks was video-taping Johnson's interview with Jeffrey.

After his confession had been taped, when the officers returned from their unsuccessful search, Jeffrey offered to return to the country road and assist the hunt for the murder weapon.

"It was wrapped in a blue and white gym sock," he said. Sergeant Anderson remembered seeing a sock hanging in a tree, back from the road. They returned to that spot and resumed their search.

At around 1 a.m. an officer spotted the black handle of a .38-calibre revolver. Also recovered in the early morning hours were a leather holster, a box of cartridges and several spent shells. Jeffrey said he always wrapped the gun and holster in the old gym sock after he cleaned them. He was now charged with four counts of first-degree murder.

Friends and relatives simply refused to believe that he

had committed the crimes. "I know Jeff, and he could not do anything like that," said one of his friends.

Melissa was in the habit of writing down her thoughts and feelings when she was confused or unhappy; it was like a letter to herself. "The Jeff that I talked to didn't hurt his parents," she wrote in her journal.

Michael Lerner volunteered his services as Jeffrey Sloan's attorney. Asked about the defence he would offer, he replied, "We'll offer a plea of insanity. Anyone would have to be insane to commit such a crime."

Tim Finnical, an assistant state attorney for Missouri, was called in to conduct the prosecution.

Trooper Richard Johnson and Sergeant Miles Parks took the stand to describe the two sessions during which Jeffrey's confessions were taped. A TV was rolled into the courtroom and the jurors and spectators listened as Jeffrey told of the slaughter of his family. The gun, holster and bullets lay on the table before the young man as he spoke.

"I sat up all night trying to decide how to kill them — My mom told me to do it — She didn't want to live in that environment any more — She asked me to kill them so they wouldn't have to suffer — I couldn't do it for a long time —"

For the first time friends and relatives heard the story of Jeff's addiction to drugs and his voluntary incarceration in a drug rehabilitation centre in July before the murders. Jeff also told of writing cheques on his father's bank account.

"Mom gave the gun to me and told me to hide it under the bed — I pointed it at Dad — I couldn't do it — I walked in circles — I pointed the gun at Dad again — It went off — Mom looked at me, I had to shoot — She said, 'Shoot me again, Jeff, I ran in the living-room — Shot Timothy — Shot Jason — Back into the bedroom — I shot my mom again in the back of the head — I heard Timmy run out — I shot him again."

Jeffrey, tall, slim and handsome, sat impassively throughout the trial, except when the tape was shown. At that point he covered his face with his hands and put his head on the table.

"My mom had cancer — She was going to die — she didn't want to die like that —" continued the tape.

The defence's primary witness was Dr. William Langley, a psychiatrist. He had interviewed Jeffrey as well as family members, and had come to the conclusion that Jeffrey and his mother were victims of "shared paranoia," or "double insanity."

Dr. Langley said he believed Judy Sloan was the dominant partner in this shared insanity, and Jeffrey had been drawn into it by his closeness to and dependence on his mother. The doctor also testified that after the murders Jeffrey became schizophrenic.

Assistant State Attorney Finnical attacked Langley's hypothesis, presenting reports from two other psychiatrists who had stated that Jeffrey was not insane.

Defence Attorney Lerner could produce no witnesses who would testify that Judy had shown any signs of insanity in the weeks preceding the killings. Furthermore, all witnesses agreed that Judy would never under any circumstances have told Jeffrey to kill Jason.

It took the jury less than an hour to bring in a verdict of murder in the first-degree. In the second phase of the trial they had only two choices of penalties: life imprisonment with no parole, or death in Missouri's gas chamber.

Relatives and friends waited in the courthouse corridor for the outcome.

"People just don't believe me," said a relative, "but Jeffrey was such a good boy — He was so close to his mom — He loved and protected Jason — I never ever, ever saw him angry."

"Why? Why did he do it?" asked another relative. "I go round and round in my head, but I just can't understand why."

"There's only one answer," a friend commented. "Drugs! Jeff took something, and it ruined his mind."

The jury were out for six hours. They returned to recommend the death penalty.

Jeffrey Sloan's face was blank, but a muscle in his jaw began to twitch, and under his too tight sports jacket he began to quiver.

On Wednesday, February 21st, 1996, just over 11 years after the horrific murders, Jeffrey Sloan was executed at the Potosi Correctional Centre by lethal injection; lethal injection having superseded the gas chamber as the method of dispatching condemned prisoners in Missouri.

14

THE "DAY YOU GOT ME DAY"

Terry Ecker

The crimes of mass murderer Gerald Stano

TO PROFESSIONALS like Detective Sergeant Paul B. Crow, a body was just a body, no longer a person. It was only a thing to be looked at for the problems it posed. Like the corpse he was called to on Sunday, February 17th, 1980, lying in a popular dumping area behind Daytona Beach Airport, Florida.

Crow spoke briefly to his boss, Captain Marvin Powers, then knelt and opened his briefcase. He took out a jar of Vaseline and put a dab in each nostril. He took out a respirator and placed it over his nose and mouth, adjusting its elastic strap behind his head. He took out a pair of gloves and put them on his massive hands. Then he closed and picked up his briefcase and walked over to the body.

From the west, about a mile away, came the roar of massed stock cars as the Daytona 500 started at the Speedway there. This was a hell of a way to spend a Sunday afternoon!

Crow took his time, observing and pondering each detail of the scene before touching anything. The covering over the body told him that this was a murder. And the smell told him that it had been committed many days ago — possibly even weeks. That was bad, but Crow doesn't accept the theory that if a murder isn't solved within 24 to

48 hours, you can forget it. The answers were there for a detective with the skill and patience to find them. But they had to be found now, today. Never again would the scene look exactly this way, exactly the way two target-shooting teenagers had found it.

Crow's first conclusion was that the killer was a man. A woman would have dumped the body beside the narrow dirt road and left it. Or she might have driven down the embankment to the canal — which would have been a better hiding place — and dumped it there. But the killer had dragged the body about 25 feet from the dirt road, then gone to considerable lengths to cover it, first with a canvas-like material and then with four branches torn from four nearby young pine trees. That was a man's work.

It just might have been the work of a man who wanted to get caught, too. The body had been left in a spot where it was certain to be found sooner or later, although there were better hiding places in the immediate vicinity. And why only four pine branches? They didn't hide anything — they were more like decorations.

Crow put subordinates to work sketching, photographing and scouring the area for anything that might be physical evidence, and then removed the covering from the body.

The decomposing mess, now infested with insects and maggots, had once been the body of a young woman. That had been two or three weeks ago, Crow estimated. She'd been a big girl. Not fat, just big-boned, well-proportioned and strong — probably an athlete. And probably attractive, Crow thought, studying what was left of her face. Her long, sandy blonde hair was parted in the middle.

The body was laid out almost ritualistically on its back, with the arms at the sides, the head turned to the right and tilted slightly upwards. That, Crow realised, could be significant. For some religious or ritualistic people, the turning of a corpse's head to the rising sun in the east or towards the setting sun in the west has a meaning. For Crow, the position of the victim's head raised the possibility that the killer was a religious freak.

The upward tilt of the head suggested a cut throat. But there was no way to ascertain that, because the throat was gone. There were several obvious stab wounds in the chest and one curious, gaping wound in the right thigh. There was no sign of blood on or around the body, probably because there had been several recent heavy rains.

The body was fully clothed — tight-fitting blue jeans and a white silk shirt, decorated with little zebras. Underneath those were intact panties and bra. There was no visible sign of sexual molestation. The shoes were missing. And no handbag, purse or wallet could be found. Souvenirs for the killer?

When Crow removed the shirt and turned the body over he discovered two more stab wounds in the back, between the shoulder-blades. So the killer was a woman-hater. Homosexual? Perhaps. Repeated stabbing had sexual overtones, in addition to the obvious indication of rage.

Naming the victim was going to be a problem. There was no identification of any kind on the body, what was left of the face was no help, and there were no fingers left to print. There was a simple necklace around the neck, partly embedded in the rotting flesh. One fingerbone bore a small gold ring. And on the left skeletal wrist was a self-winding Seiko watch which had stopped on Wednesday, January 30th, 1980. That was 18 days ago.

How long did it take such a watch to wind down once its owner's movements — which activate the self-winding mechanism — had stopped?

A jeweller told Crow that it could take from a few hours to four days, depending upon how active its owner had been and how constantly the watch had been worn. That gave the detective a time window upon which to concentrate. The victim's movements could have ceased as early as January 26th and as late as the 30th. With that in mind Crow returned to police headquarters, went to the missing persons' files and studied the details of all women reported missing since January 25th. He found a report on one young lady who seemed to fit the general description of the victim.

Mary Carol Maher, a 20-year-old college swimming star, had been reported missing by her mother on January 30th. She had last been seen on the evening of Sunday, January 27th, when her mother left her in front of a Holiday Inn in Daytona Beach. There was a significant difference, however. According to the mother, Mary had been wearing a dress. The victim was wearing blue jeans and a white silk shirt. Nevertheless, the match between the physical descriptions was too close to ignore, so Crow went to the mother's home with the victim's wristwatch, ring and necklace, plus photographs of her jeans, shirt and underwear.

After the anxious mother checked her own closet she told Crow that one of the photos appeared to be of her own shirt, which was missing. Mary could have borrowed it — and the mother could have been mistaken about what Mary was wearing the last time she'd seen her. Anyway, she was able to confirm that the jewellery was her daughter's. A positive identification of the body was then made from dental records.

The grieving mother proved to be very co-operative — and, to Crow's relief, very candid about her late daughter's friends, activities and habits. "I found the mother to be a very mature person, in that she was very aware of what was going on around her," the detective recalls. "She wasn't a naive mother. None of this 'My God, my daughter does this, my daughter does that' stuff. A very likeable and very nice person."

Mary, the mother said, was a very strong, very healthy girl who excelled at swimming and loved disco-dancing and dating. There was a list of boy friends a mile long. She would give Crow as many names as she could remember. She had not been a "loose" girl. She'd been simply a product of her time — and very popular. She smoked a little pot, but had no drug problem. A happy girl, full of life — and enjoying it.

But Mary did have one habit that had bothered her mother. She hitch-hiked a lot. Her favourite rendezvous was the Top of the Boardwalk, a disco lounge on the top floor of the Holiday Inn. When it closed at 2 a.m. Mary would often go to Fannie Farkel's, a popular nightspot that stayed open until 4 a.m. And if she couldn't get a lift with a friend she would hitch-hike. It was a dangerous habit for an attractive young woman, but Mary hadn't been physically intimidated by anyone. In fact, she'd beaten the hell out of a couple of guys who had got out of line with her.

The mother agreed to lend Crow several photographs of Mary Carol Maher. She had indeed been a very attractive young woman. Armed with the photos and information supplied by the mother, Crow and Detective Tim O'Brien drove to the Holiday Inn.

The manager was a little woman of about 50, who ran the place like a military post. And she had awards on her office wall to prove that she ran it efficiently. After hearing the detectives' problem, she took them to her apartment, ordered coffee and sandwiches for them and summoned everyone from the lounge, plus the security guard and anyone else who might know anything. Within minutes they were all there.

They had all known Mary Carol Maher — and not just by sight. She had been a very popular member of the regular crowd. They knew who and what she liked and didn't like, and who she dated. Between them, they were able to add several names to Crow's list of Mary's boy friends — two of them of particular interest. Bobby Thorne, he was told, had got Mary pregnant. She had stopped seeing him after the abortion. More recently she had been seriously involved with Steve Walker who had left town in a hurry shortly after Mary was reported missing.

All the staff recalled Mary being in the club on the night of January 27th. She had left, as usual, shortly before 2 a.m., planning to get a lift to Fannie Farkel's.

Their certainty about that bothered Crow. After all, Mary had been a regular — present at the club three or four nights a week. And that had been nearly a month ago. How could they be so sure that she was there that particular night? It was vital that her presence there on that night be established beyond doubt — and Crow knew how to do that, if the staff would co-operate. He is a devout believer in hypnosis, strongly favouring it over lie-detector tests and stress analysis, because it was, in the early 1980s, the only one of the three credible in court. So would the employees submit to questioning under hypnosis?

Yes, they assured him, they would. Crow said he would make the necessary arrangements.

Then he and O'Brien drove on to Fannie Farkel's. The staff and regular patrons there had also known Mary Carol Maher well. After much discussion among themselves, they assured the detectives that she had not — although that was unusual — been in the club on the morning of January 28th.

With that the detectives called it a night.

Monday morning was devoted to Bobby Thorne, who proved easy to find and easy to question. Yes, he had got Mary pregnant. The abortion had been a mutual decision, with no animosity. They'd stopped seeing each other, but there were no hard feelings. He had spent the night of January 27th in the company of several friends who verified his alibi.

Steve Walker was another matter. By the end of the day Crow learned that he had returned to his parents' home in New York, where his father was a lawyer. Crow was able to speak only to the father, who said he wasn't sure he wanted his son to talk to the detective. That, Crow realised, was a dead-end — unless he could build a case against the young man.

On Tuesday the autopsy report confirmed that Mary Carol Maher had died from the multiple stab wounds, and Crow spent the next few days supervising the questioning of the staff of the Holiday Inn under hypnosis. They clearly remembered seeing Mary in the club on the night of January 27th. They were even able to describe a man who had got into the lift with her when she left shortly before 2 a.m. on the 28th — apparently just some guy leaving at the same time. One employee recalled over-hearing a conversation between Mary and a young man who had given her his name — Gene Blanton.

The only Gene Blanton that Crow could find in the Daytona Beach area was a college student. He turned out to be a freckle-faced Tom Sawyer type. And he'd never even seen the inside of a bar and had never heard of Mary Carol Maher.

Mary's popularity was emphasised by the size of her funeral. The investigators photographed everyone in the long procession and later spent hours studying the thick stack of photographs. Nothing came of it.

The detectives then learned that Steve Walker had been involved in several drug rip-offs and had left town owing large sums of money to some unsavoury characters. That could explain his hasty departure, but he was the best candidate Crow had, so the investigator continued trying to ascertain Walker's whereabouts and activities on the night of January 27th. Also, there were still countless names to be checked out — friends, former boy friends and would-be boy friends.

Meanwhile the case of Susan Prentiss came to Crow's attention. He assigned it to Detective Jim Gadberry on the morning of March 26th.

Susan was a prostitute, one of many working Daytona Beach's Boardwalk area. She kept a regular room in a motel near the Boardwalk and often solicited customers by hitch-hiking. Naturally, she ran into some rough trade now and then. But, like her sisters in that tough business, she was street-smart and tough herself, so she had always managed to get herself out of nasty situations.

On Tuesday night, March 25th, however, she had come close to hitch-hiking a ride with death. She told Detective Gadberry that she'd been walking seductively along

Atlantic Avenue with her thumb out when a red car with dark-tinted windows stopped. She thought she recognised the driver. She didn't know his name, but she thought he had been a previous client. Anyway, she got into the red car — a Gremlin — and took the man to her motel room.

Susan said she'd been so high on drugs that she couldn't remember the details too clearly. But somehow an argument had developed. The man didn't want to pay, or didn't like hookers, or something. Anyway, he had pulled out a knife and sliced her up pretty badly. One cut, on her right thigh, had required 27 stitches. She wanted that bastard found and put away. She said she would recognise him if she saw him again. He was of average height, a little heavy, wore glasses and had a moustache.

Gadberry went through the Derbyshire apartments, where Susan thought her assailant might live, but couldn't find a red Gremlin. About half a block away, however, parked behind a popular restaurant, he spotted a red 1977 Gremlin with dark-tinted windows. He wrote down the licence number, then went back to headquarters and ran the number through the computer. It was registered to a Gerald E. Stano, a short-order cook, at an Ormond Beach address, just north of Daytona Beach.

When Gadberry phoned the manager of the Derbyshire apartments, he was told that the place used to have a tenant who drove a red Gremlin — a man named Gerald Stano.

It turned out that Gerald Eugene Stano, 28, had an arrest record a mile long, but no convictions. A solid case had never been made against him, but he had been the prime suspect in several assaults on prostitutes. In each case the hooker had been picked up by a "customer" while hitch-hiking.

Susan Prentiss positively identified a photo of Stano as that of her attacker, then signed a complaint affidavit charging him with aggravated battery.

After Gadberry reported his findings to Crow, the detective sergeant's interest in Stano grew considerably.

Several factors stood out immediately. One, the attack on Susan Prentiss occurred in her motel room, only a quarter of a mile south of the Holiday Inn from which Mary Carol Maher had disappeared. Two, Susan had suffered a severe stab in the right thigh, as had Mary. Three, Susan, and the hookers involved in the previous attacks, had been picked up by her assailant while hitch-hiking in the Boardwalk area. Mary had left the Holiday Inn, planning to hitch-hike to Fannie Farkel's.

Stano, if guilty of these assaults, would be a repeat offender — and probably a woman-hater. The Mary Carol Maher crime scene had told Crow that her killer was a woman-hater and probably a repeat offender. The crime had been carried out too efficiently to have been committed by a first-timer.

That crime scene had also told Crow that Mary's killer was a meticulously neat man, probably compulsively so. It would be interesting to observe this Gerald Stano.

When the suspect was brought in — at 10 a.m. on April 1st — Crow watched in silence while Gadberry did the questioning and Stano did the denying. Crow was watching for two things. One was whether Stano showed any tendency towards compulsive neatness. The other was Stano's "body language." Crow had primed Gadberry with certain questions to which he knew the answers. He wanted to see what body signals Stano gave when telling the truth — and when lying.

Stano proved to be an easy subject to read. When telling an obvious truth he would pull his chair up to the desk and lean forward, carefully rearranging and straightening the objects on the desk while talking. When about to lie he would push his chair back and cross his legs, placing his left ankle on his right knee.

After more than an hour of intensive questioning by Gadberry, Stano finally confessed to the attack on Susan Prentiss. Then Crow took over. Sitting opposite Stano, he said: "Gerald, I'm Detective Sergeant Paul Crow. And I've got a problem that I think you might be able to help me with."

Stano pulled his chair close to the desk and peered at Crow for a moment. "Hey, Crow," he said, "your moustache isn't quite even. You need to trim the right side a little."

Crow went on, unconsciously fingering the right side of his bushy upper lip: "I've got a missing girl who disappeared from the Holiday Inn Boardwalk. I just wondered if you had seen her." He showed Stano a recent photograph of Mary Carol Maher.

Stano looked at it. "Yeah, I've seen her before," he said.

"Where did you see her, Gerald?"

"I picked her up one night."

"Where?"

"On Atlantic Avenue."

"Where on Atlantic?"

"By the Holiday Inn Boardwalk."

"When?"

"About a month or so ago."

"What happened then?"

Stano pushed his chair back, crossed his legs and said: "She was with another girl."

"Was she really with another girl?" Crow inquired.

"Yeah," Stano replied. "She was with another girl."

"What did you do with them?"

"Carried them down to Atlantic Avenue and University and dropped them off. That's the last time I seen them."

Knowing that the only answers that mattered were those given when Stano's chair was close to the desk, Crow changed the subject. "Gerald, what are you upset about?" he asked. "You seem to be a little off stride."

Stano pulled his chair close to the desk and started straightening up the reports Crow had placed on the desk. "Today's 'the day you got me day'," he said.

"I know today's 'the day I got you day,'" Crow replied, puzzled.

"You don't understand," Stano said. "Today's the day

my parents adopted me."

"Really?" Crow said. "I've got an adopted little boy."

With that, the conversation turned to Stano's family relationships. Crow could sense a problem there. Why couldn't Stano's parents just celebrate his birthday? Why make a big deal over "the day we got you day?"

Finally, Crow brought the conversation around to Stano's recreational activities, asking him about the previous attacks on prostitutes. Stano didn't really deny them — and his chair stayed close to the desk. Then Crow got around to the crucial question: "Gerald, didn't you pick Mary up, thinking that she was a prostitute?"

"That thought might have crossed my mind," Stano allowed.

"Bullshit!" Crow replied. "That's *always* on your mind. That's always what you're doing out there. That's your game. So where did you take her?"

"To Fannie Farkel's."

"What happened at Farkel's? Did you want to go in there? Did she want to go in? Did you just drive by?"

"Well," Stano said, pushing his chair back and crossing his legs, "I wanted to go in. But she didn't."

Crow knew that the truth would have been the opposite. Mary had loved Fannie Farkel's, but Gerald Stano would have been ill at ease in the young crowd which normally patronised the place. The important point now, however, was the route. Fannie Farkel's was on Mason Avenue, which runs east and west. Continuing westward from Farkel's, you came eventually to Clyde Morris Boulevard, which dead-ended at Mason Avenue. From that intersection southwards, Clyde Morris ran past the airport and near the dump area where Mary Maher's body had been found.

"Where did you go from there?" Crow asked.

"We went to Goodings Supermarket and got some beers," Stano replied.

Goodings was a popular 24-hour supermarket farther west on Mason Avenue, between Farkel's and Clyde

Morris Boulevard.

"She just sat in the car while you got some beers?"

"Yeah."

"Are you sure you didn't try to get in her pants, Gerald?"

Stano stared hard at Crow for a moment. Then he pulled his chair close to the desk and said: "Yeah."

"You wanted to get a little bit and she didn't? Is that right?"

"Yeah," Stano admitted. "Goddamn it!"

"She didn't want to give it to you?"

"No, she didn't!" Stano was growing visibly angry.

"She could hit pretty hard, couldn't she, Gerald?"

"You're goddamn right she could!"

"So what did you do? Did you hit out at her?"

Stano pushed his chair back and crossed his legs. "I let her out at Mason and Clyde Morris," he said. "I've never seen the bitch since."

After a moment Crow asked: "You didn't really let her out of the car, did you?"

"Yeah, I did," Stano insisted.

"No, you didn't," Crow said. "What did she do — lash out at you? Tell you to go to hell, leave her alone, didn't want you to touch her?"

Stano stared at Crow for a moment, then pulled his chair back to the desk and said: "Yeah."

"You got pretty mad, didn't you?"

"Goddamn right I did," Stano said. "I got so goddamn mad, I stabbed her just as hard as I could!"

Realising what he had admitted, Stano pushed his chair back, crossed his legs and said: "No — now wait a minute. You're confusing me."

"I'm not confusing you, Gerald," Crow said. "I'm just asking you basically what you did. You're confusing yourself, because you're trying to figure out a way to lie to me. That's what your confusion is from. Just calm down and tell me the truth. So you stabbed her. Big deal. She's bitching. She's hitting out at you. You've got to protect yourself, right?"

"Yeah, you're right," Stano agreed, pulling his chair back to the desk.

"Tell me how you stabbed her," Crow said.

"Well, I carry this knife under the seat," Stano explained. "So I pulled it out and I hit her just as hard as I could." That explained Mary's broken sternum.

"What did you do then, Gerald?"

Stano said he stabbed the victim several times, back-handed, in the chest. "She opened the door and tried to get out, but I cut her on the leg and pulled her back in." That explained the wound in Mary Carol's right thigh.

"I shut the door," Stano continued. "She fell forward and hit her head against the dashboard and started gurgling. I stabbed her a couple more times in the back, because she was messing up my car. She just went limp. So I took her —"

"Don't tell me any more," Crow said. "Let's go in the car. You direct, I'll drive."

Crow drove to the dump area, accompanied by Stano, Detective Gadberry and two other officers. Stano showed them exactly where and how he had left the body of Mary Carol Maher. When they returned to police headquarters, he gave a full tape-recorded confession and signed a typed transcript.

While that was going on, Detective Larry Lewis was struggling with a missing person case. Toni Van Haddocks, an attractive 26-year-old black prostitute, had been reported missing on February 15th. And there was pressure to find her because she had a relative in the city administration.

Knowing what was going on in Crow's office, Lewis handed him a photograph of Toni Van Haddocks and said, half jokingly: "See if he knows anything about her."

Crow glanced at the photo — a police mug-shot — and placed it on the desk facing Stano. "Have you ever seen this girl?" he asked.

Stano looked at the photograph, pushed his chair back

and crossed his legs.

"Oh, hell!" thought Crow.

Knowing nothing about the case, except that the girl was missing, Crow wasn't prepared to question Stano about it. He booked him for the first-degree murder of Mary Carol Maher, then turned his attention to Detective Lewis and the missing black prostitute Toni Van Haddocks.

Toni worked in and around an area containing a porno movie house, a porno book store and a popular bar that featured topless dancers. Quite a few hookers made comfortable livings by soliciting aroused customers as they left those establishments. Some just stood around and smiled at passers-by, waiting to be approached. Others were more forward, making active sales pitches.

For a smart cop, a hooker can be a very reliable source of information. He patrols a zone, passing a particular spot, say, twice a day. She patrols that spot and she's there all day, every day, watching and listening. She knows what's going on there, so a police officer who can gain her trust has gained a valuable asset. Paul Crow never forgets that a hooker is a human being caught up in a tough racket.

Crow and Lewis spent a considerable amount of time in that area, talking to the girls and showing photographs of Stano and Toni Van Haddocks. They all knew Toni, but none had seen her since the middle of February when she'd had a plaster cast on her left arm.

Most of them recognised the photo of Gerald Stano as that of a local jerk who often rode around the area in a red Gremlin, ogling the girls. No, they had not seen Toni Van Haddocks get into a red Gremlin.

But Crow knew that she had. He had seen Stano's reaction to her photograph. The question was, had she survived the adventure?

That was answered on April 15th, a few hours after a resident of Holly Hill, near Daytona Beach, found a human skull in his garden.

Nearby was a wooded area in which investigators were

soon finding more human bones and bits of clothing. They also found a plaster cast that had apparently once covered a human arm. The wide scattering of the bones was the obvious result of animal activity, but with the help of technicians from the state crime lab. the investigators eventually found what appeared to be the murder scene. It didn't tell them much, however, for they found no clues there to the killer's identity.

The gathered remains were identified as those of Toni Van Haddocks. The cause of death was determined to have been multiple stab wounds in the head.

Paul Crow contacted the Volusia County sheriff's office, which was handling the case, to tell Investigator Dave Hudson that he believed the killer of Toni Van Haddocks was safely in the county jail and that he (Crow) could probably get a confession from the killer, if he had some information with which to work. Hudson gratefully invited the city detective into the county's case and took him to the crime scene.

It hadn't told the county investigators much, but Crow knew what to look for. Standing at the spot where the body of Toni Van Haddocks had apparently been deposited originally, he looked around at the young pine trees growing nearby. Lower branches had been torn from four of them.

"I've got him," Crow told Hudson.

He went to the county jail, where Stano was brought to an interrogation room. After pleasantries had been exchanged the officer asked: "Gerald, how often do you pick up black girls?"

Stano pushed his chair back and crossed his legs. "I don't," he said. "I hate them bastards."

Crow put the photo of Toni Van Haddocks on the table. "You picked *her* up," he said.

Stano stared hard at the photo. "That's the only one I ever picked up," he said, without moving the chair.

Oh, my God, Crow thought. There've been others! "Anything different about her?" he asked.

"Different? Different? Let's see. Yeah, she had a plaster cast on one of her arms — her left arm."

"Why did you kill her, Gerald?"

"I didn't," Stano said firmly. "I told you about the young lady I killed. That's the only one I ever killed."

Stano kept his legs crossed and said no more. After several minutes, Crow got up and walked to the door. "O.K., Gerald," he said as he opened the door, "I'm going to let them take you back to your cell. But we're going to have to talk about this again. Because I *know* you killed that girl. You left your signature there."

Crow started to go outside. But Stano, stunned, called out after him: "Hey, wait a minute! Hey, Crow, come here! Come back here!"

Crow took a step back into the room and looked at Stano. Stano stared at him and asked: "Did I really leave my name there?"

Some hours later Crow had Gerald Stano's tape-recorded, transcribed and signed confession to the murder of Toni Van Haddocks — and his solemn assurance that there were no others. That was it. Two murders. He'd never killed anyone else in his life.

Crow went home that night with a nagging suspicion. He thought back to the scene at the dump area behind the airport. That scene had suggested to him that Mary Carol Maher's killer had murdered before. The crime had been committed so carefully, so expertly, with much thought to detail. Much ritual. Ritualistic killers don't just kill once. They have to repeat the ritual.

But Crow had already searched his department's records and found no similar unsolved murders. And Stano was apparently a man who went around picking up and beating up prostitutes. Until one night he picked up Mary Carol Maher, happily and stupidly hitch-hiking, who turned out not to be a prostitute. And paid with her young life for that fact.

But now there was Toni Van Haddocks. A dead hooker.

And Stano had repeated his ritual. Were there other dead hookers? Were there other innocent young hitch-hikers whom Stano had mistaken for hookers?

There were no others in Daytona Beach — at least no others that had been found. But Toni's body wasn't found in Daytona Beach. It was found in the county. Did the county have other such cases, lying unsolved in the files because no one had noticed the similarities? Did other nearby counties have such cases? Other states?

It didn't make sense, Crow told himself. Someone would have noticed. Look at Ted Bundy. Before the police ever heard of Ted Bundy, they knew they were looking for a mass murderer. Look at Son of Sam. The police knew that when they caught one guy, they would solve several shootings. Look at the Hillside Strangler, the Yorkshire Ripper, Carl DeGregory. The pattern was always there — and someone always spotted it. They didn't always catch the killer, but they always knew the pattern.

Crow spent the next few days reviewing unsolved murders with sheriff's investigators. He found several to be of considerable interest. And they went all the way back to 1975.

There was Linda Hamilton, a 16-year-old visitor from Massachusetts, found dead on the beach several miles south of Daytona on July 22nd, 1975. It took investigators several days to identify her, learning that she was last seen on Atlantic Avenue, near the Holiday Inn.

The body of Nancy Heard, a 24-year-old motel maid, was found in January, 1976, near a service road in Tomoka State Park, a wilderness north of Ormond Beach. According to the reports, the death scene "looked arranged." Miss Heard was last seen alive hitch-hiking on Atlantic Avenue.

The corpse of Ramona Neal, a pretty 18-year-old from Georgia, was found in Tomoka State Park, partly concealed by small tree branches, in May, 1976.

Then Crow started looking at nearby counties. In Bradford County, nearly 100 miles west of Daytona, the body of a young woman was found in a damp area, partly concealed by small tree branches. She was last seen alive in Daytona Beach, near the Holiday Inn. In Titusville, about 50 miles south in Brevard County, a young woman's body was discovered similarly covered with branches. She was last seen alive hitch-hiking on Atlantic Avenue, in Daytona Beach.

Crow took another look at Stano's background. He had lived in Florida since 1973, when his family moved there from New Jersey. For a time, they had lived near Stuart, in south-east Florida, on the Atlantic coast.

Yes, Crow was told by a Stuart police officer, there had been some unsolved murders of young women in that area. But that had been pretty far back — 1973, 1974. Strange murders, ritualistic almost. Not only unsolved, but not even any suspects.

With a growing sense of disbelief, Crow next contacted police officials in New Jersey. It took much digging into old records, but they eventually came up with the answer he'd both feared and expected. Yes, there had been a couple of unsolved murders there before 1973. Strange cases, from the looks of the reports. Young women, laid out almost in a burial pose, covered with small tree branches. No suspects.

Paul Crow decided that it was time to take a very close look at Gerald Stano's life from day one. His record showed that he had been married briefly to an Ormond Beach woman in 1976. His ex-wife was now living with her parents. Crow went to their home to question her and was invited by her father to the kitchen table. The father ate while the mother served and the ex-wife, with constant prodding from her father, rested her huge breasts on the table and tried to answer the officer's questions.

She said that Stano had never demanded any unusual sexual activity. How could he, with that little bitty penis of his? But he did have one peculiar habit. During their brief marriage he'd frequently left the house without explanation, around 10 or 11 o'clock at night. He would return in the early hours completely exhausted and drop right off to sleep.

Next came a long and emotional interview with Stano's adoptive parents. They had always known that there was something wrong with Gerald, but they'd never really faced it. They had moved a lot, always hoping to leave the problems behind. But the problem was Gerald himself. And now — well, now both felt shattered by the ugly reality and relieved that it was at last out in the open.

They had adopted Gerald at the age of 13 months, after a New York child welfare psychiatrist had labelled him "unadoptable." They didn't know why he had been so labelled, especially at that young age, but they didn't care. They enlisted aid and raised so much fuss that they were finally allowed to adopt him, over the psychiatrist's objections.

Of course, Gerald had got off to a bad start. At the age of six months he'd been taken away from his natural mother because of "horribly extreme physical and emotional neglect." Welfare workers had found him functioning as an animal, eating faecal material. And he was the fifth such child taken away from that same woman for the same reasons.

Gerald had never shown any affection. Not towards his adoptive parents, nor towards anyone else. He was always "thing" oriented. He loved things, but couldn't relate to people as anything but objects. Never did well in school. Always in trouble, getting kicked out, getting arrested. Teachers always saying there was something wrong with him. Juvenile authorities complaining about him setting off fire alarms and dropping rocks on cars from a highway overpass, threatening to send him to reform school. Sports coaches complaining about his bribing other kids to let him win. With stolen money.

Nobody liked Gerald. Fired from job after job. Always getting caught stealing from other workers.

Girl friends? Well, yes, there had been some girl friends — even a wife once. But they'd been a strange bunch, too.

Gerald never could get along with people his own age. He always associated with younger people, children. And whenever he got really involved with a girl, she'd always be younger and have something wrong with her. Deformed, crippled, retarded. Got a little retarded girl pregnant once. Married a compulsive over-eater. And that didn't last long.

Back in his office, Paul Crow pondered his next step for a long time. He had a monster on his hands — and he clearly needed help. He had been confident questioning Stano about Mary Carol Maher and Toni Van Haddocks. He'd had the evidence to work with, a suspect to work on, plus the skill and experience to put it all together. But the investigation had grown to unbelievable proportions. He was now faced with an unknown number of murders committed over an unknown period in an unknown number of places. And committed by what had become, to Detective-Sergeant Paul Crow, a mind of unknown complexity.

Crow thought back to the Carl DeGregory case. An Ormond Beach psychologist, Dr. Ann McMillan, had made a name for herself in that investigation with her "psychological autopsy" of DeGregory. Crow decided to seek her help with the mushrooming case of Gerald Eugene Stano.

As a result Dr. McMillan spent many hours interviewing and testing Stano — performing her psychological autopsy on him. The outcome was startling. Gerald Stano, the doctor reported, had a psychological profile almost identical to those of Charles Manson, Sirhan Sirhan, Son of Sam and Carl DeGregory. What's more, she said, Stano's penchant for killing could have been predicted at any point in his life — and may in fact have been, by the New York psychiatrist who'd labelled the infant Stano "unadoptable."

"In tracing Gerald Stano's case history from the post-natal stage to the present," Dr. McMillan reported, "it can be clearly demonstrated that he has never been normal — and that, in his progression from childhood to adolescence to adult abnormalities, it was logical to predict that 'murderer' would inevitably be added to his labels."

Paul Crow spent many hours with Dr. McMillan and was coached on how to deal with Stano — what kind of questions to ask, what kind of mood to maintain, phrases to avoid, signals to watch for.

By that time two other men had become deeply involved in the Stano case. Assistant State Attorney Larry Nixon, who would prosecute Stano, was working closely with Crow in his preparations. And former FBI Agent Don Jacobson, who had played a role in the movie *The FBI Story*, was assigned to defend Stano. He found it like trying to wade through quicksand.

The amount of time spent on the lengthy preparations also proved to be of value to Crow. Confined to a cell and with nothing to do but think, Gerald Stano started having nightmares about the electric chair. And he started telephoning Crow, the only person he would talk to.

Finally, the interrogations began, with Crow sometimes feeling that they would never end. He often spent eight hours a day with Stano, day after day, week after week, month after month. In some ways it became a game. Stano sussed that Crow was reading his chair movements and stopped them. But there was always some physical signal that told the investigator when the suspect was lying.

Slowly, the story unfolded. Stano had an astoundingly vivid memory of his crimes. He could recall details of murders committed years ago, including the victim's name and items of clothing. But the sheer number of victims contributed to his undoing. He would sometimes get confused about which girl was wearing what.

He would confess to a murder and describe it in great detail. He would give the girl's name, explain how he picked her up, how he killed her and how he disposed of the body. And he would describe her clothing, but would include an article or two of clothing that the victim had not worn — but that *had* been worn by the victim of another unsolved murder, to which he had not confessed.

One such case involved a body that had not even been discovered. Stano told Crow that he had picked up a prostitute on Main Street, near the Holiday Inn in Daytona Beach — and had killed her and left her body in a wooded area. He said he hadn't learned her name, but she was wearing a brown leather jacket, brown shoes and a T-shirt with a slogan printed on it — either "do it in the dirt" or "do it in the dark."

When Stano led Crow and sheriff's investigators to the scene, sure enough the skeleton was wearing a T-shirt bearing the slogan "DO IT IN THE DIRT." But it wasn't wearing a brown leather jacket or brown shoes. Three miles south, however, sheriff's officers had earlier found a skeleton wearing a brown leather jacket and brown shoes, laid out in the same manner and partly covered with branches. Stano said he didn't know anything about that one.

Eventually he confessed to four murders, in addition to those of Mary Carol Maher and Toni Van Haddocks.

There was Nancy Heard: "She started to sound like my future wife, bitching, bitching, bitching — and I wasn't about to take it from anybody. And while we were having sex I just, I just went ahead and, uh, put my arms around her neck and just strangled her."

There was Linda Hamilton: "She got a little upset because I wanted to have a little sex with her and she didn't want it. So I just put my arms around her, put my hands around her neck and strangled her in the car down there at New Smyrna Beach."

There was Ramona Neal: "She started to get sort of on the edgy side and that got me pretty mad, too. And my hands just approached her neck and I strangled her. I also believe I cut her once or twice with a knife that I had with me."

And there was an unknown victim: strangled because of "a hot and heavy conversation that was brought on between the two of us over some, uh, money that was being transacted from having sex with the girl."

He was also suspected of the murders of Bonnie Highes, who went missing from the Daytona Beach area in 1979, and Sandra DuBose, whose body was found dumped in a roadside ditch in August 1978.

There were others who Stano admitted having picked up as they were hitch-hiking, but whom he denied killing. Crow gained the impression that Stano had been instructed by his lawyer to confess to six murders and no more — enough to establish a pattern upon which to base an insanity plea.

If that was the strategy, however, it didn't work. Four psychologists, in addition to Dr. McMillan, found Stano to be abnormal, but legally sane.

Crow and Prosecutor Nixon wanted the other murders cleared up, whether Stano was charged with them or not. Beyond his punishment, there was the consideration of all those families of victims who might never know what became of their children. But Gerald Stano stood his ground. He had killed six — and only six, he insisted.

Nixon worked out an arrangement with Defence Counsel Jacobson. Stano would be taken to the University of Florida's teaching hospital in Gainesville and questioned under the influence of a truth drug. If, under the influence of the drug, he still maintained that he had killed six and only six, he would be allowed to plead guilty, in return for life sentences. But if, under the influence of the drug, he admitted to additional murders, he would accept the electric chair for the murders of Mary Carol Maher and Toni Van Haddocks.

"To hell with that!" stormed Stano.

So a plea-bargain was worked out. Nixon had only six cases, but his main concern was that Gerald Stano should never again walk the streets. The bargain he reached with Jacobson was that Stano would plead guilty to the murders of Mary Carol Maher, Toni Van Haddocks and Nancy Heard — and that his confessions to the murders of Ramona Neal, Linda Hamilton and the unidentified girl would be read into the court record without formal charges attached. Stano would receive three consecutive life sentences, each carrying a mandatory minimum of 25 years before parole eligibility.

Nixon considered the wording of the sentence important. With one eye on the sometimes weird workings of the state pardons and parole board, he spelled out the sentence very carefully in plain language: Gerald Stano is to serve a minimum of 25 years for the murder of Mary Carol Maher; after that, he is to serve a minimum of 25 years for the murder of Toni Van Haddocks; after that, he is to serve a minimum of 25 years for the murder of Nancy Heard; he is to serve an absolute minimum of 75 years, less credit for 520 days spent in the Volusia County jail, before parole eligibility.

On September 2nd, 1981, Judge S. James Foxman reluctantly accepted the plea-bargain and imposed the three consecutive life sentences. He told Stano that death in the electric chair would have been the appropriate penalty for each of the murders, but that he was accepting the plea-bargain because his confessions enabled the families of six victims to put the matter to rest. "In essence," the judge said, "you have profited because of the large number of murders committed."

With that, Gerald Eugene Stano was whisked away to the Florida State Prison to await his 103rd birthday and parole eligibility.

But he wasn't off the hook. Other murders were still under investigation, he was eventually to confess to no fewer than 41 slayings in Florida, New Jersey and Pennsylvania, and one of them was to send him to the chair.

This was the murder of 17-year-old Cathy Lee Scharf of Port Orange, who had disappeared 11 days before Christmas in 1973. Her decomposed body, covered with branches, had been found by hunters in a drainage ditch 30 miles from her home, at the Merritt Island National Wildlife Refuge near Titusville on January 19th, 1974.

In his confession Stano said he had picked up Cathy

while she was hitchhiking on US Highway 1 at Port Orange. Over a period of several hours he had repeatedly stabbed and choked her. After finally killing her and dumping her body, he had driven to a service station, cleaned-up, combed his hair, and had then gone roller-skating.

Stano also confessed to the murders of Susan Bickrest, 24, of Daytona Beach, strangled and found floating in Spruce Creek in December 1975; and Mary Muldoon, 23, of Ormond Beach, shot in the head and discovered in a ditch in November 1977.

And Stano's victims also included Janine Ligotino, 19, and Ann Arcendaux, 17, hometowns unknown, whose bodies were found in March 1973 near Gainesville; Barbara Ann Bauer, 17, of New Smyrna Beach, whose corpse was found in April 1974 near Starke; and an unidentified woman found dumped near the Interstate Mall at Altamonte Springs in 1974.

Sam Bardwell, a Titusville lawyer who represented Stano at clemency hearings, said the egotistical murderer had confessed to crimes he did not commit. "Gerry is as much a serial confessor as a serial killer."

Stating that Stano should be studied rather than executed, Bardwell proceeded to add: "Investigators lined up to get Stano's ear. I believe he is a serial killer, but a lot of cases were closed on the weakest of evidence."

Stano's attorney Mark Olive claimed that his client's confession to Cathy Scharf's murder was phony and that he had received ineffective legal representation at his trial. He also alleged that Stano's prosecutors had solicited false testimony from a prison informant, Clarence Zacke, to bolster their case.

Zacke had claimed that he and Stano were walking in the prison yard when Stano bragged that he had played with Cathy Scharf "like a cat with a mouse," choking her senseless and then waiting for her to revive so he could do it again. Stano had allegedly said, "I stabbed and choked her some. You can make it last longer. You can take your time choking, because if you turn loose, they come back to life."

Both the Florida Supreme Court and the US Supreme Court denied Stano's request for a stay of execution.

"He was more concerned about getting his car dirty than the women he killed," said Dean Moxley, now a circuit court judge, who as an assistant state attorney prosecuted Stano for Cathy Scharf's murder. "He has never, I believe will never, show any remorse for what he's done. He's done a lot of damage to a lot of people, but all those folks kind of get washed out as the years pass."

Daryl Neal, the 41-year-old brother of one of Stano's victims, said he had waited a long time to see the killer pay for his crimes. Stano had murdered Neal's sister Ramona in 1976. She had gone on a trip to Ormond Beach with friends to celebrate their graduation from high school. After a row with her boy friend she had met Stano walking along the beach. Her decomposed body was found months later, her blue polka-dot bikini covering her bones.

"I hope he says he's sorry," said Neal, "but I don't really care. It's time." The brother was one of the witnesses invited to watch Stano die.

He added: "My sister would be forty now and probably have kids of her own. You can't measure that loss, and you can't make up for it. All that you can do is make Stano pay with his miserable life. When I go to visit my mama's grave, I can't bring myself to see my sister's. I want to look at Stano, look at his face when they strap him in. I want the bad dreams to stop. As soon as he's put to death, the better we'll all rest."

Stano's execution was to be the first of four scheduled to span eight days at Florida's State Prison at Starke, and anti-death penalty activists decried the state's renewal of capital punishment.

For a year, since March, 1997, executions had been suspended after flames erupted from Florida's electric chair during the electrocution of Pedro Medina, the killer of an Orlando schoolteacher.

The protesters included Bianca Jagger, the former wife of the Rolling Stones' Mick Jagger. Claiming that the state's politicians were "killing for votes," she said: "They are using the death penalty to present a simplistic answer to a complex problem." Florida's judicial system, she said, was "beleaguered and bloodthirsty."

But prosecutor Larry Nixon said that Stano needed to die for his crimes. "With Gerry Stano it is nothing more than society acting collectively as an act of self-defence."

In the early hours of Monday, March 23rd, 1998, about 20 protesters assembled in the pre-dawn chill outside the prison, lighting a dozen white candles which they placed beside a sign referring to Florida's governor. The sign read: "Lawton Chiles, serial murderer, kills again."

"It's not a deterrent," said a protester from Gainesville. "It's vengeance. Some of the comments of our legislators have been quite rabid."

Nobody from Cathy Scharf's family, however, was at the prison for the execution. Her parents were dead, and her brother said he just wanted to forget about Stano and the pain he had caused the family.

While the protesters shivered outside the jail, in his cell Gerald Stano — now 46 and with no more birthdays to look forward to — was tucking in to his last meal: Delmonico steak, medium rare; baked potato with sour cream and bacon bits; tossed salad with blue cheese dressing; Lima beans; and for dessert, mint chocolate chip ice cream.

Then at 7.15 a.m. he went to the death chamber to become the 40th inmate executed since Florida reinstated the death penalty in 1972, and the 237th to die in the electric chair since 1924.

He made no final statement, staring straight ahead as he was strapped in the chair, and managing only a slight smile for his attorney. This time there was no visible smoke or flame when the current was switched on. Five relatives of Stano's victims sat in the front row of witnesses, one of them uttering a subdued "Yesss!" when the jolt hit.

15

OKLAHOMA'S HOUND FROM HELL

Charles W. Sasser

"I don't feel Charles deserves to die. He's too good to older people and kids"

CONVICTS ON Death Row call that short distance from the holding cell to the execution chamber "the last mile." At 8.05 a.m. on Sunday, September 9th, 1990, prison guards at Oklahoma State Penitentiary in McAlester moved convicted killer Charles Troy Coleman from his first-floor cell on Death Row to the third-floor holding cell 25 feet from the death chamber. If his execution went ahead at midnight as scheduled, he would be the first convict in Oklahoma in 24 years to walk the last mile.

All Coleman took with him to the holding cell was his Bible. The corridors were partitioned off to keep the other inmates from seeing the condemned man should he break down or become violent.

Only the faint echo of TV sets broke the silence as the prisoner and his guards marched past the steel doors behind which 114 other inmates (110 men and 4 women) waited their turn to die. Coleman did not glance back at the cell that had been his home for the last 11 years while lawyers argued his case up and down the legal chain.

In 1987 he had been 36 hours short of being executed

before the 10th U.S. Circuit Court of Appeals blocked his execution and started three more years of legal wrangling.

This time he was just 16 hours away.

Many of his fellow-inmates on Death Row believed he would still receive an 11th-hour reprieve. Others thought his time had come. Most were placing bets on the outcome.

"I got a feeling back in March that Coleman was going to be executed," one inmate declared. "I got the feeling the Lord wasn't going to allow another stay."

Coleman — in his holding cell eight short steps away from the execution chamber — still looked confident as the wait began, especially as his lawyers expressed hopes of a last-minute stay.

Meanwhile, the debate on capital punishment continued. While it was the Supreme Court that reinstated the death penalty, it has never resolved the argument that continues to rage over the appropriateness of sentencing criminals to die.

Opponents of the death penalty claim that in convicting and sentencing criminals to death the state itself is committing murder. They believe it is implicitly unfair for official bodies to execute a fellow-human being.

The American Civil Liberties Union, according to a spokesman, "opposes the death penalty for all crimes under all circumstances because it denies equal protection of the law, is cruel and unusual punishment, and denies due process of law . . .

"The death penalty discriminates against the poor, the uneducated, the mentally and emotionally ill, members of minority groups and the weak and voiceless members of our society in general."

Mandy Welsh, the attorney who with her lawyer husband Don Ed Payne guided Coleman through much of his lengthy appeals process, added, "To execute Charles would be a sign that society has failed. It would be a sign that society cannot cope with a sick or damaged individual other than by silencing him forever."

Death penalty proponents on the other hand argue that execution deters crime, and that it is the only appropriate response by which a crime-embattled society can show its abhorrence to acts of horror committed against citizens. Anything less would be a mockery of justice.

When in 1977 Gary Gilmore became the first killer executed under the new Supreme Court guidelines, a national newspaper columnist pointed out that Gilmore "has no claim upon the people of Utah to feed, clothe, house, entertain and rehabilitate him the rest of his natural life ...

"In the decade the death penalty has fallen into disuse our criminals have become the best protected, defended and treated in history; and our citizens the most terrorised of any civilized society on earth."

Gilmore should be executed, the columnist declared, "First, because, given the repugnant and horrendous character of his crimes, death is the only punishment suitable and just. Second, so that his execution will begin to alert murderers, muggers and rapists in our midst that they are no longer dealing with the marshmallow state. And thirdly, Gilmore should face that firing squad as public witness to the value placed upon lost lives ..."

The same argument could be made for the execution of Charles Troy Coleman. His criminal career began when he was a teenager. From the age of 17 — when he pulled a gun on a deputy and threatened to kill him — until he was apprehended for murder at 32, he had been convicted of 15 separate crimes.

His last crime spree piled up 20 more felonies and five corpses in addition to the accusation of an earlier murder for which he had been acquitted.

Now he awaited his execution, a few steps away from the death chamber. He refused breakfast, taking only a cup of coffee. Until noon he was visited by friends and family, and consulted attorneys Mandy Welsh and Don Ed Payne.

Payne was firm in the belief that the execution would not occur. "I believe that anyone that hears his appeals will want to do the right thing," he said.

In the 11 years since Coleman's murder conviction his case had gone through more than 20 appeals. The U.S. Supreme Court had declined to hear the case on five separate occasions, and his attorneys now claimed in last-minute petitions that Coleman had not received a fair trial because the state withheld documents about his troubled mental history.

They were also demanding that the execution be stayed because the state parole board had refused to hold a special commutation hearing.

During the last week alone the case had bounced up to the 10th U.S. Circuit Court in Denver and back four times. It was on its way back to Denver again, along with a similar request to the U.S. Supreme Court that the execution be halted. Defence Attorneys Welsh and Payne were never far from a telephone in case Henry Bellmon, the Governor of Oklahoma should respond to their pleas for clemency.

Welsh said that arguments drawn in legal terms "did not address in much depth Charles as he is today, the good that he has done since entering prison, and the good that he will do if allowed to live.

"First, it is obvious that Charles has changed because he is in an environment that has allowed him to recover his self-esteem and develop his skills. Second, the reduction in stress has eliminated the danger that he could again resort to "violence."

A detective involved in the Coleman investigation scoffed at the claims. "Coleman's in prison!" he exclaimed. "How many people has he had the opportunity to victimise on Death Row?"

"Following his baptism into Christianity," Welsh continued, "Charles has become a man who is loved and admired by many with whom he comes into contact."

Conversion to Christianity is nearly 100 per cent on Death Row. Killers and criminals of the vilest order suddenly discover halos when faced with their own execution.

"One of the most frustrating things to me now looking back," said Welsh, "is realising how distorted the people's picture of Charles is. I know how far removed that picture is from what I know now to be the truth about Charles's life.

"When I met him I found him to be a very sensitive person who was not at all self-centred; who focused far more on people's problems and sufferings than he did on his own convictions. He frequently called to try to get help for people who were ill in prison or who were being mistreated in prison — people he was genuinely concerned about."

Four Oklahoma assistant attorney generals worked to counter the defence efforts to halt Coleman's execution.

"Cannot the parties consider this last-minute claim for clemency for what it really is?" they argued. "It is a last-ditch, calculated effort to further extend the already elongated labyrinth of multiple appeals and reviews designed to keep hope and the petitioner alive . . ."

"The appeals process has been fully utilised in Coleman's case," announced Governor Bellmon. "It has come to a conclusion and the sentence will be carried out."

Nevertheless, Bellmon said he would closely monitor the case in the event of a last-minute reason or evidence should arise to halt the execution.

Meanwhile, penitentiary officials continued preparing for Coleman's execution Prison spokeswoman Linda Morgan said the authorities could not sit back and wait, even though another delay was possible. They had the details to work out, such as selecting clothing for Coleman to wear to the death chamber, preparing for media coverage and overseeing security.

McAlester City police and Pittsburg County deputies would guard the prison grounds outside the gate and provide traffic control.

Several anti-capital punishment groups were planning

vigils and protests outside the prison gates on the Sunday of the execution.

"I find it a bit frightening that Oklahoma wants to embark on its path of using execution as a method of dealing with the very serious problem of violent crime," said a spokesman for Amnesty International. "What can only result is just one more senseless death."

Sunday, 1.00 p.m. Eleven hours of life remained for Coleman.

Warden James Saffle turned over control of the prison to Deputy Corrections Director Larry Fields while he concentrated on the execution details. Extra guards were called in. Other prisoners would be allowed normal Sunday visitors until 7.00 p.m., at which time the prison's front gate would be shut and movement inside the prison restricted.

In Coleman's cell guards sent out for hamburgers. Coleman ate one and chatted to the guards. He sounded positive and cheerful and told a reporter that he would keep a Monday morning interview appointment.

"I'll see you during regular visiting hours next week," he assured his wife.

Coleman had already been on Death Row for nearly three years when he got married in the prison visiting room on April 9th, 1982. The bride told reporters that she and Coleman had known each other as children in Muskogee. A relative of hers, an ex-convict, reintroduced her to the condemned killer. Although the couple never actually lived together, she visited Coleman in prison and phoned him frequently.

She visited him for two hours in his holding cell on Sunday morning, and again in the afternoon. In between visits, she stayed at a nearby hotel.

"I don't feel Charles deserves to die," she told a reporter. "He's too good to older people and kids. I never saw him be cruel to anyone. Charles is the kindest, gentlest man I've ever met. He gives me a sense of peace.

"The cruel part is putting him to death when he has become a Christian and repented."

Clemency papers filed before Governor Bellmon by Coleman's attorney pointed to the convicted killer's growing-up period as one in which he suffered abuse, beatings and other hardships. At 16 he married, becoming a father at 17. At the age of 19 he was in prison in Alabama. From then on he was in and out of penitentiaries in Oklahoma, Arizona, Alabama and California.

On the afternoon of what was to be Charles's last day on earth, people were still saying how personable he was. A woman involved in her church's prison ministry said, "I consider myself a friend of Charles Coleman. I have found him to be a very thoughtful, sensitive, caring person and I want to see him get the kind of care he needs."

At 5.00 p.m. Coleman refused a "last meal."

At 6.05 the U.S. Supreme Court rejected Coleman's last appeal. Any stay at this point depended upon either the governor or the 10th U.S. Circuit Court of Appeals. Time was running out.

"People are really touched by my pending execution," Coleman told a reporter. "I've seen a big movement in people's attitudes out there away from the death penalty."

If Coleman entered the death chamber at midnight and was executed, he would become the first person in Oklahoma history to be executed by the injection of a lethal drug.

After years of hangings in county seats, the state of Oklahoma took over executions in 1915 and introduced the electric chair — which was considered humane.

During the next 51 years, 83 men went to their deaths in "Ol' Sparky," as the chair became known. The last was James Donald French, who in 1966 received his 2,200 volts of electricity philosophically: "I killed the victim, right? Now they kill me, right? Simple."

No one had been executed in Oklahoma since then.

Tulsa State Representative Bill Wiseman instigated the bill calling for death by lethal injection, or the "happy hour," as it is known to inmates, following the reinstatement of the death penalty in 1976.

Officials explained to your author how the system works...

As midnight approaches Warden James Saffle and a prison chaplain will accompany Coleman to the death chamber, where he is to be strapped to a medical gurney and an intravenous tube is inserted into a vein in his arm. The I.V. tube leads over a low wall to where three anonymous executioners await. Coleman is given the opportunity to utter his last words while 30 invited witnesses watch through a window from an adjoining viewing room.

When Saffle gives the order for the execution to begin, each of the executioners beyond the wall injects a different solution into the intravenous tube. The first solution puts the inmate to sleep; the second stops his breathing; the third stops his heart. In all, the execution takes about 10 minutes.

As the September darkness fell over the prison at McAlester, supporters and opponents of the death penalty began to gather outside the prison gate. About 60 candle-carrying marchers from a nearby Catholic church chanted, "Lord, save our people!"

"What really hurts," said one of them, "is that it is too late now to begin caring about this man. If only someone had cared twenty years ago ..."

Those with the opposite point of view carried signs proclaiming: "One down, 114 to go; Oklahoma don't need a noose, we got the juice."

One man in the crowd said his seven-year-old daughter had been abducted and stabbed to death in March. "I would rather see people support the victim than the criminals," he said. "What about the victim's rights? Coleman gave up his rights when he pulled the trigger."

Meanwhile, on Death Row, only the low hum of TVs tuned to a single news channel broke the tense silence. In his holding cell Coleman continued chatting to his family, friends and lawyers. All visitors were ushered out of the cell at 9.00 p.m. and Coleman switched to the telephone.

Three hours to go.

The condemned man's attorneys hovered over a phone connected directly to the state governor's office. Defence Attorney Welsh spoke to a congregation of execution opponents outside the gate.

"Coleman said that when you start down a road, a lot of times you get a long way down it before you realise it's a one-way street ..."

Coleman's had been a one-way road.

On the afternoon of February 9th, 1979, elderly John and Roxie Seward of Muskogee, Oklahoma, surprised Charles Coleman burgling a relative's house near Brushy Mountain. Coleman marched the couple into the basement and coldly executed them — first the husband, then the wife — with a 28-gauge shotgun. So much for his being "too good to older people."

Police captured Coleman later that same night after a high-speed chase. From his truck they recovered the victims' bloodstained wallets plus loot from the burglary. Society, however, had not yet seen the last of the man who'd been nicknamed "the Hound from Hell."

On Monday, April 23rd, 1979, Coleman escaped from the 70-year-old Muskogee County jail while awaiting trial. His freedom left a trail of blood from Oklahoma to Arizona.

At 6.00 a.m. on Tuesday, Patrolman Tommie Dotson of the Oklahoma City suburb of Luther stopped a vehicle for speeding. The driver was Coleman in a stolen car. Coleman slit the officer's throat with a knife, stole the policeman's .357 revolver, and handcuffed the cop into the back seat cage of his patrol car.

Coleman was apparently satisfied that the policeman's jugular vein had been cut and he would bleed to death. That took care of his being "the kindest, gentlest man."

Coleman's next victim was 40-year-old Russell Lewis Jr., whose body the police recovered from the base of a cliff in Tulsa's Chandler Park. Coleman stole the man's wallet and blue Ford truck, then marched the victim to the edge of the wooded precipice so the body would fall over the cliff when he was shot.

It was discovered that Lewis had two bullets from Officer Dotson's .357 lodged at the base of his skull when he was found. So much for Coleman, the "thoughtful, caring, sensitive person."

The trail of the Hound from Hell next led to Howard County, Texas. On Friday, April 27th, a 39-year-old woman and her 15-year-old son disappeared from the service station they ran on the outskirts of Big Spring. Later that day, police recovered their nude bodies in a remote area nearby. They had been executed with bullets in their heads. The woman had also been raped.

Evidence soon pointed to the escaped Oklahoma fugitive Charles Troy Coleman, later described as "a very gentle person, mild-mannered, personable."

At 5.00 p.m. on April 28th, Deputy T. B. Parish of Pima County, Arizona, stopped Russell Lewis's stolen truck on Interstate 10. Coleman pulled Patrolman Dotson's gun on Deputy Parish and handcuffed the policeman inside the built-in cage of his patrol car, saying, "You've been a good boy. I'm not going to kill you."

After Coleman continued his flight, Parish escaped from the cage and sounded the alarm. Shortly afterwards the authorities recaptured Oklahoma's Hound from Hell after a desperate helicopter and car chase across the desert.

So far Coleman had been accused of murdering at least six people, including his girl friend's father in California, John and Roxie Seward in Muskogee, Russell Lewis in Tulsa, and the petrol station attendant and her son in Texas.

He had also kidnapped two policemen, slitting one's throat, stolen at least three vehicles, committed at least two armed robberies, three burglaries and a score of lesser offences.

Yet Charles Coleman, the Death Row inmate, was now "admired and loved by many."

Meanwhile, the wait at McAlester Prison continued,

where his wife still described Coleman as optimistic. "He doesn't think it's going to happen. I just hope God brings us a stay or a reprieve; anything but darkness."

"The question is, should a man like this ever be let back into society?" mused Governor Bellmon. "I think the answer is no."

Attorney Welsh pleaded with corrections officers to ask Governor Bellmon at least to speak to Mrs. Coleman. The governor refused to do so.

The clock on the wall in the execution chamber read 11.45 p.m. Time had finally run out.

Charles Troy Coleman wore new prison jeans and a blue shirt as he walked those few feet that made up "the last mile" from the holding cell to the death chamber. He was crying and simultaneously praying with the chaplain.

"He was very nervous and appeared to be afraid," noted Warden Saffle.

There was not going to be a last-minute stay and Coleman's final few minutes passed quickly. He was strapped to the gurney while the chaplain stood at his feet praying.

Attorney General Robert Henry then issued a brief statement: "It is our duty to uphold the law ..."

Coleman, lying on the gurney with the intravenous tube in his arm, was asked if he had any last words.

He replied nervously, "Just tell everybody I love them and I have a peace and a quiet heart."

"Let it begin," ordered Warden Saffle.

As he lay there about to die the condemned man asked Chaplain Hawkins to read Matthew 7: "Judge not, that ye be not judged ..."

As the verse was read out Coleman turned his head towards the witnesses on the other side of the window, smiled, and whispered, "I love you, Mandy."

A moment later he closed his eyes and muttered, "Praise God" and exhaled quickly several times.

Charles Troy Coleman was pronounced dead at 12.35 a.m.

On Death Row an inmate said, "We here are only thinking of one thing — ourselves. We're fighting to live."

In Muskogee a policeman observed quietly that the Hound from Hell had finally gone to hell.

16

DEATH TO THE FREEWAY KILLER

Lester Fox

Released early from prison, he claimed another 10 victims

WILLIAM G. BONIN had it all worked out. "If you want to kill someone," he told a potential accomplice, "you should make a plan and find a place to dump the body before you even pick a victim."

He knew what he was talking about. As a serial killer he was already into double figures. But on this occasion he'd decided to spare the life of the 14-year-old boy in whom he was now confiding.

It was 1975. The two had attended a party in their hometown in California, and as the gathering broke up Bonin had offered the youth a lift in his van. But instead of driving him straight home Bonin produced a gun and drove the boy to an isolated area. There he forced his victim to strip, took off his own clothes and then raped the defenceless youngster.

But the boy was lucky compared with some of Bonin's other victims ... the ones who'd had spikes driven into their skulls and rectums, or had simply been hog-tied and strangled. The present victim had not been spared out of sentiment, Bonin told him as he drove him back to his neighbourhood. He'd been spared because the two had been seen leaving the party together.

Bonin went on to tell the boy that he liked to pick up young male hitch-hikers, using their T-shirts to strangle them. He suggested that the teenager might like to help him with his next killing ...

But the youth couldn't get out of the van quick enough. Back home he wept and sat in shock for several hours before he phoned his mother at work. A few days later, acting on the boy's information, the police picked up William Bonin. The rapist was convicted and sentenced to one to 15 years in prison. Three years later, in October 1978, he was released. In April 1980 his parole supervision ended.

It was at about that time that the police began broadcasting appeals for information on a slayer who had become known as the Freeway Killer. Young male hitch-hikers were his speciality. Picking them up, he overcame them by brandishing a knife or gun. Then he bound and killed them in one bizarre way or another, dumping their corpses alongside southern Californian freeways. There the bodies were soon found, but it was suspected that others had been taken into the mountains and dumped in hiding-places where they would never be discovered.

By now the boy victim Bonin had spared in 1975 was at a juvenile detention centre at Los Padrinos, serving time for car theft. He heard the police appeals on the radio and read about the Freeway Killer's exploits in the papers. He recognised the *modus operandi* which Bonin had described to him five years earlier. He had a word with the authorities, and Detective John St. John was sent to question him.

Recalling his nightmare encounter with Bonin, the boy told the detective that the suspect had said he went out looking for young men to kill on Friday and Saturday nights. This, Bonin had confided, left him free to take his girl friend roller-skating in Anaheim on Sundays.

St. John turned up Bonin's rap sheet. He found that the

suspect had received his first criminal conviction at the age of 10. At 22 he had notched up his first conviction for a sex offence. Between 1969 and 1978 he'd been at liberty for only a few months, being continually imprisoned for sexually assaulting young boys. He was now 33 — and he had yet to be nailed as a killer.

Detective St. John promptly had him placed under surveillance. A week passed uneventfully, and then the police pounced. On June 11th, 1980, they saw Bonin pick up a youth. They tailed him as he drove to a dark side street in Hollywood. Then, breaking into his van, they found him sodomising a 17-year-old boy.

With the suspect safely behind bars on a sodomy charge, detectives now began probing his links with the string of freeway murders. Tragically, if his one-to-15-year sentence imposed in 1975 had been served full-term, at least 10 youths would still have been enjoying life. Instead they had ended up sprawled along freeways, stuffed into dustbins or interred in mountain graves.

At first Bonin was suspected of killing at least 21 young men discarded over six Californian counties. At a later stage the toll mounted to nearly 40, dating back to 1972 when the earliest of the strikingly-similar murders with sexual overtones was first noted. But the police and the district attorney's office could only go on what they felt they could prove. And the grim tally eventually boiled down to an even dozen in Los Angeles County, where Bonin would stand trial.

Vernon Robert Butts, 22, was arrested in connection with the Freeway Killer case and identified as one of Bonin's sidekicks. He was a cadaverous-looking labourer with long stringy blond hair, who posed as a magician and in whose apartment police found two empty coffins and a horde of novelty spiders that dropped from the ceiling on visitors.

Detectives claimed that Butts was an accomplice of Bonin's in at least half a dozen of the murders. Two months after the pair were charged James Munro, 19, was booked for taking part in the murder of young Sean King, whose death was also attributed to Bonin.

Finally, a fourth suspect, Gregory Matthews Miley, 19, was taken into custody in Houston, Texas. He was charged with the murder of two boys, aged 12 and 14, whose nude bodies were found in February 1980.

Miley admitted the killings and told in grisly detail how he and Bonin strangled the two boys within hours of each other in the van. He said that the 14-year-old was a homosexual they picked up on a street in Hollywood.

According to Miley, Bonin sodomised the youngster. He said he held the boy while Bonin tied him. Then Bonin grabbed the victim's shirt, tied it over his head and began twisting it until the boy was dead. They dumped the victim and drove around until they picked up the 12-year-old. Miley said the boy entered the van voluntarily and got in the back with Bonin. Then he heard crying sounds being made by the victim.

According to police, Miley said he helped Bonin hold the boy down, "but it didn't seem too hard to hold him because he was so small." They then dumped the body by a skip.

Before Bonin's trial Miley pleaded guilty to two counts of murder and agreed to testify against Bonin and thus save himself from the gas chamber. When he took the witness-stand it was pointed out that he had an IQ of 56, which classified him as mentally retarded. He would face 25 years in prison.

Another of Bonin's accomplices to testify for the prosecution was James Munro, also mentally deficient, who pleaded guilty to one count of second-degree murder and faced 15 years in prison.

Miley told how he and Bonin picked up a young boy as he was leaving a cinema in Hollywood. He said that Bonin had some sexual activity with the boy in the van. Then, for no reason, Bonin started beating him. Bonin tied him up and Miley said he joined in beating the youngster.

He said Bonin got a tyre-lever, pressing it against the

boy's neck until he could hear the bones cracking. Miley continued: "The kid vomited. I jumped down on him the same way, killing the guy."

Then came the confession of Vernon Butts, the aspiring magician. He said he had been on several murder forays with Bonin, but insisted that it was Bonin who did all the killing. He told how most of the victims were strangled with their own T-shirts, some were ripped with knives — and one met death by having an ice-pick driven into his ear.

But Butts could not be sure whether the ice-pick killed him or if it was the chlorohydrate acid he was forced to drink. Butts also told of the night Bonin showed up at his flat drenched in blood and asked for help in cleaning himself up. Facing six counts of murder, Butts added that Bonin had boasted of having killed 21 young men.

But still more gruesome details would be exposed for all to hear. And that was more than Vernon Butts could face.

On a Sunday morning in January 1980 he hanged himself in his cell in the Los Angeles County jail ... with a towel instead of a T-shirt.

Correspondence found in his cell indicated that Butts was getting upset about the impending release of evidence he had given behind closed doors at the preliminary hearing. He was particularly concerned that it would shock his friends and relatives. In his testimony he had claimed that Bonin had a "hypnotic" way about him. Speaking of the killings, he said: "After the first one I couldn't do anything about it."

Coroner Thomas T. Noguchi said there was no doubt that Butts *had* committed suicide. There were no injuries on the body, no signs of a struggle.

When the trial of William G. Bonin began on November 5th, 1981, evidence shown to the jury included an assortment of gory colour pictures displaying the horribly slashed and emasculated body of a 13-year-old boy.

The teenager died of a severe slash wound to his throat that extended nearly to the back of his neck. He also had a stab wound in his chest that had pierced his liver and pancreas. His skull had been crushed by a blow from a blunt instrument. The boy's sex organs had been cut off and there were bite-marks on his penis, found a few feet from his body.

Another of Bonin's victims had been slashed and stabbed more than 70 times. And in one boy's pockets police had found the tickets to Disneyland his mother had given him the afternoon he came up against Bonin — and died.

Bonin sat quietly at the counsel table throughout the grisly recitation, conferring with his lawyer from time to time, coldly eyeing the witnesses and spectators, but seeming unperturbed by the charges against him.

Deputy District Attorney Sterling Norris told the court that nothing less than the death penalty would satisfy the State of California. "We will prove that he is the Freeway Killer, as he has bragged to a number of witnesses — bragged that he killed in excess of sixteen such victims . . .

"We will show you that he enjoyed the killings. Not only did he enjoy it and plan to enjoy it, he had an insatiable demand, an insatiable appetite — not only for sodomy, but for killing."

Norris said that immediately after one murder Bonin had told his companion in the crime: "I'm horny. Let's go and get another one."

The jury were told that James Munro and Gregory Matthews Miley would be called upon to testify, in exchange for escaping the death penalty. Each had pleaded guilty to murder charges, and both were awaiting sentencing.

On December 8th there was a dramatic interruption in the trial. At about 9.40 a.m., as Bonin was getting ready to go up to the 15th-floor courtroom, one of the jailers heard a pounding on the wall of the cell occupied by Bonin and two other prisoners. Bonin was holding a piece of tissue paper to his bleeding nose. The jailer asked him what had happened.

"Nothing," Bonin replied. "I just want to be changed to another cell."

He was taken to hospital where he was treated for cuts and bruises and he was unable to attend the court that day. Bonin claimed that he had injured himself in a fall while he was in a cell with the accused Hillside Strangler Angelo Buono and John W. Stinson, a convicted murderer awaiting sentencing.

It seemed that either Buono or Stinson had dealt out a dose of jailhouse justice to Bonin for committing crimes against children.

When the trial resumed the spotlight was focused on TV newsman David Lopez, to whom Bonin had reportedly confessed in the county jail that he had killed 21 young men and boys. Previously Lopez had sought shelter under California's "shield law," which protected him from revealing anything not mentioned in his newscast.

But he now declared that he'd had a change of heart — that he was a citizen first and would no longer seek the protection of the shield law. He testified that he'd had seven conversations with Bonin, beginning in December 1980 and continuing into early the following year. On January 9th, 1981, Bonin confessed to him that he had killed the 21 boys and young men. Bonin also told him that he had led the police to the remains of victim Sean King, 14, whose whereabouts had been a mystery until then.

Bonin added that he'd done so in response to a letter from the boy's mother, in which she pleaded: "I am a born-again Christian. But I want my baby buried for Christmas." The mother now wept as she sat in the court.

Bonin also told Lopez that he was confessing because he wanted to clear Eric Wijnanedts, 21, who had been falsely accused of killing one of the victims. Lopez was told how Bonin picked up the King boy at a bus stop. And he quoted Bonin as saying: "I got the kid in the van and I killed him the way I did the others."

Bonin also told Lopez that it was Butts who thrust an

ice-pick into the right ear of Daren Lee Kendrick, 19. "Vern got really weird that night and stuck ice-picks in his head."

The witness revealed that Bonin told him the murders began in August 1979 and ended on June 11th, 1980, when police caught him sodomising a 17-year-old.

Lopez told the court: "He said that if the cops had not got there and arrested him, he would have killed the kid in the van."

Asked what he would be doing if he were still on the street, Bonin had promptly replied: "I'd still be killing. I couldn't stop killing. It got easier each time."

Prosecutor Norris told the jury that Bonin had such an insatiable urge to torture boys and young men that murder became a habit. The *modus operandi* was always the same — get the victims in the van, overpower them, tie them up, have perverse sex with them, torture them with knives, spikes, ice-picks, garottes and guns, then reach the climax of the orgy by inflicting death.

After six days of deliberation the jury found William G. Bonin guilty of 10 counts of first-degree murder and 10 counts of robbery.

But if he had any fear of the death sentence which followed, he didn't show it, sitting calmly at the defence table and displaying no emotion.

Fourteen years later — on Friday, February 23rd, 1996, with the appeals process exhausted — William G. Bonin at 49 became the first man to be executed by lethal injection in California.

17

LOVER OF THE DEAD

Turk Ryder

"I know I'm sick. I just can't help myself. I just want the killing to stop"

ROUND ABOUT 8 o'clock on a chilly December morning, Dallas detectives burst into an apartment and arrested the sole occupant — a 42-year-old former mental patient recently released from a halfway house. He put up no resistance. "I got no reason to protest," he told the detectives.

The formalities of arrest were duly carried out. He was patted down for weapons, his hands were handcuffed behind his back, he was read his legal rights, then taken to Dallas police headquarters. The suspect was taken through a side door, past a bored dispatcher taking down squad car numbers.

The handcuffs were removed and he was again read his constitutional rights. One of the detectives identified himself and said he was investigating the murder of a 32-year-old woman, found raped and half-naked outside a tavern. It was the first time since the lawmen knocked on his apartment door that the man had been told the reason for his arrest.

"Tell us what happened," the detective said.

"O.K.," the man said, running a hand through his long, dark hair. He asked for a cigarette and a soda.

One of the detectives shook a cigarette from his packet. Another spent 50 cents to buy a soda from a machine and slid it across the table.

"I can tell you right now that I need some help," he told detectives. "I'm with a woman — and then something comes over me and I kill her."

The detectives looked at each other. They weren't really expecting this, a full confession. One of the men grunted: "Go ahead."

The man said he met the woman in a bar on a cold, wintry October night. They had a couple of drinks and went back to her place. One thing led to another and he found himself on the bed with his hands around her neck. He couldn't recall whether her clothes were on or off. He also couldn't remember if he had sex before or after he killed her. He woke up next morning with the worst hangover of his life and a stiffening corpse lying next to him. He slept with her for three days. Then he left.

The detective asking the questions felt a jolt halfway through the statement. The man was confessing to a murder no one but the killer knew anything about.

"Now, about the girl in the bar," the detective asked when the suspect was through. "Tell us about her."

"Which one?" the suspect asked — and the lawman felt another jolt.

The confessions lasted well into the night. When they were over, the suspect had finished several soft drinks, a hamburger dinner — and confessed to a string of ghoulish murders that crisscrossed the south-west portion of the United States.

A Dallas prosecutor would describe the grisly confessions as "something like you might read in one of those detective magazines." A *Dallas Morning News* story described him as a "character from last night's horror movie" that included such infamous killers as Ted Bundy, Albert DeSalvo and John Wayne Gacy.

The story made headlines in a town noted for sensational murder cases. In November, 1980, however, there was no publicity. Just a routine murder case that needed solving and a detective out doing his job ...

The call lit up the Dallas police switchboard early on the morning of November 12th, 1980. The caller announced: "I found a young woman in a car park. She doesn't have any clothes on. I think she's dead."

Police cars and an ambulance converged on the nearly-empty car park in east Dallas. The pretty brunette lying face-up on the asphalt was not exactly nude — she still wore a blouse and a bra — but the rest of the observation was correct.

Investigator Gerald Robinson arrived at shortly before 6 a.m. He was followed by the police photographer, lab. assistants and a medical examiner.

The brunette, in her late 20's or early 30's, had probably been very pretty. She wasn't any more, though. The vacant brown eyes stared sightlessly up towards the sky, while her full, tulip-shaped lips were crusted with blood that spilled from the sides of her mouth.

The medical examiner tilted the victim's head to one side and pointed to purplish marks on her slender neck. "Strangled," he said. "Not long ago, either. Maybe just a few hours."

Behind a clump of trees about 20 feet from the body were a pair of women's slacks. They'd been ripped in front, apparently when the garment was forcibly pulled from her body. And they held identification naming the victim as Wanda Fay Roberts, 32, of Dallas.

Tracing her whereabouts before she was killed took a little more doing. Initially, Robinson thought the woman had been strangled somewhere else, then dumped here. The car park was bordered on three sides by tall buildings. But an examination of the body revealed marks on the back of the legs and buttocks, indicating that her body had been dragged. About 10 feet from the slacks, detectives discovered shoeprints and drag-marks in soft dirt behind a bush at the edge of the car park. More searching revealed partial shoeprints leading towards the bush.

The partial prints and the drag-marks from the bush ruled out the use of a car. The young woman had been walking when attacked.

As the medical examiner had observed at the scene, the victim had died as a result of strangulation. The post-mortem, however, also determined that the woman had been drinking heavily before she died.

To Robinson, this meant that she had probably been in a bar the night she died. And probably somewhere close, since she had been on foot and walking through a deserted car park when attacked.

The detective took morgue photos and showed them to bar staff. Midway through the afternoon, he got lucky. A barman at a club about a block from where the body was found remembered Wanda Fay.

"She's a regular here," he said. "She was in here last night."

Did he see her leave with anyone?

"She might have left with Cole," he went on. "They were talking and drinking together most of the night."

Cole was Carroll Edward Cole. And the barman said that Cole had been in on each of the previous three nights. "He talks to all the women when they come in," the barman added. "I think he sees himself as something of a ladies' man."

The barman didn't have an address for Cole. Robinson ran a motor vehicle check, but it came up empty. But the Department of Prisons had records that concerned him. So did the Department of Mental Health.

From 1963 to 1970, Cole had been arrested for car theft, buying liquor for minors, pimping, arson and assault with intent to kill. He spent two years in a Texas prison, having pleaded guilty in 1965 to setting fire to a Dallas motel, in an attempt to kill his first wife.

Cole's record showed that he had been in state mental hospitals in California, Missouri and Nevada. He also had a brief stay at a mental hospital in Dallas in 1967, following an unsuccessful suicide attempt.

One psychiatrist described Cole as acutely disturbed and a menace to society. Another was more to the point. "The female figure is very threatening to him and he wants to kill it," this psychiatrist said. "He dare not rape the woman of his obsessions. He must kill her first, then rape her."

Robinson let out a whistle. This was the same guy the barman took for a ladies' man? The guy who talked all night and later left with Wanda Fay Roberts?

Robinson learned that Cole had served a short stretch in federal prison in Missouri for forgery and had been paroled to a halfway house in Dallas. The social worker at the halfway house reported that Cole had dropped out of the course three days before. No one knew where he was.

The investigator put out an all-points bulletin for the federal parolee, noting that Cole was a convicted sex offender and was a suspect in a murder case. He was to be considered armed and dangerous, particularly to women.

It seemed crazy that a man who had an obsession with killing females so he could rape their bodies would have been returned to society. But that appeared to have been what happened.

The barman and waitress at the honky-tonk were told to call police immediately, should Cole return to the bar. Detectives checked in regularly to talk to other patrons, hoping to get a lead to Cole's whereabouts.

Several women remembered talking to Cole. They described him as an honest, well-mannered man, with an earthy sense of humour. One said that Cole looked like a "good catch" and that she would have gone if Cole had asked her for a date. She was thankful he hadn't now.

Police learned from Cole's ex-wife and others who knew him that he was a drifter who had been back and forth across the country a couple of dozen times in the past 10 years. Born in Sioux City, Iowa, he was raised near San Francisco.

Cole had bragged that he had experienced his first "heterosexual encounter" with a girl when he was just seven years old. He also claimed to have developed a habit as a youngster of choking the family dog into near-unconsciousness.

He dropped out of school to join the navy. Just 20 months later, he was court-martialled and dishonourably discharged for stealing two .45-calibre pistols from an armoury. He told psychiatrists that he stole the pistols to kill a woman he mistakenly believed had given him a venereal disease.

Released from the Napa State Hospital for the Insane in Imola, California, after a 90-day observation, Cole bounced from one town to another. He found work, but always quit or got fired after a couple of months. His favourite pastime was hanging around honky-tonk bars and picking up women.

Police discovered a few who found Cole to be a nice, witty guy who liked to have a good time. They apparently never saw the dark side of his personality.

"We dated a few times, then he would just disappear," one woman said. "I always wondered what happened to him." So did Dallas police, who wondered whether the Iowa-born itinerant had gone back to Nevada, California, or Oklahoma.

Cole was something of a handyman who could frame a house, work on a car, or fix a leaking tap. He would find a job, work a couple of weeks, then disappear before his name ever reached police computers. He could also knock over liquor stores and filling stations to keep himself alive. It was conceivable that years might go by before he was caught. By then the case might be so old that when he was stopped inevitably for the routine traffic violation or public intoxication, police wouldn't know about the murder warrant that was hanging over his head.

And that almost happened.

Shortly before midnight on Sunday, November 30th, 1980 people on a quiet, tree-lined residential street in north-west Dallas heard screams come from the apartment of 43-year-old Sally Thompson.

They rushed to the apartment and pounded on the door. A minute or so later, a stranger answered. He looked dishevelled and reeked of liquor, but appeared coherent. The neighbours said they had heard screams and wanted to talk to Sally. The man showed them in.

Sally lay on the living-room floor, near the couch. She was face-down on the carpet — and her jeans and panties were down to her knees. She didn't appear to be breathing.

Police and paramedics were summoned. The victim was rushed to hospital, where she was pronounced dead.

The stranger in the apartment gave his name as Carroll Cole. He said he had met Sally in a bar earlier that evening. They'd had a few drinks and gone back to her place. One thing led to another and they started to make love. He had her pants half off when Sally suddenly collapsed on the floor. He said he'd been about to call for help when the neighbours pounded on the door.

Cole was taken to a police station, but was released a few hours later, after the initial medical examiner's report indicated that he could be telling the truth. The pathologist had found no external marks on the body, no signs that she had been poisoned or strangled. He did find a great deal of alcohol in her blood and signs that she might have died from an alcohol-related death.

There seemed no reason to hold the man, so he was released on his own recognisance. It was only later that morning that police learned that Carroll Cole was wanted on an outstanding warrant.

Detective Robinson cursed his misfortune as he read the report made out by the police officers responding to the call by the neighbours. The report listed an address on Lemon Avenue. Robinson imagined it to be fictitious — until he knocked there on that Tuesday morning and Carroll Cole opened the door.

Cole was dirty and unshaven. There were pouches under his brown eyes. And he appeared to have been drinking, but not drunk. "What can I do for you?" he asked as Robinson and other officers shouldered their way in.

Three hours later, he was confessing to a string of gruesome sex murders that made just about everyone who read the headlines wonder if there was any limit to human depravity. Cole confessed to eight murders, but said that the toll might be three or four times that many.

Some of the murders were never substantiated. Others weren't officially murders, but were classified as "death by natural cause." Even so, it was an impressive list. One detective described it as "a one-way ticket on a terror train."

It began in San Diego in 1971, when Cole picked up 39-year-old Esther Buck in a San Diego bar, strangled her in his car and tossed her corpse beside a road out in the country.

Cole said he once woke up in an apartment in Oklahoma City. In the bed with him was the nude, strangled body of a woman he had met in a bar the night before. Cole said he had sex with the corpse, then ate portions of her flesh, before stuffing the dismembered corpse into several garbage bags and disposing of them in a convenient skip. In May, 1977, Cole was living in Las Vegas. He said he went to a bar off the Las Vegas strip where, over drinks, he met 26-year-old Catherine Jo Blum. Cole said they started back towards his car around midnight, when the urge came over him to have sex. He said he strangled her to death behind a house, then dragged her body through several backyards to a tree that grew at the mouth of an alley. He stripped off her clothes and had vaginal sex with her body, managing to climax several times.

"I remember dragging her through the grass underneath this tree," he recalled. "I took off her cowboy boots and then we did it there. She was pretty well naked. I know she was dead."

His next victim was his wife, Diana Faye, 36, whom he married in Texas in 1974. On December 4th, 1980, police burst into the couple's one-bedroom apartment in San Diego and found her naked corpse leaning against the closet door. The coroner estimated that she had been dead about a week.

Cole said he went back to Las Vegas where, in November, 1979, he murdered 51-year-old Marie Cushman at the Casbah Motel. "We had sex in the bathtub," he said. "I strangled her on the bed."

A year later, Cole was sipping whisky in a Dallas honky-tonk when the urge to kill overcame him. The unlucky victim this time was 51-year-old spinster Dorothy King. Cole said he took her back to her place, strangled her, raped her, then slept and made love to her dead body for three days. Her decomposing corpse was found by police on November 11th.

Next day, he strangled Wanda Fay Roberts and raped her corpse beneath a bush in the Dallas car park. Two weeks later, the string of murders came to an end, after Cole was found standing over the half-naked body of Sally Thompson, who he now claimed to have strangled to death.

In a confession made shortly before his trial, Cole claimed that he had probably murdered 35 women or more since 1971. Police still don't know whether this was an idle boast to get his name in the record books, or if Cole was actually telling the truth.

The three women he claimed to have murdered in San Diego, including his wife, all had high levels of alcohol in their bodies and had been ruled by the coroner's office as having died of natural causes. Authorities have ruled out the possibility that Cole murdered the women in Wyoming and Oklahoma, as he claimed to have done. And the Dallas medical examiner disputes the claim that Sally Thompson was murdered, saying that the 43-year-old woman's death was probably alcohol-related.

One detective who investigated the three deaths in San Diego said it was possible that the deaths ruled as either accidental or from natural causes might actually have been murders that went undetected by the deputy coroners doing the autopsies.

"The women had high levels of alcohol in their blood and were probably comatose or unconscious when Cole killed them," the investigator noted. "It doesn't take much to choke to death a person in that state and not leave any marks. Cole just might have found the way to commit the perfect murder."

Perfect was not the right word, however. For Cole was to stand trial for the murders in Dallas and Las Vegas. Yet he didn't seem to care where he went on trial, or when. Even the death sentence hanging over his head didn't get much more than a grunt out of him. "I have been in and out of institutions all my life," he said. "I know I'm sick. I just can't help myself. I just want the killing to stop."

At his trial, which began in Dallas in March, 1981 before Judge John Mead, Cole told the jury about his decade-long reign of terror. He said he murdered the Dallas women after each of them "came on" to him in bars. He said he was "repulsed" by what he called his victims' loose morals. He killed them, he said, because "they reminded me of my mother. I think I kill *her* through *them*."

He said that fantasies of strangling women had sexually aroused him for "20 or 25 years," ever since he saw his mother in a bar in San Diego with another man and learned that she was a regular customer there.

His attorney, Doug Parks, told the jury that Cole was a "mighty sick man, who was a victim of the Texas psychiatric system. Carroll Cole has been asking for help for 20 years and has yet to receive it," Parks added. The jury was asked to return a verdict of innocent by reason of insanity, so that Cole could receive the treatment he needed.

The jurors, however, believed that Cole was claiming mental illness to save his skin. "His argument didn't sell at all," the foreman said. They took just 25 minutes to find him guilty of the first-degree murders of Dorothy King,

Wanda Fay Roberts and Sally Ann Thompson.

On April 9th, 1981, Judge Mead sentenced Cole to three life sentences, to run concurrently. This meant, in real terms, that the honky-tonk Romeo would not be eligible for parole until after he had served 25 years behind bars.

Cole, unhappy with the verdict, told the press that he did not want to spend any more time in prison. If he could not receive treatment at a state mental hospital, then he preferred to receive the death sentence.

In Nevada, it looked like he might get his wish. In early summer, 1984, he arrived in Las Vegas to stand trial for the murders of Catherine Jo Blum and Marie Cushman. Now plump and 46, Cole told reporters that he would plead guilty to the murder and request the death sentence. "I believe in capital punishment — and I believe it's warranted in this case," he said.

He pleaded guilty to the two Las Vegas killings on August 17th, 1984, before Judge Myron Leavitt. He then requested a panel of three judges rather than a jury to return a verdict in the penalty phase of the trial. "I figure that, with a panel of judges, I got a better chance of getting the death sentence," he said.

His chances were cut in half when the three-judge panel ruled, on October 11th, 1984, that Cole could not receive the death sentence for the murder of Catherine Blum, because she was murdered in 1977 — before the state enacted the death penalty.

Then, two days later, Judge Leavitt announced that the three-judge panel had reached a verdict. Ushered into the Clark County courtroom, amid reporters and spectators, Cole looked up as Judge Leavitt announced the sentence — death by chemical injection at the state penitentiary in Carson City.

Carroll Edward Cole burst into a smile and exclaimed: "Thanks, judge!"

He was led back to the jail cell, where he waited until his transfer three weeks later to Carson City. It appeared that

Cole's odyssey of violence and death had finally come to an end.

And, to all intents and purposes, it *had*. For, on Friday, December 6th, 1985, the serial killer who so badly wanted to die was granted his wish, even as protesters opposed to the death penalty held a candlelight vigil outside the prison in Carson City.

The 47-year-old convicted killer of five women — though he himself confessed to murdering 35 females — spent his last hours on this earth playing poker with the chaplain and gobbling Valium tablets to steady his nerves. In a Death Row interview, he told a reporter: "I know I'll kill again if I get out of prison. So why prolong the life of a despicable person who acted as the judge, jury and executioner to the people he murdered?" He added that he'd given doctors permission to examine his brain following his death.

After he was strapped to a table in the converted gas chamber, three lethal drugs were injected into his arm. And Carroll Edward Cole, the "ladies man" who could only make love to women if they were dead, was no more. He got his wish and dozed into eternity.

18

AN EYE FOR AN EYE

Franklin Sharpe

An inexperienced hangman, and a hefty client

LIGHTNING doesn't strike twice in the same place ... so they say. But no that's not what locals think any more in Clearview, Washington State. Not after what happened to Renae Wicklund. She had the kind of luck that makes you think she was fated. And years after her story was over, it was to have a strange sequel ...

None of this might have happened if she hadn't decided to wash her windows in her swimsuit. But on December 11th, 1974, the sun was shining; it was warm, and it seemed a good idea to give those windows a clean before she put up the Christmas decorations.

Spreading a blanket on the lawn for her baby daughter, Shannah, she slipped into her swimsuit, fetched her bucket and leather, and set to work.

It was then that she saw the tall, curly-haired young man come out of the woods behind the house. It wasn't until he was within a few feet that she saw the knife in his hand. He swooped to pick up Shannah and put the blade to the child's throat.

"Get inside and do what I tell you — or I'll cut the kid's throat!" he snarled.

The next half an hour was a nightmare for Renae as the man with the knife forced her to perform a series of revolting sex acts.

When the rapist left, disappearing into the woods, Renae ran screaming from the house with her daughter in her arms. Her cries attracted the attention of her neighbour Barbara Hendrickson, who called the police.

Mrs. Hendrickson had seen the man who'd just fled from the Wicklund home in the small community of Clearview. The two women were able to give a good description of the rapist. He was in his late teens or early 20's, very tall, with reddish-brown hair parted in the centre, large dark eyes and prominent ears.

One of the officers thought he recognised the description, and the women were taken to the sheriff's office in Everett. There they picked out a photograph of 19-year-old Charles Rodman Campbell, who lived in nearby Edmonds. He was out on parole from a 15-year sentence for burglary, and he was now taken into custody.

Both women picked him out of a police line-up. Campbell denied the rape, claiming that he had never even been in Clearview.

He continued to protest his innocence at his trial a year later. Renae Wicklund faced the ordeal of relating the sordid details of the sex acts she had been forced to perform. A jury found Campbell guilty of sodomy and assault, and on January 26th, 1976 he was sentenced to serve 20 years in the state reformatory.

But Renae's troubles weren't over. The rape became a barrier between her and her husband, and eventually it led to a separation. Renae remained at the house with Shannah, and Jack Wicklund moved into a flat in Seattle.

A year later, disaster struck again. An intruder broke into Jack's apartment, tied him to a chair, robbed him and poured petrol over him. Then, striking a match, the gunman shouted "Merry Christmas!" and turned Wicklund into a torch.

Despite third-degree burns over 40 per cent of his body, Wicklund managed to survive.

Horribly scarred and in constant pain, Wicklund had to

wear a rubber-type suit to protect the healing wounds. Four months after the attack he was driving to his parents' home, when his car left the road, struck a telegraph pole and killed him.

To support herself and her daughter, Renae ran an accounting business for beauty parlours from her home. It was successful, allowing her to be with Shannah through her toddler years, and later when she went to school. Her closest friend was still Barbara Hendrickson, who was 20 years older.

When Barbara's husband came home from work just after 6 p.m. on April 15th, 1982, he was surprised to find that his wife was not there and preparations for the evening meal had not been started. He looked to see if she'd left a note, but couldn't find one. He assumed she'd soon phone to explain her absence.

After waiting for a while he looked across the road to Renae's home. Her car was in the drive. He also saw Shannah's bicycle, which meant that they were at home. He phoned Renae to see if she knew where Barbara had gone, but there was no reply.

It was dusk but there were no lights in Renae's house and that disturbed him. He walked over and rang the doorbell. There was no response, and as the door was unlocked he walked in, switching on the lights and calling out to Renae.

There was no one in the living-room, so he went towards the kitchen, looking down the hall towards the bedrooms. Then he froze in horror.

Sprawled in the hall was his wife, her throat slashed from ear to ear, her blood lying in pools on the floor. He saw at a glance that she was dead.

Stepping gingerly past Barbara's corpse, he looked into the bedroom. Renae lay on the bed, her throat slashed. And that wasn't all. Some of her clothing had been removed and it seemed that a knife had been used to mutilate her genitals. Eight-year-old Shannah was on the floor. Her throat had also been slashed.

The first police to arrive questioned the stunned neighbours about anything they might have heard or seen. It was believed that the attack had taken place in the late afternoon, after Shannah had come home from school at about 4 p.m.

There were no indications that any of the rooms had been ransacked, or that anything of value had been taken. Renae's handbag containing money and her car keys was on the kitchen table, and there were no signs of a struggle. Bloody footprints were found in the hall, leading out via the back door. They appeared to have been made by one person.

Detectives speculated that Renae had probably been killed first, while she was in the house alone. It would be light outside, and the doors would have been unlocked as she waited for Shannah to come home.

While the killer was still in the house Shannah had arrived. She had probably been the second victim as the killer dragged her into the bedroom, slashed her throat and left her lying beside her dead mother. Barbara Hendrickson might have heard Shannah scream and hurried to investigate, only to be caught by the killer in the hall.

The police interviewed a girl who'd come home with Shannah on the school bus. She had walked with Shannah as far as the driveway to her own house.

The girl was almost positive that she had seen only one car in the drive — the one owned by Renae Wicklund. She said: "I'm almost sure that if there'd been another car Shannah would have noticed it and wondered who was visiting them."

Neighbours who had driven past the Wicklund home in the late afternoon and early evening were unable to recall having seen a second car parked at the house. In fact they could not remember seeing *any* strange car in the vicinity.

Detectives wondered how the killer had reached the house, and why if he'd been on foot he hadn't taken Mrs. Wicklund's car. It was possible that he had parked his vehicle some distance away and then walked through the wooded area at the rear of the house.

Tracker dogs picked up a scent from the bloody footprints in the house and led the handlers through the back garden and into the woods, following a trail for almost half a mile to the Snohomish River, and for a short way along the bank — until it ended in the water.

It seemed that the killer had waded into the water to wash the blood from his shoes and clothes. In case he'd thrown the knife he used into the river, arrangements were made for divers to conduct a search.

Two of the detectives on the scene had investigated Renae's rape eight years earlier. On the chance that the youth sent to prison for the assault might have escaped, Sheriff Robert Dodge asked for a check with the state reformatory to determine whether Charles Campbell was still in custody. Word soon came back that Campbell was still there.

So far there were only two pieces of solid evidence. One was the bloody footprints that had left a distinctive pattern. The other was a bloody palm-print on a glass. The killer had apparently stopped to take a drink of water after the murders.

Sheriff Dodge was still at the crime scene the next morning when he received a call from his office. A deputy told him: "We just got a call from the reformatory. It seems that when we asked for a check on a guy named Campbell last night, he was there, all right."

"So?"

"He was there — but he didn't get there until ten o'clock," the deputy said, explaining that the person who had phoned from the reformatory told him that Campbell was on a work-release scheme which allowed him to come and go at a facility in Everett almost at will, as long as he checked in every night.

And according to the reformatory official, Campbell had been away from the facility the previous day. But when he returned at around 8 p.m. he was drunk, so the authorities there had returned him to the reformatory.

Sheriff Dodge hurried back to his office and phoned the reformatory. He requested that Campbell be put in maximum security and that his clothes and shoes be impounded. He also wanted to know why his office had not been informed that Campbell was on a work-release scheme in an area where he had been convicted of rape.

Detectives learned that Campbell had a car and worked during the day for a landscape company. He was under the supervision of a parole officer and had got drunk once before, when he had been warned that if it happened again he would be returned to the reformatory.

"He came in staggering drunk last night," an official said. "He couldn't talk coherently. When we tried to sober him up he became belligerent, so we took him back to the reformatory."

Asked if anyone had noticed whether Campbell's clothes or shoes had been soiled or wet, officials said they weren't sure. It seemed that he might have fallen into some dirt in his drunken condition.

But the big break came when detectives interviewed a young woman Campbell had been seeing while he was on the work-release scheme.

She said that when Campbell came to her home at mid-morning on the day of the murders he'd been drinking heavily. He'd asked her to have sex with him, and when she refused he'd wrestled with her and tried to undress her. She had managed to talk him out of it, and after having several more drinks he left.

More to the point, she said that after his departure she noticed that a large carving-knife was missing from her kitchen. She assumed that Campbell had taken it.

Then Sheriff Dodge received a report from the FBI crime lab. It identified the palm-print on the glass in the Wicklund home as Charles Rodman Campbell's.

Following the announcement that Campbell had been charged with the murders, a placard outside a Clearview store declared in capital letters: "AN EYE FOR AN EYE." The sign was replaced a few days later with a new one: "WE WANT THE DEATH PENALTY." There was also an invitation to sign a petition to be handed to the prosecutor.

Campbell responded by sacking his court-appointed lawyers and demanding to be allowed to represent himself. Then he asked to be taken to hospital for psychiatric evaluation. This was suspected to be a move which would later let him change his plea to not guilty by reason of insanity.

Next, accepting two lawyers to represent him, Campbell appealed to have the charges against him dismissed because he had not received a prompt trial, as required by law. The petition was rejected.

On November 26th, 1982, he was found guilty on all counts. But at the conclusion of the penalty phase which followed, Campbell seemed to be the only relaxed person in the courtroom.

In dark brown trousers, a tan sports jacket, light-coloured shirt and patterned tie, he sat half-sprawled in his chair, grinning at the jury.

They decided that he should be put to death for his crimes, either by hanging or by lethal injection.

Then, as the judge checked with each juror to ensure that this was their unanimous decision, Campbell turned to his lawyer and growled: "Do we have to go through all that crap again?"

The sequel, as is the way on Death Row, was a long time coming. It was not until May 1994 that the appeals process was completed and Charles Campbell at last went to his execution.

But his hanging wasn't the end of the story. A hefty client for the inexperienced hangman, he was nearly decapitated. And when another Death Row veteran heard of it, he was quick to turn it to his advantage.

Mitchell Rupe, awaiting execution in the same prison for shooting two women dead during a bank robbery, promptly claimed that he was too heavy to be hanged. If Campbell, weighing a mere 16 stone, was nearly decapitated, Rupe argued, what would happen to *him* . . . turning the scales at nearly 30 stone?

Rupe declined to choose between the gallows and lethal injection, so under Washington state law he had to hang. But his lawyers came forward with medical testimony that if their client hanged, he would probably lose his head. And in September 1994 a court ruled that Rupe shouldn't be hanged because, of all things, losing his head would be "cruel and unusual punishment" and is therefore illegal.

19

PLEASE PUT HIM TO DEATH

Michael Jason

She told the court of the wasted life she had endured

THE JEWELLER took life sitting down. Severely disabled by arthritis, he had no option. Nevertheless, 50-year-old Kenneth Staton had established a successful shop in Van Buren, Arkansas, where he cheerfully served customers from his wheelchair.

He was married with three daughters, the oldest of whom — 24-year-old Suzanne Ware — worked in the shop with him. On September 10th, 1980, Ken and Suzanne were to join the rest of the family for dinner at six o'clock. When the two didn't turn up or answer the phone Mrs. Staton and the other two daughters went to the shop, arriving at about 7 p.m.

Suzanne's jeep wasn't in the parking area, but the lights were on in the shop. There were no signs of activity. The front door was ajar.

The two girls stepped inside and called out for their father and sister. They walked through the deserted shop to a workroom at the rear and pushed the door open.

The bodies of their father and sister were lying on the floor! Each had their hands roped behind their back. Each had been gagged with gauze. And each had two bullet holes in the head.

Van Buren Police Chief Virgil Goff, an old friend of the

Statons, arrived moments after the phone call. The store was in a shopping centre, and crowds were already gathering. Goff instructed his men to question anyone who might have seen or heard anything suspicious.

Investigator Don Taylor of the Arkansas state police joined the search of the premises. His quick check of the death scene turned up three .22 bullet casings on the floor beside the bodies. A fourth shell was found beneath Suzanne Ware.

It seemed that the crippled father had been shoved out of his wheelchair and thrown on the floor beside his dead or dying daughter. A white tablecloth with what looked like powder burns on it lay near the victims.

An assistant from a nearby shop said she had seen two men who arrived in a white van with Florida licence plates enter the jeweller's around 5 p.m. "There was nothing special about their appearance or manner," she said. She had not noted the van's number.

It was impossible to determine how much had been taken from the shop without an inventory. Yet it had clearly been ransacked — many jewellery trays were missing. The victims' family were too grief-stricken to be of immediate help. But Mrs. Staton did note one special missing item as she held her dead husband's hand for the last time. His wedding ring was not on his finger.

"Ken always said he would never take it off as long as he lived," the sobbing widow told Goff as the bodies were handed over to Dr. Fahmy Malak, the state medical examiner.

As the investigation widened, a cruising patrol car spotted Suzanne's missing jeep parked near an apartment complex. It was impounded, minutely searched and dusted for prints.

Working on the theory that the murderers might have cased other jewellery stores, investigators canvassed the whole area with their very skimpy description of two possible suspects. Two pawnbrokers reported having visits from two men fitting the general description, who had said they were gold-buyers. "But they didn't buy any gold. In fact, they didn't seem to really know what they were talking about," was the reason both shop-owners gave for remembering the visitors.

Officers began checking motels in the Van Buren area, which is in the Ozark Mountains and at that time of the year was popular with tourists flocking to see the autumn colours. But no leads to the killers materialised. Then local camp-sites were checked.

A park ranger remembered seeing a white van with a camping trailer, bearing Florida licence plates. "There were two couples. The girls were young. The guys had a motorcycle they rode a lot. They had a couple of parties I had to keep an eye on. They stayed several days — checked out on September eleventh or twelfth, I think."

The ranger at the park's exit had noted the van's licence number. An alert went out for the van, which was registered in the name of Damon Peterson. The second man was identified as Richard Phillip Anderson. FBI files showed that both had lengthy criminal records. And an inventory of the jewellery shop by now showed about $100,000 missing...

On September 23rd, in Jacksonville, Florida, a dimly lit bar rocked to the beat of country-western music. The booze flowed, tempers flared — and more than a dozen shots rang out.

When the lights came on and the smoke cleared three men lay on the floor, severely wounded.

Police moved in and arrested two men. They were identified as Richard Phillip Anderson and Damon Peterson. Peterson had a gunshot wound in his right arm. The two were also identified as being wanted for questioning in the Arkansas jewellery shop murders of a fortnight earlier.

Peterson could not raise bail, so he was held in the Jacksonville jail. Anderson posted bond and was told to return to police headquarters. But the next report the authorities had on him was that he was seen getting on a

Greyhound bus, heading north. An all-states pickup request went out and the FBI joined the search.

Damon Peterson had many aliases, but it was finally determined that he was Eugene Wallace Perry, a 36-year-old native of Florida. He pleaded guilty to one count of attempted murder on the Florida charges and received a 10-year sentence.

Perry was then returned to Arkansas and charged with two counts of capital murder. For his own safety he was remanded to the Sebastian County jail, a county bordering Crawford County where the murders had taken place. The community had been so enraged by the slaying of the crippled jeweller and his daughter that threats had been made against Perry . . .

On January 10th, 1981, the thief who robbed the Bank of Nova Scotia in Vancouver, British Columbia, got only four blocks away when the Canadian Mounties got their man. A routine check identified him as Richard Phillip Anderson, wanted in Arkansas on two counts of capital murder. The Canadian authorities released him to Arkansas and he was returned in early February. Like Perry, he pleaded innocent to all charges brought against him.

After Judge David Partain agreed to separate trials for Perry and Anderson, Perry's court-appointed attorney, Ron Harrison, asked for the return of $2,000 in cash confiscated from his client when he was arrested in Jacksonville. Harrison said Perry wanted the money to use in his defence. The request was granted.

When Perry's trial began on July 13th, 1981, he wore a conservative business suit, and his hair was cut short. He appeared tense, and did not look at the jury. He claimed he was in Alabama on September 10th, the day Ken Staton and his daughter had been robbed and murdered. Furthermore, the defence asserted that not only had Perry not been in Arkansas on September 10th — he had never been in the state at all!

Dr. Malak, the medical examiner, told the court:

"Suzanne was bound and shot twice. The first shot entered the right temple and went into the brain. The second wound was in the right forehead, above the right eye. The muzzle of the gun was in touch with the skin. She was shot first.

"Kenneth Staton was shot twice in the forehead, above the right eye. The muzzle of the gun was placed against the skin." Dr. Malak explained that he could tell when a gun had been pressed against a body by the gunpowder residue left on the skin.

The prosecution called the shop assistant, who testified that she had seen Perry and another man in the car park at the shopping centre on September 10th. "I'm ninety-nine per cent positive that was one of the men I saw," she said, pointing at Perry. But the defence forced her to admit that she had seen the two men from a distance — and only briefly.

A motel manager verified that he had rented a room on September 9th to a man named Damon Peterson, whom he pointed out as Perry. But he also admitted, under cross-examination, that he had at first told officers that he didn't remember Perry, and he'd recalled him only after seeing a picture of him.

The pawnshop owners said that Perry resembled one of two men posing as gold-buyers who appeared in their stores "on or about September 10th." But neither could definitely say that Perry was the same man, only that his general appearance was the same.

A dramatic moment came when the weeping widow held a gold ring cupped in her hand. "This is Ken's ring, one that I gave him. He vowed he would never pull it off as long as he lived." The ring had been in Perry's possession when he was captured, the police alleged.

"I remember him," Mrs. Staton said of Perry. "He and a young lady came in the store a week or so before the robbery. They browsed around and looked through all the jewellery. But they left without buying anything."

The next prosecution witness was a local girl. She was

very slim, very blonde, very frightened. She knew her testimony would ruin her reputation and could cost her her life. Perry had bragged to her about his Mafia connections, but her conscience wouldn't let her remain silent.

She testified that she'd first met him at the shopping centre car park near Staton's jewellery shop. "He called himself Damon Peterson. We talked for a while, then another guy came up — a guy he called Rick. They had come to town on a motorcycle. They invited me back to their motel for a beer. Damon and I drove back there in my car and Rick followed on the motorcycle.

"We drank a six-pack of beer. Then I told them I had to leave. Damon tried to make me promise I would come back. He was a real good talker. I did come back a couple of hours later — and I spent the night in the motel room with him." The night, she said, was September 9th.

The next witness wasn't local — and some might not call her a lady. She crossed her shapely legs, looked directly at Perry and said: "He told me he was a jewellery dealer and his name was Damon Peterson when he picked me up in Kansas City. He had a trailer he was pulling behind a big old Cadillac. We drove to Beaver Lake, in northern Arkansas.

"We all camped there together — me and Damon and Rick and another girl. We all stayed in the trailer together, but the guys would go off and talk together, where we couldn't hear. They did this several times. Then one day they just packed their stuff and left."

The items the men packed, she said, included two guns, some rope and a change of clothing. The men left on the morning of September 9th, telling the women to remain at the camp-site until they returned.

"The guys came back late next night — September tenth — with two bags full of jewellery and watches.

"They told us to pick out some pieces we liked. They had a lot of really nice watches and stuff, so me and the other girl took a couple of rings and bracelets."

The defence attorney asked: "What did you think had happened? Where did you think they got the jewellery?"

The witness hung her head. "I didn't ask no questions."

The jewellery had shop tags on it. The women were told to burn them and make sure that no tags or watch boxes were left. "Damon told me several times to be sure all the tags were burned — and I thought I'd done a good job."

The Kansas City witness continued her saga. "We broke camp and drove to Rogers, Arkansas, where we traded Damon's car. Then we stored the trailer in a Fayetteville garage. We all went on to Atlanta." But in Georgia they ran out of luck. "While we were out having a drink some bastard broke into our motel room and stole most of the jewellery!" she testified indignantly.

She said she then decided to go back to Kansas City. "They let me go home, but they said that if I ever uttered a word to anyone they would come and get me. And if *they* couldn't, they knew someone who would."

She insisted that she knew nothing about the robbery or the double murder. She had gone along for the ride. But under cross-examination by the defence counsel she agreed that Rick and Damon might have been away longer than overnight — they might not have returned to the camp-site until September 12th.

Among expert witnesses the prosecution called Berwin Monroe, a state crime lab. technician who testified that charred rope found in ashes at the camp-site matched that which had bound the victims' hands. And Investigator Don Taylor described his search of the trailer left by two men at the Fayetteville storage facility. A small price tag, similar to those used in Staton's jewellery shop, had been stuck to the floor. And a page torn from a Fort Smith-Van Buren telephone directory, also found in the trailer, had Kenneth Staton's home address on it.

The defence presented five witnesses. Perry's ex-wife and two daughters testified that he had been with them in Oxford, Alabama, from September 8th until the 10th. His petite 14-year-old daughter said: "My sister and I went shopping with Daddy on the eighth and ninth. Then he left to visit Grandma and came back on the eleventh." She showed the jury the notes she had made in her diary.

Then Perry's mother testified that she and her husband had been at a prayer meeting on the night of September 10th. "My son came in late that night and we stayed up and talked. He spent the night with us. Then he left the next day, saying he was going back to Oxford to spend more time with his children."

The wedding ring that Perry had in his possession at the time of his Florida arrest had been given to him by his girl friend, his mother claimed.

Closing arguments were brief, as was the jury's deliberation. Eugene Wallace Perry was found guilty and sentenced to death.

Richard Phillip Anderson was tried a few months later. He admitted that he had participated in the robbery and was present when the Statons were killed. But he swore that he did not pull the trigger — and that he begged Perry not to kill the victims.

The jury nevertheless found him guilty of first-degree murder. He was sentenced to life in prison and fined $15,000.

Eugene Wallace Perry spent the next 16 years fighting for a reprieve. Then in July 1997, when the appeals process had run its course, the Arkansas State Clemency Board sat to decide Perry's fate. It was then that Ruth Staton, the victim's widow, appeared before the board to argue in favour of execution for Perry.

Weeping as she gave evidence, she told the court of the wasted life she had endured since her husband and daughter were murdered by Perry: "Please put him to death! He took my life. Now take his!" she said with emotion.

It took less than 15 minutes for the board to come to a decision and vote to recommend that Perry be executed, and on August 7th, 1997, Perry was put to death by lethal injection.

20
THE BUCHENWALD
EXPERIENCE

L. C. Schmuhl

"Ah," he snarled, "My old Nazi friend"

THROUGH breakfast I'd tried to catch the early
newscasts. Failing, I had a nagging curiosity when I
arrived at work at Indiana's old state prison.

Warden Ralph Howard, who had good old-fashioned
ideas about early hours, was already at his desk. I paused
to chat a moment.

"Heard anything about the trial?" I asked.

He smiled, knowing my interest was both personal and
professional. "No," he said. "The case went to the jury
last night. The jury was still out when I went to bed."

"Me too," I replied.

I must have let a trace of petulance creep into my voice
because a twinkle came into Warden Howard's wise old
eyes and he said, "Don't fret. They'll be back — and
probably in your building."

I nearly replied, "I hope so!" Instead I said, "I expect
you're right. We'll see."

As deputy warden I had helped to execute more than 30
men. I didn't like it, but it was my duty — a disagreeable
part of my life's work.

But I had never been wholly convinced that capital
punishment was right, and I had certainly never wished

death for any man — including the deadliest of the men I guarded.

Yet of Robert Oscar Brown I had almost said, "I hope he gets the chair!" Walking towards my office that cold, blustery Saturday, November 22nd, 1947, I tried to sort it out in my mind — scarcely noticing the grey prison stirring around me.

Brown, a bitter, psychopathic master of invective, had got under my thickened hide more deeply than I realised, but I would find it no easier to help execute him than any of the others.

Feeling better — but still plagued by that nagging curiosity — I finally picked up my phone and called Al Spiers, an old friend who edited the Michigan City newspaper.

"What happened at the trial?" I asked.

"They got the works," Spiers replied.

"Death?"

"Yep!"

"Both of 'em?"

"Yep! The jury reported at two-fifteen this morning after a six-hour session. They'll appeal, of course, but it looks like they'll be your babies."

I put down the telephone slowly, wondering what Death Row would do to the toughest, meanest, most bitter criminal I had ever known.

I had encountered thousands of criminals — large and small, mean and mild — in 20-odd years in Indiana's big house, including the entire Dillinger gang.

It was in our prison, in fact, that John Dillinger first met his deadly cohorts — Pierpont, Hamilton, Makely, Shouse, Clark, Dietrich.

But none of the Dillinger gang possessed the volcanic hatred, explosive violence and sadistic venom that perpetually simmered in the soul of Robert Oscar Brown. And Brown was one of the two men now coming to Death Row.

He was no stranger. We'd held him before — always

with perpetual grief. If he wasn't plotting to escape, he was fighting with guards or other prisoners.

My mind drifted back to the grey dawn of a morning some years before, and the sight of a yard officer all slashed, bloody and beaten. He'd been jumped in the darkness and left to die.

There was a rope dangling from a hook flung onto the top of the wall, but footprints below showed that our man was still inside.

"He wore a guard's coat and hat," the officer said weakly from a hospital bed as the doctors fought to save his life.

I remembered how grimly we'd worked that day — sifting out all the prisoners who had been at early jobs. I remembered putting them into officers' coats and hats and sending them into that hospital room, one by one.

It was late afternoon before we got around to Bob Brown, who had been assigned to the breakfast mess crew. When Brown walked into the hospital room the yard officer half rose, weak as he was, and pointed an accusing finger.

"That's him. That's the rat!" he cried.

Brown stared back at him with cruel eyes, and sneered.

We put him in solitary for that caper, and I talked to him there.

The prison board had decreed that he should serve his whole long robbery sentence as punishment for the abortive break. "You'll do it all," I told him. "You'll do every day of it."

"You won't keep me, you fat rat," Brown snarled. "I'll get out of this bird cage one way or another."

I held my temper with an effort.

"One of these days," I told him quietly, "you'll leave this bird cage feet first — on a stretcher going out of the death house."

Brown laughed, curled his thick lips and said tauntingly, "You'd like that, wouldn't you? But Old Smoky will never get me. You can bet on that."

Brown did his time the hard way — a lot of it in solitary confinement. Once he slashed another prisoner so badly it took 125 stitches to close the wounds. Another time he slugged a guard.

As time passed he grew more bitter and deadly. His hatred for us and for the police became a fiery passion — almost psychopathic.

Between the world wars I was a reserve infantry officer. Early in 1942 I was ordered back to active duty. The grapevine told Brown, who was doing another stretch in solitary at the time. He called to me as I passed his cell on one of my final days at the prison.

"Don't you want to say goodbye, Schmuhl?" he asked, a mean note in his voice.

"I'll be back," I told him bluntly.

"I hope not," Brown said maliciously — meaning every word. "But I won't be here, anyway. My full time is up in '44. They can't keep me after that — no matter what I do."

I knew that was so, but I replied, "I'll be back — and so will you. You haven't got sense enough to stay out of trouble."

I saw the familiar rage creep into his face. Then he snarled, "Not me! You'll never see me again, you dirty screw!"

"I'll see you," I told him quietly, and walked away.

I was in Germany, a major attached to a military government unit, early in 1944 when Brown was finally released. He was back in prison before the year was out.

In September 1944 three burglars raided the home of a Michigan City gambler. Surprised in the act, they shot their way out. The gambler was wounded and his bodyguard killed. Two months later Brown and two partners were arrested. A grand jury indicted them for first-degree murder. Brown came to prison for safekeeping while awaiting trial.

"This is a bum rap," he told my successor, A. J. Funk. "I'll beat it."

Brown was a prison "guest" for several months while his case pended. He was as mean and ornery as ever. Once he tore all the plumbing out of his cell. He took a swing at a guard and poured vicious invective at Deputy Funk.

But in the end he did beat that rap. The three men were tried separately. The first of Brown's pals got a hung jury. The prosecutor decided he couldn't win a second trial. Two of the men were wanted elsewhere on other charges, so they were released. Brown, momentarily unwanted, went scot free.

"I said you'd never keep me again, and I was right," Brown gloated when he left.

"You'll be back. Guys like you always come back," Funk said quietly.

"I won't!" Brown snarled.

He was wrong again.

It started as a simple car theft. Brown had drifted to Indianapolis. There he made contact with another of our old convicts, Frank Ray Badgley, a dour man of 50 — cringing, mixed-up, and with little taste for violence. I knew him well — a shifty, whining veteran of crime alley.

Badgley had a queer mind. One corner of it was brilliantly photographic. We had learned that, to our dismay. During his long stay in prison Badgley got into petty trouble several times. Once when he was in solitary we discovered on him a crude key, fashioned from a pipe stem, broom straws and adhesive tape.

We tried the key in his cell door. Although it wouldn't stand the pressure of use more than once or twice, it actually opened the door.

"Who gave you a key to copy?" I asked.

Badgley smiled proudly. "Nobody," he said. "I just looked at the key when the guard used it. I made this one from memory."

"You're lying," I accused him.

"No, I'm not," he said calmly. "Try me. Show me any key and I'll draw an exact duplicate of it on paper."

I tried him. He did it. We learned then that he could

read a book and recite it, almost page for page — although a month later he would have forgotten the whole thing.

But the rest of Badgley's mind was utterly criminal. His prison record went back to 1914. It was impossible for him to think or reason like a normal, law-abiding human being. He was an ideal partner for Bob Brown.

The night it all began they'd picked up a car near a theatre in Hammond. They'd driven it to a dark, obscure street, intending to switch number plates.

Before they could get out a cruising patrol car drove up, containing three officers — veteran Jon Gerka with Rudy Mamala and Don Cook, two five-day rookies Gerka was training.

To Gerka a car on a dark, obscure street containing two men was good for a practice shakedown. He stopped the prowl car, briefed the rookies and approached the vehicle.

Gerka was careful, alert and watchful. He had in fact just warned Mamala and Cook that more cops are killed shaking down suspicious cars than any other way.

So he was ready when one of the two men whipped out a gun instead of a driving licence. Gerka snatched the gun, shouted a warning and ducked low.

The second man began shooting from the other side of the car.

In the wild battle that followed, Gerka and Cook were fatally wounded, one slug hitting high on the left door of the patrol car. Mamala, unarmed, grappled with one of the gunmen — and was slugged after tearing off his foe's coat.

The gunmen got away on foot — but they left a multitude of clues: clothes, guns, flashlights, knives, tools.

One of the guns finally led to Badgley, and Badgley, talking fast in the hope of ducking the chair, promptly fingered Brown.

The police built a solid case against them, including identification of both of them by Officer Mamala.

That was the case which had ended with two convictions on the night of November 21st. The next job would be mine — keeping the killers until their final moment.

As I sat in my office that morning I wondered if I could do the job without losing my temper.

Between their capture in January and their trial in November, Brown and Badgley, too tough for county jails, had been lodged in our prison for safekeeping. I'll never forget the day they came in. Badgley as usual was morose, but a malicious, satanic glee had flashed in Brown's face when he confronted me again.

"Ah," he snarled. "My old Nazi friend. Schmuhl — the Butcher of Buchenwald!"

A good deputy warden learns early to control his emotions behind a poker face — but Brown's crack caught me off guard. I exploded out of my chair and started around the desk.

A colleague restrained me. He stepped between us and said, "Easy, deputy!"

I stopped, my neck red, my face livid.

"There'll be no more of that, Brown," I said.

The malice in his face intensified. Bowing, he replied, "Yah, der Fuehrer!"

"Take him away," I snapped.

"Heil Hitler," cried Brown over his shoulder.

I sat down, trembling with anger, aware that I had made a painful mistake. I had let Brown know that his barb had got home.

My ancestors were German, but I fought Germans in World War I and again in World War II. My son Bob, a lieutenant, had led an infantry group through rugged fighting almost to the Rhine before a sniper shattered his knee.

If that wasn't enough to give me an undying hatred for everything Nazi, I had the misfortune to be the only officer available to take over that unbelievable horror Buchenwald, after General Patton liberated the foul prison and swept on.

For nearly 10 days I was the only American at Buchenwald. I recruited a crude staff from among prisoners who could still walk in that living hell where

400 to 500 died daily. I had mass graves dug — and other mass graves opened for checking.

When I was finally relieved I almost collapsed — partly from exhaustion, partly from the emotional strain of simply being in that awful place.

When I came home I was interviewed about Buchenwald. I told the story and it was printed. Apparently Brown had read the interview and now sensed that the Buchenwald experience had left an enduring horror in my mind.

So he had driven a fiery needle into that memory. Caught off guard, I had let him know how it burned.

Sitting there, letting my anger slowly subside, I knew Brown would be hell incarnate from then on. And he was. Bob Brown made the next few months the worst of my two decades in penal work.

He was quartered in a seclusion cell near my office. If I walked past he'd come to the door and shout: "Were you at Buchenwald before or after we took it?"

He'd listen for my office door to open so he could shout: "Heil Hitler! There goes the Butcher of Buchenwald!"

I learned to take it. I had to, because I soon perceived that Brown had a subtle, secondary reason for baiting me.

He hated me, of course, and relished his taunts. But more to the point, awaiting trial as he was, he wanted me to slug hell out of him so he could go into court battered and bruised and play upon the sympathy of the jury.

Badgley didn't join in this psychological devilry. He whined, complained and wheedled, but did nothing to infuriate me or his guards.

Somehow the months passed, and in time the two were taken away for their trial.

I breathed a deep sigh of relief.

"Maybe," I told a colleague hopefully, "Brown will change if he is sent back to Death Row."

Well, the trial was over now. In a few days Brown would come back to us. I got up from my desk and looked thoughtfully out of my office window.

Would Brown be changed? Would the nearness of death

soften him? How would two hardened criminals like Brown and Badgley act in their final days and hours?

I soon got the answer to one of my questions. On December 2nd, Brown and Badgley were sentenced by Judge Robert Thompson to die on March 19th. Badgley took the sentence silently, but Brown snarled, "My own attorneys sabotaged my defence!"

Two weeks later, after their appeals were arranged, Brown and Badgley came back to our prison. As soon as they were booked in I had them brought to my office. I wanted to know whether the trial had changed Brown.

"Hello, you Buchenwald bastard!" he snapped, the moment he stepped into my office.

This time I was ready.

"You can stow that stuff now, Brown," I said. "It'll get you only misery."

"Like a beating from your storm troopers, eh?" he sneered.

"I won't need storm troopers," I warned him. "For your own good, behave!"

Brown spat out a single, expressive four-letter word.

I saw it was useless to say more. If Brown had changed, it was for the worse. I waved them out, and the guards tucked the two men into Death Row cells upstairs.

In the weeks that followed I stayed as far away from Brown as my official duties permitted. I had to. His jibes were getting under my skin again.

There was always the faint hope that approaching death would soften him. That's the way it happens in books and movies. But this was real life and Brown and Badgley were both lifelong criminals. Their minds and ideas had long been twisted out of shape. They reacted like cornered rats and began a desperate battle to escape the chair.

Brown trusted no one, not even his own lawyers. He had a queer idea that he could study law and ultimately spring himself. Accordingly he got money from relatives to buy law books, and demanded to be allowed to study them.

I wanted to refuse this unprecedented request, but

Warden Howard, a kindly man, said, "Let him. It will do no harm."

So Brown got his law books, which he shared with Badgley in order to make future use of the latter's photographic memory. Together they studied avidly. But Brown wasn't satisfied with our acceding to this request. Next he wanted a typewriter in his cell so he could type out legal briefs and notes. This we refused, for we knew that many other things besides words might be fashioned out of the metal and parts of a typewriter.

The turning down of this request brought a scurrilous letter addressed to me, dated August 13th, 1948. Brown wrote:

"Heil!

Despite all that you and the rest of the 'Hoosier Gestapo' can do I am going to get a new trial and beat this rap.

Since you seem to be too yellow to act like a man I will take this method of telling you that I don't like the way you and Warden Howard run this damn 'Buchenwald' and I warn you that unless you stop your underhanded attempts to delay and obstruct my efforts to obtain justice you will some day pay for your unjust and illegal actions.

As for the typewriter you can stick it — you know where! And I am sure that the Warden has room for one too!

Brown No. 24276"

The attorneys of Brown and Badgley meanwhile finalised their appeal and took it to the Indiana Supreme Court. Several times the lawyers conferred with their clients in Death Row, and I chatted with one of the attorneys after such a visit.

"That Brown thinks he knows more law than we do," he said wryly. "He wants us to do everything his way." He shook his head. "I guess it doesn't matter much ..."

"Doesn't matter?"

"No. There's not a chance in a hundred that the Supreme Court will reverse the conviction. The evidence was sound, the procedure proper ..."

"But Brown still insists he's innocent," I said.

He looked at me quizzically for a long moment, and then smiled. "Of course," he murmured.

Despite Brown's interference, the attorneys undertook a long, hard fight for a reversal. The battle gained only time for the doomed man. Two stays of execution were granted so that the case could be completed.

But in the end, months later, the court affirmed the convictions. Only the governor could now save the two men — and everyone, including Brown and Badgley, knew he wouldn't intervene.

"Get into federal court," Brown snapped at his lawyers when they told him the bad news.

"That's impossible," they replied. "There's no issue . . ."

"The hell with you," Brown raged. "I'll do it myself."

If anything Brown was more difficult to handle after that. He was a volcano of anger, and he erupted almost without provocation. He cursed the Death Row guards, demanded impossible concessions and even raged across Death Row at Badgley.

When I came near, Brown continued to needle me. I finally silenced him as I yearned to do with a bunched fist, but in a simple, obvious way I should have spotted earlier.

After firing his attorneys he had resumed his law studies. It dawned on me that he still hoped to beat the case himself. So after one of his outrageous outbursts I went to his cell.

"Would you like to spend the rest of your time in solitary?" I asked.

"Why not the gas chamber or cremation ovens, you Nazi butcher?" he snarled.

"No — just solitary," I said quietly. "Solitary — without your law books."

His mouth was open, ready to spew more hate — but it suddenly snapped shut. His eyes became murderous, but fear lurked in their depths.

He licked his lips and stared at me. Finally he muttered, "All right, you Nazi rat. You win!"

"And you can stow that Nazi Buchenwald stuff, too," I continued. "One more crack like that and down to the hole you'll go."

"Yes, sir," Brown said. His tone was mild and obedient, but there flashed in his eyes at that moment the most intense hate I have ever seen.

I went away, knowing I had silenced his tongue but fanned his malevolence.

As February of 1949 began, Brown started writing a long, laborious, legal brief by hand. He was determined to get his case into federal court — to buy time if nothing else.

I knew it was a futile hope, but these men were driven by self-preservation. Unless I was mistaken, they would fight right to the end.

I wondered if I could shed new light on the case by obtaining last-minute statements. Brown, I was sure, would never crack. So I tried to get closer to Badgley.

He was friendly — even grateful for the attention I gave him. He talked eagerly about inconsequential things — but clammed up tightly whenever I steered the conversation to the police murders.

In time I sensed that Badgley too might have something up his sleeve.

Chaplain Robert Hall was attending both men.

"Are you getting close to them?" I asked one day.

The chaplain shook his head. "It's too early," he said. "Besides, they seem preoccupied with something besides religion."

I sensed it too, and worried a little. As a precaution I had them both stripped and minutely searched. I had their cells shaken down and when the guards were finished I double-checked personally. I wanted no abortive escape or suicide attempt. We found nothing — yet I was sure something was cooking.

What appeared to be their last big pitch developed the week before the scheduled execution. Brown sent word to his mother and brother to come to the prison.

They arrived on Friday, February 18th. Brown gave them a 20-page handwritten petition for writ of habeas corpus.

"Take this personally to Judge Luther Swygert in Federal Court at South Bend," he instructed them. "File it with him. Then contact Bob Buhler at Fort Wayne. Hire him. He's the best criminal lawyer in the state."

I had to examine the document as a customary precaution. It was a rambling brief, couched in legal phrasing. In it, Brown protested his innocence, alleging police brutality, denial of rights and anything and everything else he deemed pertinent.

Brown's mother and brother delivered the brief to Judge Swygert at 2 o'clock that afternoon. The judge immediately scheduled a hearing for the next day.

In prison Brown and Badgley waited tensely, sweating it out.

The Saturday hearing was brief. The lawyer Buhler argued long and hard, but in the end Judge Swygert said, "There is no new evidence here."

The word got back to Brown.

"Appeal," he told Buhler.

Now I began to see Brown's strategy. Their death date, February 23rd, was a legal holiday — Washington's birthday. Unless the Appeal Court chose to act swiftly, the brief would probably win a stay of execution.

On Monday, Attorney Buhler sped to the U.S. Court of Appeals in Chicago and presented his case.

But if winning time was Brown's intent, Judge Sherman Minton foiled him.

"We'll hear the case tonight," he decided promptly. At 6 p.m. the appeal was argued.

"There's nothing on which this court can act," Judge Minton ruled.

And that, I thought, ends the big pitch.

I was wrong!

Tuesday, execution day, was hectic. In the morning Buhler conferred with his clients, giving them the bad news. There was nothing more he could do. I spoke to him briefly as he was going out.

"They told me to stick around," he said.

That was curious. I asked why.

Buhler shrugged. "I don't know. They didn't say." He told me he'd be at a Michigan City hotel if they wanted him. Then he left.

Both men had final visits from relatives that morning. When the visits were over, Brown called for Chaplain Hall and was baptised.

I checked the two at noon. Both were calm, quiet and courteous. Yet I sensed a tension between them and wondered . . .

After dinner we moved them into death cells on the first floor, pausing en route to have them shaved and readied for the chair.

Both were still calm and quiet — yet after my own lunch I could feel a tension building up. I couldn't put a finger on it, but it was there.

Here were two complete criminals who had made a long, relentless fight to escape the chair. My long prison experience told me they would still be fighting desperately — with every kind of dodge and device.

Yet they were docile and relaxed. It didn't add up.

Then it happened.

At 2.45 Badgley sent word that he wanted to see me. I went to his cell — a few feet from Brown's.

"I want to make a sworn confession," Badgley told me.

"All right," I said. "I'll send pen and paper."

"No," Badgley protested, "I want my lawyer here. I want witnesses. I want this very legal."

"Why?" I asked. "Legally the case is over. A confession won't change it."

"It might."

"In what way?"

"In Brown's way. I was in on that Hammond job. I helped kill those cops. But Brown didn't. He wasn't with me. It was someone else."

"Who?" I asked abruptly.

"One of my kin," Badgley replied, naming a relative. "You'd better get my lawyer."

I knew then why they'd told Buhler to hang around. I called Warden Howard immediately and told him what had happened.

"I think he's lying, trying to buy time," I said. "But you'd better summon Buhler."

The attorney came quickly. We gave him a stenographer and witnesses. He conferred with Badgley at length.

By 5 p.m. we had the full statement — signed, witnessed and very legal.

Brown, in a nearby cell, knew something was going on. But we didn't tell him what it was. There'd be plenty of time for that later.

When the statement was finished I talked with Buhler.

"What do you think?" I asked.

He shook his head slowly. "It doesn't add up," he said. "There are some contradictions ..." He frowned for a long moment, then snapped his fingers.

"Two of Badgley's relatives are waiting outside," he said. "They are decent, honest women. Badgley visited them — with his companion — earlier on the night of the murders. I'm going to talk to them ..."

He hurried away.

Brown and Badgley ate their last meals at 6.30. Both seemed tense and watchful, and only picked at their food.

At 7 p.m. Buhler called. "My work on this case is done," he said.

"What about the confession?"

"I went over it at great length with Badgley's relatives," he said.

"What did they say?"

"They said they couldn't understand how a man could lie when so near to death. You can tell Badgley the case is over."

The sad-eyed old criminal looked up hopefully when I walked into his cell a few moments later.

"It's all over, Frank," I told him.

"But," he blurted, "you're killing an innocent man. Brown wasn't with me, I swear he wasn't ..."

"The law says he was," I replied gently. "We aren't the law. We are only its servants. There's nothing we can do now."

"But ..."

"It's no use," I interrupted. "It was a good pitch, Frank, but it failed. You're going to meet your Maker tonight. Why don't you tell the truth before you go?"

Badgley lowered his head. "Brown wasn't with me," he muttered. He turned his face back to mine. "I swear he wasn't with me," he repeated.

I looked into his frightened eyes and saw a mixture of death and defeat.

"You've got a few hours," I said. "Think it over. We'll be close by if you want to talk."

"Brown wasn't with me," Badgley muttered again.

A little later Brown asked me to come to his cell. His face was calm and composed and he was almost friendly.

"This may surprise you," he said quietly, "but I want to apologise for the bad time I've given you."

It did surprise me, and I took a chair opposite the bunk on which he was lounging. I was suddenly hopeful that Brown might have softened at long last, and that he might want to talk.

"That's decent of you," I said slowly. "Now why don't you be completely decent and honest and clear up this whole business?"

Brown's eyebrows rose, and a mocking light came into his pupils.

"Didn't Badgley tell you the truth?" he asked quickly.

"He said you weren't with him, if that's what you mean," I said calmly.

"I wasn't with him," Brown snapped, some of the old anger returning. "And you're going to kill me."

"We are," I replied, looking straight into his smouldering eyes. "Nothing can save you now. It's all over and done. Why not tell the truth? Were you with Badgley?"

"No!" he snapped.

"How about that Michigan City murder?"

"I wasn't near this burg the night the gambler's bodyguard was bumped off."

I shrugged and got up. "Have it your way," I said. "I'll be here if you change your mind."

"S'long, deputy," Brown said with a cold grin.

I stayed in my office, marking time as the night progressed — slowly for me, swiftly for those two men.

Brown wrote several letters to relatives and friends. Each one began with the same paragraph. It went like this:

"There is an old saying that 'Murder will out!' But in this case the truth was learned too late to save me from an unjust death ..."

Badgley, who had earlier scorned religion, became more devout as midnight neared.

I sat waiting and thinking as the pressure of fleeing time and nearing death built up. At 11.45 I glanced at my watch and thought, about five more minutes. But I realised that if there was a pitch to make at 11.49 they'd make it. Even knowing that, I wasn't prepared for the weird cry that echoed through Death Row a few minutes after 12 o'clock.

We took Brown first, simply because his was the lower prison number. Badgley's cell door shut off his view, but he could hear the footsteps clatter on the hard floor as the swift, short death march started.

At the top of his voice he shouted, "You're killing the wrong man!"

It was an eerie thing, and I saw some of the official witnesses wince.

When it was over we took Badgley. With Brown dead, you might have expected Badgley at long last to change his story.

He didn't! There was scant time, and he was too busy praying. He was just a tired, frightened old man at the end of a long criminal road.

At 12.30 the undertaker took away the bodies — Badgley to be buried in the prison cemetery, Brown to be cremated because he had said, "I've been caged up all my life. I don't want to be locked in a hole after death."

Did we execute an innocent man? I'm quite sure we didn't. In 20-odd years in the Big House I'd come to know a little about how the criminal mind functions. This was simply a classic, chips-down example.